COPYRIGHT LAW AND THE DISTANCE EDUCATION CLASSROOM

Tomas A. Lipinski

THE SCARECROW PRESS, INC.
Lanham, Maryland • Toronto • Oxford
2005

SCARECROW PRESS, INC.

Published in the United States of America
by Scarecrow Press, Inc.
A wholly owned subsidary of
The Rowman & Littlefield Publishing Group, Inc.
4501 Forbes Boulevard, Suite 200, Lanham, Maryland 20706
www.scarecrowpress.com

PO Box 317
Oxford
OX2 9RU, UK

British Library Cataloguing in Publication Information Available

Library of Congress Cataloging-in-Publication Data

Lipinski, Tomas A., 1958–
    Copyright law and the distance education classroom / by Tomas A.
Lipinski.
        p. cm.
    Includes bibliographical references and index.
    ISBN 0-8108-5171-7 (pbk.: alk. paper)
    1. United States. Technology, Education, and Copyright Harmonization
Act of 2001. 2. Distance education—Law and legislation—United States. 3.
Computer-assisted instruction—Law and legislation—United States. 4.
Copyright and distance education—United States. 5. Copyright
infringement—United States. I. Title.
KF4209.E38.L57 2005
344.73'077—dc22

                                                    2004011642

This book is dedicated to my parents,
E. J. (1919–2004) and Jeannette Lipinski, for the
many countless and immeasurable instances of support
over the years. Thanks, Dad! Thanks, Mom!

Contents

List of Tables   vii

Foreword   ix

**Part I: Understanding the Limitations on Exclusive Rights
      for Educators**

1   Performance and Display Rights in the Live Classroom and the
    Remote Classroom: The Need for Reform   3

Part II: Understanding the New TEACH Distance Education Law

2   The Scope of the Privilege for Educators: Excluded Materials   35
3   New Rights and Limitations Regarding Use of Copyrighted
    Material: Section 110(2) and Subsections (A), (B), and (C)   53
4   New Responsibilities for the Institution: Section 110(2)(D)   89
5   Summary of Part II: The Section 110(2) Requirements in
    a Nutshell   109

Part III: Completing the TEACH Puzzle

6   The Ephemeral Recording Privilege in
    Distance Education: The Old and the New   115
7   Fair Use of Copyrighted Material in the
    Distance Education Classroom   155

Appendix A A TEACH Q&A Compliance Audit   189

Appendix B Model Distance Education Copyright Policy   201

Appendix C Copyright Statute Sections (Selected)   209

Selected Bibliography   217

Case Index   221

Subject Index   225

About the Author   227

List of Tables

1.1   Current Law: 17 U.S.C. § 110(1)   18

1.2   Section 110(2), Pre-TEACH Law Limitations on Exclusive
Rights: Exemption of Certain Performances and Displays   23

2.1   Comparison of Section 110(2)(A) Teaching Activity versus
MIA   37

3.1   Section 110(2), Limitations on Exclusive Rights: Exemption
of Certain Performances and Displays   57

3.2   The Potential Mismatch of Performance Rights in a Musical
Work and a Sound Recording   67

6.1   The Ephemeral Recording Right under Section 112(f)   130

6.2   Discerning the Meaning of "Available to the Institution"
through Market Incentives   140

7.1   Making a Performance of an Audiovisual Work, in Excess
of the Section 110(2) Limitation   177

Foreword

Now is an exciting time for educators involved in the distance education environment, with new technologies offering a variety of tools and delivery mechanisms. However, conflict often accompanies change. In the distance education classroom, new technological protocols may challenge traditional practices, raise pedagogical issues, and fuel change. So, too, it is with law and technology. It might even appear that technology and copyright law, for example, are in a constant tug-of-war, between reality and ideology, between applying existing legal concepts to emerging technology and designing a legal infrastructure with foresight for change. It is fortunate that copyright law was amended in 2003 to accommodate some of these dynamics. Only time and personal opinion will tell how successful that foresight proves.

The current reality is that the Technology Education and Copyright Harmonization (TEACH) legislation provides sweeping changes in the way educators must act in the distance education environment. These changes are the focus of this book, the specific purpose of which is to provide a step-by-step explanation of the law involved. To a lesser extent, this book addresses related concepts in the distance education classroom, such as instructor ownership issues and a general application of fair use but not in as much detail, for several reasons. First, the related problems have always existed, whether the educational context is "distance" or not. For example, issues surrounding instructor ownership of classroom materials can arise in traditional or face-to-face instruction as well as the distance or online environments. These issues have some legal pedigree and have been discussed elsewhere in the courts or by commentators, often extensively by the latter. This is not to suggest that those issues are settled but that detailed presentation here would be redundant. Second, the law and legislative history for some of these related issues provide scant assistance. For example, there is little discussion, if any, about the creation of e-reserves in the legislative history, and only small handfuls of copy-shop course-pack cases have been reported. Thus, much of the discussion by commentators applying fair use to these concepts is supposition, even if informed supposition. Further, while there is as yet no case law on these new distance education provisions (a good sign, perhaps, as well), there is a detailed legislative history in the form of a Conference Report (as both the House and Senate passed versions of the legislation); a Conference Committee was formed, and its report, the Conference Report, serves as the significant source of that history throughout this text and supporting documentation.

First, a word about reading legal text and the nature of the developing law: As observed above, the law is so new that there is no case law interpreting these provisions, nor, for that matter, is there case law applying fair use (§107 of the copyright law) to distance education; we have only the words of the statute and the legislative history from which to discern legislative intent. Here it should be mentioned that using legislative history to interpret the text of a statute has its limitations. Some judges, for example do not like to rely upon it, Supreme Court Justice Scalia being the most famous example. However, in my experience, courts do often use the legislative history of the copyright law more often than not when it appears on point. Furthermore, with respect to the new distance education law discussed herein, the legislative history is extensive and offers explanation and context not offered by the text of the statute. Moreover, I have some experience with researching and writing on copyright issues in library and educational settings and have brought to bear that insight such as it is gained thereby on interpreting and applying the legislative history to the present task.

Some of the discussions of related issues and concepts herein do cite case law. I have emphasized recent copyright cases discussing digital environments and hypothesized a "qualified" trend in educational fair use. But again, with a dearth of case law, it is difficult to state with certainty the state of the law. In this climate the few cases that do exist often take on more significance than they otherwise might. For the same reason, a particular case or two may not necessarily represent "the law" of the entire country, as only a decision of the U.S. Supreme Court can do that. In legal actuality, a particular case only represents the law in the jurisdiction to which it applies; it may, however, represent the start of a trend, or at least would serve as persuasive precedent if a similar case were to arise in another jurisdiction. In an attempt to provide some inkling of the mind-set of recent court decisions, breadth is offered instead of depth. As a result, this discussion of the anti-circumvention and anti-trafficking rules of §1201 in chapter 2 or of fair use in chapter 7, for example, is not meant to be a comprehensive treatment of those related issues, as is the main discussion of TEACH §§110(2) and 112(f) in chapters 2, 3, 4, and 6. If it were, its bulk would defeat the purpose of this work, which is to make needed information accessible to a targeted readership. In the end it was a tactical decision to include at least an introductory discussion of some of the related provisions and background context of the new distance education copyright law in order to assist the reader in understanding that new law and the changes it brings, and more important, the issues the new distance education law does not address.

Any library that directly provides or indirectly supports the provision of distance education or materials therefore, or any educational entity itself, such as a school district, technical school, college, or university so engaged, should be aware of copyright considerations. More particularly, it is often the library or the media, computing, or information center that either by design or by default is the ombudsman of copyright compliance within the educational institution. I know of several books that discuss copyright issues in the educational realm, though most target particular communities such K–12 or higher education alone. This book applies to all settings, from primary to tertiary. Moreover, no book I know of is specific to distance education (save for a few scattered articles in the literature), and fewer still incorporate the new changes brought about by TEACH.

Copyright Law and the Distance Education Classroom is best viewed at an intermediate level, with perhaps the discussion of §112 at an intermediate to advanced level. This advice should not discourage the distance educator or administrator from spending time with it, as 17 U.S.C. §§110 and 112 are your educational "bread and butter," just as §108 is to librarians and archivists. If you know nothing about copyright law, do not become discouraged and reluctant to read on, but be aware of some limitations. While written here in as straightforward a style as possible, make no mistake, any rendering of copyright law can be tough stuff, especially for the novice and especially in light of the complexity of the new distance education provisions. The TEACH Q&A (appendix A) might be a good place to begin; at the end, it can serve as a review and implementation tool.

On the other hand, and by the same token, *everyone is in the same boat.* These provisions are still "newborn" in terms of copyright years, the legislation having been enacted in late 2002.

As a novice copyright reader, you have several choices for improving your grasp of the concepts and consequences of this newly enacted law. You might want to read and review one of the works listed in the bibliography to gain a basic understanding of copyright law concepts such as exclusive rights, fair use, and so on, which I do not cover in great detail here. Or you could have such an item at the ready when you feel the need to pause, back up, and breathe (a copyright sigh of relief of sorts). In the alternative you can press ahead, but be aware that there may be gaps in background or context information. These gaps, while disconcerting to some readers, should not inhibit you from proceeding and gaining a measure of success in understanding the copyright law as it applies to distance education. Moreover, endnotes supply some help with brief digressions regarding the background and context of a referenced concept.

I

UNDERSTANDING THE LIMITATIONS ON EXCLUSIVE RIGHTS FOR EDUCATORS

1

Performance and Display Rights in the Live Classroom and the Remote Classroom

The Need for Reform

W HEN MATERIALS ARE TO BE USED in the distance education classroom, copyright considerations can be approached through a series of steps. The first step is to determine whether the work is in fact protected by copyright or by some other legal right. (The latter category, including a trademark, trade secret, or contract [license], is beyond the scope of this book.)

The work in question may consist of material that is uncopyrightable. Facts, for example, are not protected by copyright, though the selection, coordination, or arrangement of those facts into some creative pattern might itself be copyrightable as a compilation.[1] This is the concept behind the copyright protection afforded to statistical and other fact-containing databases. Extraction of the unprotected fact would in theory be legal (though in practice often prohibited by contract), but since copying the database would capture the protected selection, coordination, or arrangement of those facts as well, it might be an infringing use of the database.[2] There is some case law to suggest that copying as an intermediate and noncompeting step to extraction is a fair use,[3] but the law is still under development here. Moreover, there have been legislative proposals to protect extraction of unprotected material.[4] Other material, such as titles or recipes (though the former might be protected by trademark), is not protected by copyright, either. And the duration of copyright protection, while substantial, is not indefinite, so the copyright on a protected work may have expired, with the result that the material has fallen into the public domain. (The concepts of copyright formation and duration are important but not possible to include within the confines of this book.)

Once it is established that the work is protected by copyright, the second step is some review of the scope of the copyright, starting with determining the exclusive rights of the copyright owner. While the exclusive rights of the copyright owner are extensive, they are not without limit.

Copyright owners have the following rights under §106:

1. to reproduce the copyrighted work in copies or phonorecords,
2. to prepare derivative works[5] based upon the copyrighted work,
3. to distribute copies or phonorecords of the copyrighted work to the public by sale or other transfer of ownership, or by rental, lease, or lending,
4. in the case of literary, musical, dramatic, and choreographic works, pantomimes, and motion pictures and other audiovisual works, to perform[6] the copyrighted work publicly,
5. in the case of literary, musical, dramatic, and choreographic works, pantomimes, and pictorial, graphic, or sculptural works, including the individual images of a motion picture or other audiovisual work, to display[7] the copyrighted work publicly, and
6. in the case of sound recordings, to perform the copyrighted work publicly by means of a digital audio transmission.[8]

Looking at it from the copyright user's perspective, this second step looks to whether the use an educator desires to make of the work somehow impinges or steps on the rights of the copyright owners. If the use does not, then there is no "copyright issue" even though the copyright law in fact protects the work. A simple example would be the viewing of a copyrighted audiovisual work (DVD) at home by an educator in conjunction with class preparation. While the viewing is a performance of a copyrighted work, it is not a "public performance." Thus, there is no copyright issue, because the right of the copyright owner extends only to public performances. In copyright law, these rights are known as exclusive rights.

The most important step is next: seeking support within the copyright law for the desired use. This entails examining whether any of the limitations on a copyright owner's exclusive rights apply to the intended use. These limitations come in two forms, specific and general. The *general limitation* is "fair use," found in §107 of the copyright law. (See chapter 7 for a discussion of the application of fair use principles to the distance education classroom.) For educators, a *specific limitation* is found in §110, with §110(1) designed specifically for face-to-face instruction and §110(2), the major focus of recent legislative reform and of this book, designed for distance education. In addition, a second supporting provision, §112(f), which offers a limitation on the exclusive reproduction right of copyright owners for material that is the subject of authorized uses under §110(2), is also part of the new TEACH law, discussed in detail in chapter 6.

The trick, so to speak, is to understand which exclusive right is impacted by an intended use and whether a specific limitations such as §110 or §112 applies. Alignment of rights and limitation not only indicates when a use is permissible but also suggests when recourse to a general limitation of fair use under §107 is otherwise necessary.

Consider the following basic distance classroom activities that an educator might undertake: read a story, show a movie clip, play a piece of recorded music, or discuss a portion of an assigned reading. Do any of these activities infringe on the exclusive rights of copyright owners? What if the instructor recorded his reading, made a copy of the movie and the recording to place on the institution's distance education server, and scanned and then loaded the text of the article onto the course website, all in order to facilitate access by students at a time convenient to the student? The nuances of these acts both in face-to-face and distance settings (the law is different for each!) are discussed in detail later, but a brief answer to this hypothetical case is presented here in order to demonstrate the importance of understanding the process.

First of all, a story is a category of literary work[9] known as a nondramatic literary work.

The copyright law recognizes eight categories of works[10]: literary works, including computer code; musical works, including accompanying words; dramatic works, including accompanying music; pantomimes and choreographic works; pictorial, graphic, and sculptural works,[11] so-called static-visual works; motion pictures and other audiovisual works, so-called active visual works; sound recordings; and architectural works.[12] Audiovisual works are "works that consist of a series of related images which are intrinsically intended to be shown by the use of machines or devices such as projectors, viewers, or electronic equipment, together with accompanying sounds, if any, regardless of the nature of the material objects, such as films or tapes, in which the works are embodied."[13] Notice that an audiovisual work need not have audio. This might appear illogical, but consider a silent film, which has no sound, obviously, but as a motion picture, a category of audiovisual work,[14] it is still protected as an audiovisual work.

Reading the story to a class would be a public performance,[15] but because educators have performance and display rights granted to qualifying classroom uses under §110, reading it in front of a class face-to-face or to online students is allowed. Making a recording of your reading is arguably a derivative work, as are most recorded performances of copyrighted material, as the educator created a sound recording of the work, itself a category of copyrighted work.[16] Keeping a copy of it for subsequent classroom use is arguably allowed under §112(f) or possibly §112(b). Showing the movie clip or playing the recorded music to a class is a public performance of an audiovisual work or musical work, respectively. In addition, the performer of the original recording may have a right in his or her recorded performance of it; that is, in the sound recording. However, there is no performance right in a sound recording unless it is by digital transmission. So playing the recording to a face-to-face class or broadcasting (a nondigital transmission) to remote students would be allowed under the same provisions that allowed the reading, because the only exclusive right impacted would be the performance of the nondramatic musical work (the score of the music that underlies the recording).

In order to distinguish between a sound recording (a category of copyrighted work),[17] and a recording of sounds (a "copy" of the sounds), the copyright law uses what might appear at first glance to be an odd term to encompass this latter concept: *phonorecord.* A phonorecord, used in many statutory phrases in conjunction with "copy," is defined as a "material object . . . in which sounds, other than those accompanying a motion picture or other audiovisual work, are fixed by any method now known or later developed, and from which the sounds can be perceived, reproduced, or otherwise communicated, either directly or with the aid of a machine or device. The term 'phonorecord' includes the material object in which the sounds are first fixed."[18] Recording each of these onto the server would be making a copy, and so the reproduction right is triggered. However, the ephemeral recording of the work under §112(f) as a precursor to a performance or display authorized under §110(2) is permitted. Scanning the article is also a reproduction, and its placement on the server would be a display, again both potentially covered by §§112(f) and 110(2), respectively. For example, an abridged book on tape would be a derivative work of the novel on which it is based. There is a sound recording copyright in the reading of it. The phonorecord of it is the cassette tape on which the sounds are fixed.

This simple example demonstrates the analysis that must be undertaken when an educator desires to use copyrighted material created by someone else. At other times the educator might desire to use material that he or she created—a series of case studies, lesson plans, exercises, quizzes, and tests, for example. Depending on the level at which the educator operates and the circumstances of the creation, ownership issues may arise between the educator as copyright owner and the institution—school or school district, college or university—as owner.

Who Owns Copyrights Used and Created in the Distance Education Classroom?

Deciding who owns what with respect to instructor-created material, either in the face-to-face classroom or the distance classroom, entails discussion of the work-for-hire doctrine. What is the nature of the relationship between instructor and institution? If the instructor is an employee, then the work-for-hire doctrine within the copyright law operates to vest the ownership rights over the material to the employer for works produced within the scope of employment.[19] However, there is some case law, discussed below, that suggests some courts are willing to read an exception for an instructor of higher education, even though the instructor is an employee of the institution. Often a tertiary institution may have a policy that grants to faculty the ownership rights to their scholarly and instructional creations. The legal alternative to employee status is categorization as an independent contractor. It is important to understand the implications of this difference.

The law in this area developed in the analog, face-to-face teaching environment, but its application to online instruction should occur without hesitation. Though some institutions may believe that the increased expenditure in the distance education classroom should impact the analysis—that is, the more the employer spends, the stronger its claim of ownership—nothing in the copyright law suggests that result. Of course, the case for employee ownership in distance environments remains just as tenuous with respect to online instructional material as it does with respect to face-to-face instructional material or to material first developed for face-to-face instruction that is now placed online.[20]

Understanding the Work-for-Hire Doctrine

Determining an educator's legal status for purposes of the copyright law and the work-for-hire doctrine requires not merely asking if the person is called an "employee" but asking, as well, whether or not the instructor is in fact an employee for purposes of the copyright law. The United States Supreme Court has addressed this issue and concluded that "the general common law of agency, rather than on the law of any particular State" should control.[21] The Court held that the Restatement of Agency,[22] Second (1958) is instructive in determining whether or not a person is an "employee" under general rules of agency. Drawing from agency concepts, the Supreme Court considered the following factors instructive when making that determination:

1. the extent of control over the details of the work, including the ability to assign other work to the hired party and the hired's ability to in turn hire and pay assistants,
2. the distinctness of the occupation or profession of the hired party,
3. the locality of the work (and whether the work is performed with or without direct physical supervision),
4. the skill level required,

5. which party supplies the instrumentality, tool, or place of work,
6. the duration of the work or project,
7. the method of payment (by time or by the entire project), including the provision of employee benefits, and the tax treatment of the hired party,
8. whether the work is part of the regular business of the employer,
9. the perception in the minds of both parties, and
10. whether the principal is in business as a matter of course.

It would appear that most faculty, lecturers, instructors, and teachers are employees for the purposes of the copyright law "work made for hire" doctrine and not independent contractors. Faculty hired to consult in some capacity at another institution (or even at their own institution) during summers, for example, might fall into independent contractor status for purposes of that consultation.

What about situations where the instructor works on his or her own time to create copyrighted instructional material? The work-for-hire doctrine appears to create a rather harsh result. When and where are less factors than inquiry into whether the work is of the kind the employee would create; that is, was employed to perform. Certainly the reader should agree with the legal logic that concludes that, if the employee as a part of his or her instructional duties is required to create a curriculum but chooses to write it at home, after work hours, or because of the practical time constraints of the job is forced to write it at home, "Neither case law nor the legislative history suggests that a person can avoid the 'work for hire' doctrine merely by preparing the work during non-working hours or in a facility not controlled by the employer. The mere fact that preparations were done outside an employee's office or normal working hours does not remove such preparations from the scope of employment."[23] The Restatement of Agency suggests that a servant's conduct is within the scope of employment "only if: (a) it is of the kind he is employed to perform; (b) it occurs substantially within the authorized time and space limits; [and] (c) it is actuated, at least in part, by a purpose to serve the master."[24] Now it might seem that an instructor who creates a series of exercises (a workbook) or subject tests or a complete curriculum, even if never used in the classroom (i.e., the instructor wanted to submit the work to a publisher) would not meet either of the last two criteria, and should be able to claim the copyright of the work as his or her own. However, as acknowledged by commentators, courts have not seen it that way.[25] Rather, when work is "of the kind" of work the employee is hired to create—and arguably in the above example, the exercises, test, or complete curriculum would surely fit—"[w]hen that element of the Restatement test is met, courts have tended not to grant employees authorship rights solely on the basis that the work was done at home on off-hours."[26]

Viewing Faculty as Independent Contractors

Since faculty would for purposes of the copyright law be considered employees, faculty work product falls under the work-for-hire doctrine, with ownership in the work created belonging to the school, school district, college or university, or other employer. However, this does not end the discussion. A faculty member may also be considered an independent contractor, even if performing duties similar to the duties undertaken, and for the same employer, for whom he or she is an employee.[27] However, this exception should not be relied upon by faculty seeking to have the work product of extracurricular activity classified as their own because of the reality of the all-consuming "publish or perish" environment in higher education. It would seem logical that a high school mathematics teacher who wrote a mystery novel on the weekends would own the copyright to the book, as it is not material of a kind he or she is normally employed to perform. However, it does appear that, under a reading of the statute as interpreted under the case law, the same teacher writing a workbook or test book on algebra on the weekends would not own the copyright in the work because it would surely be a "work prepared by an employee within the scope of his or her employment."

In those cases where someone other than an employee (that is, an independent contractor) prepared the work, then the ownership of the work can still reside in the school, school district, college or university, or other employer under an extension of the "work for hire" doctrine. This might occur where the instructor consults for another school, district school, school district, college or university, or other educational entity. The work produced by the independent contractor faculty may be treated as a work made for hire if the technical requirements of §101 are met. First, the educational institution or entity and the faculty must execute a written contract to that effect. Second, the work must fall within a limited number of nine statutory categories. The categories are as follows:

> ... as a contribution to a collective work, as part of a motion picture or other audiovisual work, as a translation, as a supplementary work, as a compilation, as an instructional text, as a test, an answer material for a test, or as an atlas.[28]

In independent-contractor cases outside those statutory categorizations, the most that can be hoped for is an assignment of copyright, or some portion of it, from the educator to the educational institution or employing entity. This option could include the sharing of ownership rights between the faculty member and the educational institution.

The Courts, Faculty Work Product, and the Development of a Faculty Ownership Right

When a faculty member is in fact an "employee," the work-for-hire doctrine operates to vest ownership of that work product—scholarly, curricular, and administrative (i.e., that work product that would fall within the scope of employment)—with the employer institution. However, this is not the end of the analysis, as persuasive precedent suggests that there is a recognized "teaching" exception to the work-for-hire doctrine for faculty at institutions of higher education.[29] Under the academic (scholarly work-product) or teaching (curricular work-product) exception to the work-for-hire doctrine, faculty hold the copyright associated with scholarly and curricular material produced, not the college or university. One commentator believes that this exception might also extend to the K-12 environment,[30] but the cases that have discussed this "exception" to the work-for-hire doctrine have applied it to faculty in higher education. Moreover, as developed by the courts, the exception applies only to faculty, not to other employees of the academy who would continue to have their work product governed by the work-for-hire doctrine.[31]

The issue of the existence of a teaching or faculty exception to the work-for-hire doctrine is by no means settled. The case law supporting such an exception appears only in one federal appellate circuit, the Seventh (covering the states of Wisconsin, Illinois, and Indiana), in opinions written by two former University of Chicago Law School faculty turned federal appellate judges. Moreover, the discussion appears as dicta and not as the holding of either case. In addition, an interpretive issue among the discussion of the courts and commentators is whether the doctrine survived either the 1976 Copyright Act or the Supreme Court's subsequent decision in *Community for Creative Non-violence v. Reid*. However, two commentators argue that there may be works created by employees that simply do not fall within the scope of employment and are therefore not covered by the work-for-hire doctrine, suggesting that those works might include scholarly and curricular work product.[32] Perhaps it is a distinction without a difference; the result is the same: Faculty own the copyright, either because the scholarly and curricular work product of employee faculty simply is not viewed as being within the scope of employment, or because it is within the scope of employment but an exception exists to otherwise remove it from the normal work-for-hire rules. Yet, the distinction is important. First, the former rule lacks the appeal of common sense, in that scholarly and curricular work product would be the obvious sort of thing faculty are employed to create. The latter rule also mitigates an illogic of institutional ownership of scholarly productivity: It might make invalid all the transfers of copyright that faculty have routinely executed upon publication of their respective articles and other works, as the copyright was not theirs to transfer. Second, it would not matter by which logic faculty come to own their scholarly and curricular work product if everyone played by the same rules. Wadley and Brown admit that an interpretation whereby some scholarly and curricular work product falls outside the scope of employment entails determination on a "case-by-case" and "task-by-task" basis, reflecting the expectations of both parties.[33] The problem with this approach is that not all employers have the same expectations, as some institutions assert stronger ownership claims than others do. (It is assumed that all faculty have the same expectation: ownership of their scholarly and curricular work product.) This would introduce a variable determination of authorship into the copyright law. Recognizing faculty ownership of scholarly and curricular work product by exception presents a "clean" resolution of the issue.

In contrast, there is recent precedent rejecting this exception, though with little discussion, if any, of it. In *University of Colorado v. American Cyanamid*, the district court observed that the "[p]laintiffs maintain the Regents 'are quite obviously the owner, because the article is a "work made for hire" by the coauthors done within the scope of their employment.' Plaintiffs argue Cyanamid has offered no evidence to rebut such ownership. I agree."[34] Subsequently, in *Vanderhurst v. Colorado Mountain College District*, in an opinion by a different judge of the same district court, the work-for-hire doctrine applied to the ownership of curricular material as well:

> It is undisputed that Vanderhurst prepared the Outline on his own time with his own materials. However, there is no genuine dispute that Vanderhurst's creation of the Outline was connected directly with the work for which he was employed to do and was fairly and reasonably incidental to his employment. Further, creation of the Outline may be regarded fairly as one method of carrying out the objectives of his employment.[35] I conclude, therefore, that pursuant to the "work for hire" doctrine, as of 1995, any copyright remaining in the Outline did not belong to Vanderhurst. Thus, I will grant defendants' motion for summary judgment on claim eight.[36]

It should be noted that while these cases represent more recent precedent, the cases are from a district court. If this issue arose in another circuit, the appellate decisions from the Seventh Circuit might have greater weight, though either series of cases would represent persuasive precedent only in courts outside of Colorado and the Seventh Circuit, respectively. What is in the mind of federal judges is difficult to discern and predict. Yet as recently as 2003, in *Foraste v. Brown University*, a district court looked to Seventh Circuit appellate precedent when commenting upon the faculty exception to the work-for-hire doctrine in an almost matter-of-fact reference, as if it were considered a widely acceptable doctrine.[37] Moreover, the majority of courts that have had occasion to discuss the concept have recognized the doctrine, citing public policy, the tradition of the academy, and the impracticalities of ownership over all faculty work product vesting with the employer. However welcome the result for college and university faculty, recognition of the exception contradicts the plain language of the statute. This contradiction underscores the equitable nature of the doctrine, and like other equitable concepts in the copyright law, such as fair use, its recognition by subsequent courts would not be "unprecedented" in the copyright law.

In addition to scholarly work product, faculty might also desire to assert a copyrightable interest in the lecture notes created to support a teaching endeavor and in the other fixed expressions of that teaching made by others as well, for example, student notetakers.[38] The copyrightability of faculty lectures can be complicated, as no copyrightable work is created until all the requirements of the statute are met: an original work of authorship fixed in a tangible medium.[39] Again, there is limited support in the case law for this position: "We are, however, convinced that in the absence of evidence the teacher, rather than the university, owns the common law copyright in his lectures."[40] This would by logic extend to a situation in which the lecture is routinely recorded as a part of the delivery of course content, for example, as simultaneous recordation during a distance education broadcast or live Web stream. Since the original and creative content of either recorded broadcast lectures or Internet Web-based instruction involves the fixation of teaching expression, the requirements for a valid copyrightable work are met (i.e., it is an original work of authorship fixed in a tangible medium).[41] Once the lectures are taped or transcribed, the work exists. The faculty is the author of the lecture regardless of whether the recording is made by the faculty, student, or third-party note-taking service. The issue, as with scholarly work product, is whether the faculty employee or the college or university employer owns the copyright in the recorded lectures. Therefore, in a jurisdiction recognizing the faculty exception to the work-for-hire doctrine, copyright should logically extend to cover the Web-based equivalent of lecture notes and, under the teaching exception to the work-for-hire doctrine, vest that ownership with the faculty. As a result, the ownership of that work, under the copyright law, belongs to the faculty, and storage of the work on an institutional facility should be at the direction or under the control of the instructor or faculty member. Consideration should be given to the subsequent storage and use of that protected expression by faculty and the educational institution. Can the faculty "take" those lectures and use them at another university, or sell the lectures to a commercial service in the same way faculty would a textbook? These issues remain unsettled in the courts. The important fact is that, if a broadcast or streamed lecture (or other analogous lecture note material) is recorded and stored on institutional facilities, a copyrighted work has been created.

University Copyright Policy and Faculty Ownership Issues

It should also be pointed out that many universities have a copyright policy in place similar to the one at issue in *Weinstein*, which defines conditions under which faculty output would be considered a work-for-hire and when it would be considered to belong to the faculty. Typically such a copyright policy is considered part of the employment contract with the university. In fact, for public institutions, it may be part of the state's administrative code. However, the unilateral nature of these documents makes them suspect as valid contracts,[42] even though they may be incorporated by reference into the actual employment contract, and, as discussed below, such policies remain invalid instruments of copyright transfer. Moreover, "the copyright statute seems to assume that there is no jurisdiction over copyrightable works under the statute until after the works are created and fixed, making an advance blanket release somewhat problematic."[43] In *Weinstein* the State of Illinois incorporated its copyright policy into each professor's contract. According to the policy, faculty retained the copyright to his or her scholarly output unless the work fell into one of three categories:

(1) The terms of a University agreement with an external party require the University to hold or transfer ownership in the copyrightable work, or (2) Works expressly commissioned in writing by the University, or (3) Works created as a specific requirement of employment or as an assigned University duty. Such requirements or duties may be contained in a job description or an employment agreement which designates the content of the employee's University work. If such requirements or duties are not so specified, such works will be those for which the topic or content is determined by the author's employment duties and/or which are prepared at the University's instance and expense, that is, when the University is the motivating factor in the preparation of the work.[44]

It is not clear from the policy whether the University of Illinois was merely recognizing faculty ownership then carving out exceptions to it or was asserting its rights under the work-for-hire doctrine but granting faculty ownership in works outside the three articulated categories. The appellate court appears to split the difference, acknowledging the work-for-hire concept in the faculty setting but implying that some works are not included by it. What remains unclear is whether the court felt the exclusion was by operation of law or operation of the policy. If the latter, the court ignored the validity of a transfer of copyright vis-à-vis an institutional policy with the result that such policies are insufficient to effect such transfers.

In light of the "publish or perish" atmosphere of the university setting (with scholarly writing a condition of tenure), the district court interpreted that the third provision covered scholarly work product. However, the Seventh Circuit disagreed. According to the appellate court, the trial court had misinterpreted the university's work made-for-hire policy. According to the Seventh Circuit, the University of Illinois work made-for-hire policy appeared to apply "more naturally" to administrative reports than to journal articles or other scholarly work product.[45] Therefore, there is some legal support for the argument that faculty scholarly output, even when it is employment-dependent with respect to tenure requirements, is not within "employment duties" nor is it prepared at "the University's instance and expense," as those terms are used in an institutional policy and at least according to the Seventh Circuit. For faculty at institutions with similar policy language, such a policy would at least not stand in the way of ownership rights vesting in the faculty as the scholarly work product of the faculty, if not included by those terms of the policy.

Another factor to consider is that a university copyright policy may contain language indicating that if the university incurs extraordinary expense in the support or production of faculty output then the university shall have ownership rights in the works produced. A university may want to argue that the investment in distance education programs would meet these somewhat specious standards. However, the case law from the Seventh Circuit again suggests otherwise. In *Hays v. Sony Corporation of America*, the court commented:

> Although college and university teachers do academic writing as a part of their employment responsibilities and use their employer's paper, copier, secretarial staff, and (often) computer facilities in that writing, the universal assumption and practice was that (in the absence of an explicit agreement as to who had the right to copyright) the right to copyright such writing belonged to the teacher rather than to the college or university.[46]

The point can be made that in the technology-infused classroom of the twenty-first century, as well as in distance education environments, the use of expensive technology should not be seen as "extraordinary" and trigger policy provisions vesting ownership with the institution. The high price of new technology is simply another cost of doing business in the distance education environment, much like the photocopier or overhead projector in days past or more recently the personal computer and LCD projector.

Many university policies granting copyright ownership rights to faculty are based on the implicit presumption that the work-for-hire doctrine operates to vest the institution with ownership of all faculty work product and that the university "hands over" copyright to the faculty pursuant to its policy instrument as a benevolent gesture (I am not entirely objective on this point). For the moment, assume that the work-for-hire doctrine does indeed control all faculty work product and, further, that no faculty exception exists. Then the use of a policy to transfer copyright actually raises more problems for the university and its faculty than it attempts to solve, as the unilateral nature of policy formation may not constitute a valid contract for purposes of the copyright law, with the result that no transfer has occurred and the institution still retains the copyright.

This would call into question the validity of the intended transfer of copyright from faculty member to publisher. Judging from the industry tumult that resulted when many newspaper publishers realized that existing contracts with their authors failed to vest publishers with electronic republishing rights, so that subsequent transfers the newspapers made to online database vendors were invalid,[47] the impact of this reality upon the scholarly publishing industry would be incalculable.

Exacerbating this scenario is recent precedent indicating that a unilateral statement in an institutional policy is *not* an adequate instrument of transfer under the copyright law, if in fact the initial ownership lies with the university vis-à-vis the work-for-hire doctrine and the university so desires to transfer that ownership to the faculty, in the benevolent gesture scenario. The work-for-hire doctrine, articulated in §201, does not allow an employer to revoke its "authorship" in the "work made for hire" or unilaterally "waive" or transfer its ownership of its copyright by unilateral mechanism. If the work-for-hire doctrine truly vests the copyright ownership of all employee work product, including that of faculty, with the institution, then a statement in the institution's policy that it waives or transfers those ownership rights is *not* effective under the copyright law. This is true because the plain language of §201(b) states that:

> In the case of a work made for hire, *the employer* or other person for whom the work was prepared *is considered the author* for purposes of this title, and, unless the *parties have expressly agreed* otherwise in a written instrument signed by them, owns all of the rights comprised in the copyright.[48]

As a result, the only effective way to alter the ownership ordering of the work-for-hire doctrine would be either by court-created exception to the work-for-hire rule in the first instance, as discussed above, or by an express written instrument signed by all parties to the transfer. As the district court observed in *Foraste v. Brown University*:

> It would defy that intention [to safeguard employers' authorship and ownership rights] to accept the claim that an employer could transfer copyright ownership in a work made for hire to an employee without complying with the strict requirements of section 201(b)'s "unless" clause.[49]

Obviously, as the distance environment continues to increase the portability of faculty scholarly and curricular work product, the unresolved issues developed over the years with respect to the faculty exception to the work-for-hire doctrine will increase the importance of these issues to both faculty and institution.

Of course, these transfer issues become moot if the faculty exception operates to vest the faculty member with copyright ownership of his or her scholarly and curricular work product vis-à-vis a recognition of the faculty as author, in contrast to the §201(b) "employer . . . considered the author" with its attendant rights of ownership mechanism requiring an express written bilateral agreement. In that instance, a transfer of copyright from the faculty to the institution would be governed *not* by the strict §201(b) work-for-hire transfer rules but by the more liberal §201(d) and §204(a) rules allowing unilateral transfers through "an instrument of conveyance, or a note or memorandum of the transfer." In other words, a transfer from the employer-as-owner to the employee is effected by the strict §201(b) work-for-hire transfer rules, while an employee-as-owner to publisher or employer transfer occurs under the less strict §201(d) and §204(a) rules. Moreover, the *Foraste v. Brown University* court found the policy lacking as a §204(a) instrument of transfer as well.[50] While there is dispute among courts as to the particulars of a valid §204 transfer, even the *Foraste v. Brown University* court concluded that the nature of the works and the specific rights transferred or reserved would need to be identified.[51] It is obvious that most university polices would fail this minimum.

Again, drawing sweeping conclusions from a single district court case is tenuous at best, but it is an indication of the sort of issues entailed in any transfer from faculty to institution or vice versa with respect to a policy. Until these issues are resolved, the most prudent course of action would be to articulate the copyright status of faculty work product in specific agreements and not to rely on institutional policy to effect the desired result.

A Brief Review of the §110(1) Rights of Educators in Face-to-Face Teaching: A Starting Point

To see how the copyright law limits the exclusive rights of copyright owners, an examination of §110(1) can be made. This accomplishes several purposes. First, it is a good way to understand how a significant "limitation" provision is structured and works in practice. It also demonstrates the use of legislative history to help understand a provision of the law. Section 110(1) is relatively easy to understand—easy, compared to the complexities of the new law. Understanding the less complicated §110(1), applying to face-to-face teaching environments, will help in understanding the more complex §110(2) enacted as part of TEACH. Moreover, when compared to the brief discussion below of the prior law relating to §110(2), the need for the new TEACH should be obvious. In addition, comparing the new rights of distance educators created by TEACH (and discussed in the following two chapters) with the rights of educators in face-to-face settings might lead the reader to the conclusion that the new law did not go far enough.

In any event, recognizing the differences between the rights of educators and students in face-to-face versus distance teaching is critical as educators develop hybrid models of education in which some students are "live" and others are "remote" or some of the instruction is face-to-face and some is transmitted (through Internet technology, for example). The copyright law through §110(1) and (2) establishes circumstances under which use (performance and display) of copyright material may be made in "face-to-face teaching activities"[52] and "by or in the course of a transmission,"[53] respectively. However, the law does not care if the student receiving the transmission is two blocks away accessing instructional material from a dorm room, two miles away at home, or two continents away. In each instance the instruction is "by or in the course of a transmission" and would come under the rules of §110(2) designed for remote or distance education. In the case of our dorm student enrolled in a hybrid class (some instruction "live" and some instruction "online"), when the "live" series of lectures reconvenes later in the semester in a campus lecture hall, §110(1) will govern the performance or display of copyrighted material, not §110(2).

The most important feature of either §110(1) or §110(2) is that the limitations on the copyright owner's exclusive rights granted by its provisions apply to only two of the rights that copyright owners possess: the performance right and the display right (see table 1.1). This does not mean that other uses cannot be made, but just as when there is a performance or display beyond the limitations of §110, legal support for the use must come from some other specific limitations of the copyright, the general limitation of fair use, or license.

"To 'perform' a work means to recite, render, play, dance, or act it, either directly or by means of any device or process or, in the case of a motion picture or other audiovisual work, to show its images in any sequence or to make the sounds accompanying it audible."[54] Performance can apply to literary works, musical works, dramatic works, pantomimes and choreographic works, motion pictures and other audiovisual works, and sound recordings. In general, sound recordings have no performance right. An educator can always play an LP record, but the underlying music (musical work) of the composer and lyricist remains subject to the performance right. The performance of the musical work (i.e., the underlying melody and lyrics embodied in the sound recording on an LP, cassette, or CD) is what the §110(1) right grants. However, a sound recording has a performance right associated with it when the recording is performed by digital audio transmission.[55] But since a §110(1) face-to-face teaching encounter does not involve a "transmission" under the

TABLE 1.1
Current Law: 17 U.S.C. §110(1)

Exclusive Right of the Copyright Owner to Which the Limitation Applies	Work of Authorship: Category of Copyrighted Material	Portion of the Work that May Be Performed or Displayed	Examples in the Classroom
Performance	Any category of copyrighted work that can be performed	No limitation on the portion (amount) of a work that can be performed	
	Literary works		Reading from a book
	Musical works		Playing a tune on a piano
	Dramatic works		Acting out a play
	Pantomimes/ choreographic works		Dancing a number from a Broadway musical
	Motion pictures/ other audiovisual works		Showing a movie or a narrated filmstrip
	Derivative works		Playing a Gershwin tune on the piano that has been adapted for beginners
Display	Any category of copyrighted work that can be displayed	No limitation on the portion (amount) of a work that can be performed	
			Projecting multiple images of the . . .
	Literary works		. . . text of a poem
	Musical works		. . . the score of a song
	Dramatic works		. . . the script of a play
	Pantomimes/ choreographic works		. . . a script of dance
	Pictorial, graphic and sculptural works		. . . a slide of a painting
	Architectural works		. . . blueprints of a building
	Derivative works		. . . the score of a song the teacher adapted for a younger audience

copyright law, a §110(1) educator need not be concerned with the limited performance right in sound recordings.

Other items in the classroom may be displayed: "To 'display' a work means to show a copy of it, either directly or by means of a film, slide, television image, or any other device or process or, in the case of a motion picture or other audiovisual work, to show individual images nonsequentially."[56] Some categories of works can be performed, although others can only be displayed. For example, an educator typically does not perform a piece of sculpture; likewise one does not display a sound recording. But an educator can display the sheet music (musical work) of the song. Display can apply to musical, pictorial, graphic, and sculptural and architectural works. Some works, of course, can be both performed and displayed. For example, an educator could display and discuss the composition techniques within a particular score of music (a musical work), then perform it for students to demonstrate variations in interpretation. In either case of performance or display, there is no limitation of the portion of the work used. As discussed below, this is an important difference between the old law and the new TEACH law.

In addition, §110(1) limits who may make the performance or display. The performance or display in subsection (1) must be made by instructors or pupils and cannot be done by guest performers or students not enrolled in the class. But the legislative history suggests that a guest lecturer is covered by the exception and may perform or display works consistent with the section's other conditions.[57] The major limitation that §110(1) does impose on educators in "live" class settings is tied to the statutory language requiring that qualifying performances and displays occur within the context "of face-to-face teaching activities of a nonprofit educational institution, in a classroom or similar place devoted to instruction." Transmissions—"remote broadcasts"— are not allowed. However, the "concept does not require that the teacher and the students be able to see each other, although it does require their simultaneous presence in the same general place."[58] As long as the instructor and pupil are in the same building or general area, even though the performance might be "broadcast" via in-house, closed-circuit television, the exemption applies. Also excluded under §110(1) are works performed or displayed, "whatever their cultural value or intellectual appeal, that are given for the recreation or entertainment of any part of their audience."[59] Section 110(1) would not authorize the use of a movie as a reward or a rainy-day recess filler or to an audience outside the enrolled members of the class, such as the chess club or parents' group that might like to watch *Searching for Bobby Fisher* in preparation for the upcoming tournament.

Finally, a condition is placed on the use audiovisual works under §110(1): "[I]n the case of a motion picture or other audiovisual work, or the display of individual images" from it, the performance right granted to educators by

§110(1) does not apply if "the person responsible for the performance knew or had reason to believe [that the work] was not lawfully made."[60] The "person" could be the teacher or it could be a student. Like other provisions of specific limitation on copyright owner's exclusive rights impacting educators and librarians, the use right granted by the limitation is conditioned on the copy or phonorecord of the work used being a lawfully made copy, not a bootleg or pirated copy. Several such "lawfully made" requirements are found in §109. For example, "The transfer of possession of a *lawfully made copy* of a computer program by a nonprofit educational institution to another nonprofit educational institution or to faculty, staff, and students does not constitute rental, lease, or lending for direct or indirect commercial purposes under this subsection."[61] The rationale behind such a condition is to eliminate any incentive for making unlawful copies, as the use of those copies cannot underlie an otherwise legitimate performance and display under §110 or distribution under §109. As discussed in chapter 2, TEACH requires that all uses pass this "legitimate" copy or phonorecord test.

As the definition of "display" intimates, display includes the presentation of the work by device or process, though it could also be made by film, slide, or television image. The exemption to the exclusive right of display granted by §110(1) thus grants educators the right to use an overhead or slide projector, or LCD or other panel display device to present copyrighted material. According to the 1976 legislative history, "As long as there is no transmission beyond the place where the copy is located, both section 109(b) [now section 109(c)] and section110(1) would permit the classroom display of a work by means of any sort of projection device or process."[62]

Notice that table1.1, in the "Examples in the Classroom" column, under "Display," does not include more obvious examples of classroom displays such as holding up a map or chart or poster. This is because §109(c) provides that "notwithstanding the provisions of section 106(5) [establishing the exclusive right of display], the owner of a particular *copy lawfully made* under this title, or any person authorized by such owner, is entitled, without the authority of the copyright owner, *to display that copy publicly*, either directly or by the projection of no more than one image at a time, to viewers present at the place where the copy is located."[63] Section 109(c) gives anyone the right to make a public display of a lawfully made copy.[64] For example, §109(c) allows an educator (or anyone, for that matter) to make a public display of a map or transparency of a map to a group gathered in the same place where the copy is located, such as a library meeting or reading room or a classroom. "The exclusive right of public display granted by section 106(5) would not apply where the owner of a copy wishes to show it directly to the public, as in a gallery or display case, or indirectly, as through an opaque projector. Where the copy itself is intended for projection, as in the case of a photographic slide, negative, or transparency, the public projection of a *single image* would be permitted as long as the viewers are 'present at the place where the copy is located.'"[65] However, it would not necessarily authorize the projection of it throughout a school to numerous classrooms or the broadcast of the image to remote students. "The concept of 'the place where the copy is located' is generally intended to refer to a situation in which the viewers are present in the same physical surroundings as the copy, even though they cannot see the copy directly."[66] The display right that §110(1) grants that §109(c) does not—that without §110(1) what would still be retained by the copyright owner under the §106(5) display right might be characterized as a dual display right of sorts (i.e., why §110(1) is still needed)—is the right to display multiple images or to use "new communications media, notably television, cable and optical transmission devices, and information storage and retrieval devices"[67] to display copyrighted materials to a remote audience.

Recall that §110(1) is not a distance education provision, even though the list of technologies quoted in the legislative history might suggest that application. However, the sorts of displays covered by the §110(1) privilege that are not acceptable under the more "generic" §109(c) display right are suggested by the 1976 legislative history of §109(b)(now §109(c)); that section would not exempt "the simultaneous projection of multiple images of the work . . . where each person in a lecture hall is supplied with a separate viewing apparatus."[68] This would be an example of a face-to-face teaching display for which the generic "single" display provision of §109(c) would not be available but §110(1) would be needed and available, as the §110(1) display privilege places no limit on the number of displays (multiple projections of the same work at the same time) that could be made. So, too, the §110(1) legislative history provides for the use of "new communication media," to use the language of §109(b) (now §109(c)) legislative history, beyond that contemplated by §109. For example, the "concept does not require that the teacher and the students be able to see each other, although it does require their simultaneous presence in the same general place."[69] The same building or general area would apply; for example, a closed-circuit transmission is permitted when used to "beam" the class session and its displays of copyrighted material from the main lecture room to students gathered in adjoining or satellite rooms on other floors in the same building and at the same time. However, §109(c) would not authorize a local symphony group to host a guest lecture before a concert where the lecture and slides are "beamed" (displayed) throughout the community arts center using the facility's closed-circuit television system. Section 110(1) would not "authorize" the display of the slides, either, because §110(1) is an educators' provision, for use by schools, colleges, universities, and other educational institutions.[70] While §109(c) applies to all uses, §110 doesn't. This is the value of the §110(1) and, as discussed in chapter 2, of the §110(2) performance and display privilege, a privilege not available to other users, even other nonprofit institutions or community groups such as the local symphony in the above example or the public library.

A Brief Look at the Prior Law (or How Educators Used to Violate Copyright Law in Distance Education Settings)

Since the amendment by TEACH to §110(2) was significant, there is little need to review its original operation in detail, though a brief review can have several advantages. First, the need for reform becomes apparent, and looking to the future, an educator may conclude that TEACH did not go far enough and that further amendment is necessary. Second, several of the concepts that were reaffirmed in the TEACH reformulation of §110(2) derive from §110(1) or were carried over from pre-TEACH §110(2). Understanding the way in which §110(2) used to be applied thus can assist somewhat in determining its current and future application.

Under the old law, while there was no limitation on the portion of a copyrighted work that could be performed or displayed, that performance or display was limited to either displays or to performances of two very narrow categories of copyrighted material: nondramatic literary and nondramatic musical work (see table 1.2). A significant exclusion was audiovisual works, such as those embodied in a VHS tape or DVD. Of course, fair use could have justified showing a portion of the work, but it would unlikely have justified a public performance of an entire motion picture; more likely than not, a performance license would have been obtained by the distance educator. Thus a performance license or other permission was needed to perform a dramatic, pantomime, or choreographic work, or motion picture or other audiovisual work. According to the 1976 pre-TEACH legislative history,

> the copyright owner's permission would be required for the performance on educational television or radio of a dramatic work, of a dramatico-musical work such as an opera or musical comedy, or of a motion picture. Since, as already explained, audiovisual works such as filmstrips are equated with motion pictures, their sequential showing would be regarded as a performance rather than a display and would not be exempt under section 110(2).[71]

This exclusion is a major reason why the expansion of educator rights in TEACH was promoted by distance education advocacy groups. Moreover, §110(2), in the pre-TEACH version, also excluded from use or failed to in-

TABLE 1.2
Section 110(2), Pre-TEACH Law Limitations on Exclusive Rights: Exemption of Certain Performances and Displays

Exclusive Right of the Copyright Owner to Which the Limitation Applies	*Work of Authorship: Category of Copyrighted Material*	*Portion of the Work that May Be Performed or Displayed*	*Examples in the Classroom*
Performance	Nondramatic literary works	No limitation on the portion (amount) of a work that can be performed	Broadcast ("transmission") of the reading of a novel or short story
	Nondramatic musical works	No limitation on the portion (amount) of a work that can be performed	Broadcast ("transmission") of the singing of a song or the whistling of its melody
Display	Any work to which the display right applies	No limitation on the portion (amount) of a work that can be displayed	Broadcasting ("transmission") a display of any of the following:
	Literary works		. . . the text of a poem
	Musical works		. . . the score of a song
	Dramatic works		. . . the script of a play
	Pantomimes/ choreographic works		. . . the script of a dance
	Pictorial, graphic, and sculptural works		. . . a slide of a painting
	Architectural works		. . . the blueprints of a building
	Derivative works		. . . a Bernstein score that has been adapted for high school jazz bands

clude, for purposes of the limitation on the copyright owner's exclusive rights, §106(2) works (i.e., derivative works). For example, §110(2) "is not intended to limit in any way the copyright owner's exclusive right to make dramatizations, adaptations, or other derivative works under section 106(2). Thus, for example, a performer could read a nondramatic literary work aloud under section

110(2), but the copyright owner's permission would be required for him to act it out in dramatic form."[72] If a work itself was a derivative work (a category of copyrighted work), it could be displayed or possibly performed (if a nondramatic literary work such as a book based on a screenplay or musical work such as a poem set to music), but the educator could not under §110(2) make the derivative work him- or herself, as this is an exclusive right of the copyright owner—again, subject to a general fair use right of the educator to do so.

Similar to the requirement in the §110(1) face-to-face right provision, §110(2)(A) required that the performance or display be a "regular part of the systematic instructional activities"; that is, the performance or display must be incorporated into actual teaching. The legislative history suggests this is broader than the curriculum alone. The "concept of 'systematic instructional activities' is intended as the general equivalent of 'curriculums,' but it could be broader in a case such as that of an institution using systematic teaching methods not related to specific course work,"[73] but which would still be part of "instructional activities" overall. An example might be a technology-literacy session not tied to a specific course but designed as a preparation for students beginning a distance education degree program. Second, under prior §110(2)(B) the performance or display must be "directly related and of material assistance to the teaching content" of the class; that is, it cannot be for recreation or entertainment. According to the TEACH Conference Report, which also refers to the Register's Report,[74] and relating it to the pre-TEACH previous §110(2)(B) requirement, "this test of relevance and materiality connects the copyrighted work to the curriculum, and it means that the portion performed or displayed may not be performed or displayed for the mere entertainment of the students, or as unrelated background material."[75] In other words, the 1976 legislative history that created §110(2) did not comment on the exclusion of works for entertainment or recreational purposes, but the 2002 TEACH legislative history read such limitation into the previous §110(2) privilege and incorporated the exclusion into the TEACH §110(2) formulation as well. In terms of the evolving nature of distance education, the most debilitating requirement of the prior law was that under §110(2)(C)(i), the performance or display must be "made primarily for . . . reception in classrooms or similar places devoted to instruction." Under §110(2)(C), factors determining whether the purpose of a transmission is "primarily" for one of the permissible designated groups—(1) traditional classroom students, (2) disabled or other special student groups such as preschool children, displaced workers, illiterates, and shut-ins, or (3) government employees as part of a training exercise, the latter two categories covered in current 110(2)(C)(ii) and (iii), respectively—include the "subject matter, content and the time" of the transmission.[76] Finally, was the previous law limited to analog uses only? Language in the TEACH Conference Report suggests that a pre-TEACH distance education display could only be analog. "This limitation [the display of works under TEACH] is a further implementation of the 'mediated instructional activities' concept described below, and recognizes that a 'display' may have a different meaning and impact in the digital environment *than in the analog environment* to which section 110(2) had previously applied."[77] While the use of the word "transmission" could be interpreted broadly enough to apply to the now-prevalent distance education scenario of Web-based digital transmissions of today, the 1976 legislative history entitled the discussion of §110(2) with the words "Instructional Broadcasting," which does suggest analog. Moreover, the word "broadcast" is used repeatedly, as well as explanatory text linking it to traditional and analog television-type transmissions, throughout the legislative history of pre-TEACH §110(2). In any event, these concerns are moot with the passage of TEACH, a law that applies to both analog and digital transmissions. However, as discussed in detail below, additional requirements are forced on the educational entity when instructional content is performed or displayed by means of a digital transmission.

Notes

1. 17 U.S.C. 101 ("A 'compilation' is a work formed by the collection and assembling of preexisting materials or of data that are selected, coordinated, or arranged in such a way that the resulting work as a whole constitutes an original work of authorship. The term 'compilation' includes collective works.").

2. *Assessment Technologies of WI, LLC. v. Wiredata, Inc.*, 350 F.3d 640, 643 (7th Cir. 2003) ("But WIREdata doesn't want the Market Drive compilation. It only wants the raw data, the data the assessors imputed into Market Drive" and suggesting that if WIREdata did so desire that form, made a request, and the municipalities made such a copy of the compilation "they would be infringing AT's copyright because they are not licensed to make copies of Market Drive for distribution to others; and WIREdata would be a contributory infringer [subject to a qualification concerning the fair-use defense to copyright infringement, including contributory infringement, that we discuss later]." Id. at *6–*7.).

3. *Ticketmaster Corp. v. Tickets.com*, 2000 U.S. Dist. LEXIS 12987 (C.D. Calif. 2000) ("Reverse engineering to get at unprotected functional elements is not the same process as used here but the analogy seems to apply. The copy is not used competitively. It is destroyed after its limited function is done. It is used only to facilitate obtaining non-protectable data—here the basic factual data. It may not be the only way of obtaining that data (i.e., a thousand scriveners with pencil and paper could do the job given time), but it is the most efficient way, not held to be an impediment in Connectix [*Sony Computer Entertainment v. Connectix Corp.* 203 F.3d 596 (9th Cir. 2001)]." TM [Ticketmaster] makes the point that copying the URL (the electronic address to the Web pages)

which is not destroyed, but retained and used, is copying protected material. The court doubts that the material is protectable because the URL appears to contain functional and factual elements only and not original material. Id. at *12-*13.).

4. See H.R. 3261, 108th Cong., 1st Sess. (2003) (Database and Collections of Information Misappropriation Act); H.R. 3872, 108th Cong., 2d Sess. (2004) (Consumer Access to Information Act of 2004). See also Jonathan Band and Makoto Kono, The Database Protection in the 106th Congress, 62 *Ohio State Law Journal* 869 (2001).

5. 17 U.S.C. 101 (A derivative work is defined as "a work based upon one or more preexisting works, such as a translation, musical arrangement, dramatization, fictionalization, motion picture version, sound recording, art reproduction, abridgment, condensation, or any other form in which a work may be recast, transformed, or adapted. A work consisting of editorial revisions, annotations, elaboration, or other modification which, as a whole, represent an original work of authorship, is a 'derivative work.'").

6. 17 U.S.C. 101 ("To 'perform' a work means to recite, render, play, dance, or act it, either directly or by means of any device or process or, in the case of a motion picture or other audiovisual work, to show its images in any sequence or to make the sounds accompanying it audible.").

7. 17 U.S.C. 101 ("To 'display' a work means to show a copy of it, either directly or by means of a film, slide, television image, or any other device or process or, in the case of a motion picture or other audiovisual work, to show individual images nonsequentially."). Some categories of works can be performed, although others can only be displayed; you cannot perform a piece of sculpture, nor can you display a song.

8. 17 U.S.C. 106.

9. 17 U.S.C. 101 ("'Literary works' are works, other than audiovisual works, expressed in words, numbers, or other verbal or numerical symbols or indicia, regardless of the nature of the material objects, such as books, periodicals, manuscripts, phonorecords, film, tapes, disks, or cards, in which they are embodied.").

10. 17 U.S.C. 102.

11. Pictorial, graphic, and sculptural works "include two-dimensional and three-dimensional works of fine, graphic, and applied art, photographs, prints and art reproductions, maps, globes, charts, technical drawings, diagrams, and models." 17 U.S.C. 101.

12. 17 U.S.C. 101 ("An 'architectural work' is the design of a building as embodied in any tangible medium of expression, including a building, architectural plans, or drawings. The work includes the overall form as well as the arrangement and composition of spaces and elements in the design, but does not include individual standard features.").

13. 17 U.S.C. 101.

14. Motion pictures "are audiovisual works consisting of a series of related images which, when shown in succession, impart an impression of motion, together with accompanying sounds, if any." 17 U.S.C. 101.

15. Kenneth D. Crews, Distance Education and Copyright Law: The Limits and Meaning of Copyright Policy, 27 *Journal of College and University Law* 15, 23–24 (2000) ("The live, face-to-face classroom could arguably be a place open to the public. Even if entrance is limited to enrolled students, the assembled students in any particular course are likely beyond the customary circle of family and friends. Similarly, when the performances and displays are transmitted to other locations in the name of distance education, they may

also be received by similar groups of students constituting the 'public.' Moreover, in the case of a transmission of the educational content, received by students at their own time and place as distance education, the activity can be 'public' even though the students are receiving the content in 'separate places' and 'at different times.'").

16. Section 106(6) covers the performance of sound recordings and provides for the exclusive right by the copyright owner to "perform the copyrighted work publicly by means of a digital audio transmission." 17 U.S.C. 106(6). Sound recordings in essence capture the rendering of an original expression, the presentation of a speech or lecture, the singing or playing of a musical work, or the reading of a text or other literary work. Unless the expression is completely ad lib or spontaneous, sound recordings are often based on a pre-existing work, and are therefore a form of derivative work. For example, a CD made by Ashley Judd, Jason Patric, Ned Beatty, and others of the 2003 Broadway revival of *Cat on a Hot Tin Roof* is a sound recording, and thus by its nature, derivative of a dramatic literary work; i.e., the original Tennessee Williams play about a dysfunctional Southern family.

17. A sound recording is a "work[] that result[s] from the fixation of a series of musical, spoken, or other sounds, but not including the sounds accompanying a motion picture or other audiovisual work, regardless of the nature of the material objects, such as disks, tapes, or other phonorecords, in which they are embodied." 17 U.S.C. 101. An example would be represented by a reel-to-reel tape of a famous speech, an LP cassette of a rock group, a cassette of a Broadway show, or a CD of a dramatic reading from a classic novel.

18. 17 U.S.C. 101.

19. 17 U.S.C. 102(b) ("In the case of a work made for hire, the employer or other person for whom the work was prepared is considered the author for purposes of this title, and, unless the parties have expressly agreed otherwise in a written instrument signed by them, owns all of the rights comprised in the copyright.").

20. However, in the online setting the stakes seem to be higher. As one commentator observed: "In response to changing technology, many schools are suddenly rewriting their policies on how professors may use course material. Why the sudden interest? The answer is simple: Money." Gregory Kent Laughlin, Who Owns the Copyright to Faculty-Created Web Sites?: The Work-for-Hire Doctrine's Applicability to Internet Resources Created for Distance Learning and Traditional Classroom Courses, 41 *Boston College Law Review* 549, 556 (2000) (footnotes omitted). See also Elizabeth Townsend, Legal and Policy Responses to the Disappearing "Teacher Exception," or Copyright Ownership in the 21st Century University, 4 *Minnesota Intellectual Property Review* 209, 211 (2003) ("This notion of 'teacher exception' has been called into question in the last twenty years, in part because of the new copyright law of 1976, and in part because of new technologies that increased the potential economic interest in course content, scholarly writings, distance learning, commercial note-taking ventures, and multimedia and software projects.").

21. *Community for Creative Nonviolence v. Reid*, 490 U.S. 730, 740 (1989).

22. Restatement (Second) of Agency §228 (1958).

23. *Marshall v. Miles Laboratory, Inc.*, 647 F. Supp. 1326, 1330 (N.D. Ind. 1986).

24. Restatement (Second) of Agency §228 (1958).

25. See Ashley Packard, Copyright or Copy Wrong: An Analysis of University Claims to Faculty Work, 7 *Communications Law & Policy* 275, 280 (2002) ("Using these criteria, faculty members appear to be employees operating under the work-for-hire doctrine. Consequently, universities would be entitled to claim the copyright to professors' intellectual work, unless professors could prove their creative work fell outside the scope of their employment."); Gregory Kent Laughlin, Who Owns the Copyright to Faculty-Created Web Sites?: The Work-for-Hire Doctrine's Applicability to Internet Resources Created for Distance Learning and Traditional Classroom Courses, 41 *Boston College Law Review* 549, 575 (2000) ("Given the Miller [*Miller v. CP Chemicals, Inc.*, 808 F. Supp. 1238 (D.S.C. 1992)] and Marshall [*Marshall v. Miles Laboratory, Inc.*, 647 F. Supp. 1326 (N.D. Ind. 1986)] cases, it is hard to imagine that a court would find that faculty-created scholarly articles, books and teaching materials are not prepared within the scope of employment."); and Michele J. Le Moal-Gray, Distance Education and Intellectual Property: The Realities of Copyright Law and the Culture of Higher Education, 16 *Touro Law Review* 981, 1000 (2000) ("The work faculty members produce will normally fall 'within the scope' of the courses they teach and the field of study they have been hired to pursue.").

26. *Avtec Systems, Inc. v. Pfeiffer*, 805 F. Supp. 1312 (E.D. Va. 1992), aff'd in part, rev'd in part and remanded, 21 F.3d 568, 571 (4th Cir. 1994) (citing *Miller v. CP Chemicals, Inc.*, 808 F. Supp. 1238, 1242–44 (D.S.C. 1992)) (computer program prepared at home during off-hours, without direction or extra compensation from employer, held work-for-hire); *Marshall v. Miles Laboratory, Inc.*, 647 F. Supp. 1326, 1330 (N.D. Ind. 1986) (same result, regarding an article written for publication in a scientific journal); and *In re Simplified Information Systems, Inc.*, 89 Bankr. 538, 542 (W.D. Pa. 1988).).

27. See also *Sherrill v. Grieves*, 57 Wash. L. Rep. 286 (D.C. 1929).

28. 17 U.S.C. 101 (articulating when a work is a work-for-hire: "a work specially ordered or commissioned for use as a contribution to a collective work, as a part of a motion picture or other audiovisual work, as a translation, as a supplementary work, as a compilation, as an instructional text, as a test, as answer material for a test, or as an atlas, if the parties expressly agree in a written instrument signed by them that the work shall be considered a work made for hire.").

29. See *Hays v. Sony Corporation of America*, 847 F.2d 412 (7th Cir. 1988); *Weinstein v. University of Illinois*, 881 F.2d 1091 (7th Cir. 1987); contra, *University of Colorado v. American Cyanamid*, 880 F. Supp. 1387 (D. Colo. 1995); *Vanderhurst v. Colorado Mountain College District*, 16 F. Supp. 2d 1297 (D. Colo. 1998).

30. Melville B. Nimmer and David Nimmer, *Nimmer on Copyright*, §5.03[B][1][b][I] n. 31, at 5-17–5-18 (2000).

31. *Foraste v. Brown University*, 290 F. Supp. 2d 234 (D.R.I. 2003) (concluding that photographs taken by university photographer are works made for hire). Commenting on the faculty exception: "These equitable policy concepts do not apply here because Foraste was not working under an implicit or explicit 'publish or perish' directive, and because he was usually directed by Brown officials to photograph specific scenes." Id., at 239.

32. James B. Wadley and JoLynn M. Brown, Working Between the Lines of *Reid*: Teachers, Copyrights, Work-For-Hire and a New Washburn University Policy, 38 *Washburn Law Journal* 385 (1999) ("If these two dimension of the 'works prepared with the scope of employment'—the idea that the nature of the work is as relevant as

the nature of the employment—are applied to the work activity of teachers in an academic environment, it should be apparent that most of the work having copyright implications would fall outside the scope of the work-for-hire doctrine.").

33. James B. Wadley and JoLynn M. Brown, Working Between the Lines of *Reid*: Teachers, Copyrights, Work-For-Hire and a New Washburn University Policy, 38 *Washburn Law Journal* 385, 404 (1999).

34. *University of Colorado v. American Cyanamid*, 880 F. Supp. 1387, 1400 (D. Colo. 1995) (quoting Plaintiff's Reply Brief for Supplemental Motion for Partial Summary Judgment at 29 n. 55) (citation and footnote omitted).

35. Citation to Restatement (Second) of Agency §228 (1958) omitted.

36. *Vanderhurst v. Colorado Mountain College District*, 16 F. Supp. 2d 1297, 1307 (D. Colo. 1998) (citing Restatement (Second) of Agency §228 (1958)).

37. *Foraste v. Brown University*, 290 F. Supp. 2d 234, 239, at n. 5 (D.R.I. 2003) ("The Court notes that the traditional 'faculty exception' to the work made for hire doctrine, 'whereby academic writing [is] presumed not to be work made for hire, see *Hays v. Sony Corp. of America*, 847 F.2d 412, 416 (7th Cir. 1988), is inapposite here. That exception is meant to protect the 'scholarly articles and other intellectual property' created by university professors while in the employ of an academic institution. *Weinstein v. University of Illinois*, 811 F.2d 1091, 1094 (7th Cir. 1987). Various equitable considerations often mandate that a scholar retain the copyrights in his work, notwithstanding the work made for hire doctrine.").

38. Melville B. Nimmer and David Nimmer, *Nimmer on Copyright*, §5.03[B][1][b][I] n. 31, at 5-17 – 5-18 (2000) ("Thus, if a professor elects to reduce his lectures to writing, the professor, and not the institution employing him, owns the copyright in such lectures.").

39. See 17 U.S.C. 102(a). See also 17 U.S.C. 101 ("A work is 'created' when it is fixed in a copy or phonorecord for the first time; where a work is prepared over a period of time, the portion of it that has been fixed at any particular time constitutes the work as of that time, and where the work has been prepared in different versions, each version constitutes a separate work.").

40. *Williams v. Weisser*, 78 Cal. Rptr. 542, 544 (1969). Based on this reasoning, one commentator believes it supports faculty ownership of scholarly work product as well. Roberta Rosenthal Kwall, Copyright Issues in Online Courses: Ownership, Authorship and Conflict, 18 *Santa Clara Computer & High Technology Law Journal* 1, 19 (2001) ("The same reasoning surely should apply to faculty members' scholarship and other work products, although some commentators have argued to the contrary." [footnote omitted]).

41. 17 U.S.C. 102 ("Copyright protection subsists, in accordance with this title, in original works of authorship fixed in any tangible medium of expression, now known or later developed.").

42. See Ashley Packard, Copyright or Copy Wrong: An Analysis of University Claims to Faculty Work, 7 *Communications Law & Policy* 275, 313–314 (2002) (questioning whether a written university policy satisfies the more general section 204(a) copyright transfer requirement of a unilateral writing, signed by the transferrer, much less the more stringent section 201(b) requirement of a bilateral writing, signed by both parties); Todd A. Borow, Copyright Ownership of Scholarly Works Created by University Faculty and Posted on School-Provided Web Pages, 7 *University of Miami Business Law Review* 149, 166–167 (1998) ("handbooks are unlikely to be considered signed writings by courts").

See also Sandip H. Patel, Graduate Students' Ownership and Attribution Rights in Intellectual Property, 71 *Indiana Law Journal* 481, 498 (1996) (Commenting with respect to inventive creations; i.e., patent: "Most faculty are . . . unaware that, as a matter of law, they have original ownership rights to many of their creations. . . . Moreover, universities have an economic interest in keeping this vital information from faculty members. Therefore, faculty could argue that there is no meeting of the minds between the university and themselves, one of the first requirements for a binding contract.").

43. James B. Wadley and JoLynn M. Brown, Working between the Lines of *Reid*: Teachers, Copyrights, Work-For-Hire and a New Washburn University Policy, 38 *Washburn Law Journal* 385, 409 (1999).

44. *Weinstein v. University of Illinois*, 811 F.2d 1091, 1094 (7th Cir. 1987).

45. *Weinstein v. University of Illinois*, 811 F.2d 1091, 1094–1095 (7th Cir. 1987).

46. *Hays v. Sony Corp. of America*, 847 F.2d 412, 416 (7th Cir. 1988).

47. *New York Times Co., Inc. vs. Tasini*, 533 U.S. 483 (2001).

48. 17 U.S.C. 201(b) (first, second, and third emphasis added).

49. *Foraste v. Brown University*, 290 F. Supp. 2d 234, 239 (D.R.I. 2003).

50. *Foraste v. Brown University*, 290 F. Supp. 2d 234, 241 (D.R.I. 2003) ("This Court finds that the Policy fails as a section 204(a) transfer instrument.").

51. *Foraste v. Brown University*, 290 F. Supp. 2d 234, 240 (D.R.I. 2003) ("The Court finds it significant that the Policy fails to make any reference at all to the subject matter of the rights to be transferred, the recipient of the transferred rights, the timing of the transfer, or any other particulars of the deal.").

52. 17 U.S.C. 110(1).

53. 17 U.S.C. 110(2).

54. 17 U.S.C. 101.

55. 17 U.S.C. 106(6). When Congress amended section 106 in 1996, adding the performance right in sound recording via a digital audio transmission, it added a definition of digital audio transmission to mean "a transmission in whole or in part in a digital or other nonanalog format." This definition is not terribly helpful but "plausibly implicate[s] most of the major conduits by [which] Americans now receive information, including television and radio broadcast, telecommunications, cable and fiber optics, direct satellite services, and even online interactive services." John W. Hazard, Jr., *Copyright Law in Business and Practice* §4:41, at 4–58 (2004).

56. 17 U.S.C. 101.

57. H. Rpt. No. 94-1476, 94th Cong., 2d Sess. 82 (1976), reprinted in 5 United States Code Congressional and Administrative News 5659, 5696 (1976) ("However, the term 'instructors' would be broad enough to include guest lecturers if their instructional activities remain confined to classroom activities. In general, the term 'pupils' refers to the enrolled members of a class.").

58. H. Rpt. No. 94-1476, 94th Cong., 2d Sess. 81 (1976), reprinted in 5 United States Code Congressional and Administrative News 5659, 5695 (1976).

59. H. Rpt. No. 94-1476, 94th Cong., 2d Sess. 81 (1976), reprinted in 5 United States Code Congressional and Administrative News 5659, 5695 (1976).

60. 17 U.S.C. 110(1).

61. 17 U.S.C. 109(b)(1)(A) (emphasis added).

62. H. Rpt. No. 94-1476, 94th Cong., 2d Sess. 82 (1976), reprinted in 5 United States Code Congressional and Administrative News 5659, 5696 (1976).

63. 17 U.S.C. 109(c) (emphasis added).

64. H. Rpt. No. 94-1476, 94th Cong., 2d Sess. 79 (1976), reprinted in 5 United States Code Congressional and Administrative News 5659, 5693 (1976) ("Section 109(b) [now section 109(c)] adopts the general principle that the lawful owner of a copy of a work should be able to put his copy on public display without the consent of the copyright owner.").

65. H. Rpt. No. 94-1476, 94th Cong., 2d Sess. 79–80 (1976), reprinted in 5 United States Code Congressional and Administrative News 5659, 5693 (1976) (emphasis added).

66. H. Rpt. No. 94-1476, 94th Cong., 2d Sess. 80 (1976), reprinted in 5 United States Code Congressional and Administrative News 5659, 5694 (1976).

67. H. Rpt. No. 94-1476, 94th Cong., 2d Sess. 80 (1976), reprinted in 5 United States Code Congressional and Administrative News 5659, 5694 (1976) (Commenting on the limits of section 109(c): "In other words, the display of a visual image of a copyrighted work would be an infringement if the image were transmitted by any method (by closed or open circuit television, for example, or by a computer system) from one place to members of the public located elsewhere." Id.).

68. H. Rpt. No. 94-1476, 94th Cong., 2d Sess. 80 (1976), reprinted in 5 United States Code Congressional and Administrative News 5659, 5694 (1976).

69. H. Rpt. No. 94-1476, 94th Cong., 2d Sess. 81 (1976), reprinted in 5 United States Code Congressional and Administrative News 5659, 5695 (1976).

70. H. Rpt. No. 94-1476, 94th Cong., 2d Sess. 82 (1976), reprinted in 5 United States Code Congressional and Administrative News 5659, 5696 (1976) (Clause (1) [17 U.S.C. 110(1)] makes clear that it applies only to the teaching activities 'of a nonprofit educational institution,' thus excluding from the exemption performances or display in profit-making institutions such as dance studios and language schools.").

71. H. Rpt. No. 94-1476, 94th Cong., 2d Sess. 83 (1976), reprinted in 5 United States Code Congressional and Administrative News 5659, 5697 (1976).

72. H. Rpt. No. 94-1476, 94th Cong., 2d Sess. 83 (1976), reprinted in 5 United States Code Congressional and Administrative News 5659, 5697 (1976).

73. H. Rpt. No. 94-1476, 94th Cong., 2d Sess. 56–57 (1976), reprinted in 17 U.S.C.A. 110, Historical and Statutory Notes.

74. U.S. Copyright Office, *Report on Copyright and Digital Distance Education* 80 (1999).

75. Conference Report, H. Rpt. No. 107-685, 107th Cong., 2d Sess. 230 (2002).

76. H. Rpt. No. 94-1476, 94th Cong., 2d Sess. 83 (1976), reprinted in 5 United States Code Congressional and Administrative News 5659, 5698 (1976).

77. Conference Report, H. Rpt. No. 107-685, 107th Cong., 2d Sess. 2279 (2002).

II

UNDERSTANDING THE NEW
TEACH DISTANCE EDUCATION LAW

2

The Scope of the Privilege
for Educators

Excluded Materials

L ET US EXAMINE EACH CLAUSE of revised §110(2) and use the legislative history to help understand what is being required of qualifying educational
entities. At this point I recommend making a copy of §§110(2) and 112(f)
from appendix C to follow line by line with the discussion (never fear, the
U.S.C. is in the public domain, so no copyright law is violated by copying any
of it) or at least flagging the pages for easier reference. Line-by-line reading of
the copyright law might seem intimidating, but it is a good systematic way to
learn about the law and its internal logic. It is also good practice, and it will
assist you when you strike out on your own to read and research other provisions of importance to you. Finally, it allows you, the reader, to understand
why I make the conclusions I make. As we work through the various provisions I will digress from time to time to explain related concepts.

The Nature of the Privilege Provided Educators

Recall that each subsection of §110 operates, as its section title suggests, as a
"Limitation on exclusive rights: Exemptions of certain performance and displays." The opening clause of §110 reads: "Notwithstanding the provisions of
section 106, the following are not infringements of copyright." This indicates
that each of the activities described in the successive subsections of §110 do
not impinge upon the exclusive rights of copyright owners. In other words
each subsection of §110, such as §110(1) and §110(2), the live and remote education subsections, respectively, are exceptions to the control copyrighted

owners exercise over their works vis-à-vis the exclusive rights granted to owners in §106. Like the general "exception" of fair use in §107, sections such as §110 operate as a legal privilege of sorts, granting users the right to make certain uses of copyrighted material.

Three Ways for Works to Be Ineligible for Section 110(2) Transmissions

New TEACH §110(2) begins with the word "*except*" to indicate that the opening two provisos of §110(2) operate as exceptions to a privilege. In other words, the rights granted to educators in §110(2) to remove ("exempt") certain performances and displays from the control of copyright owners vis-à-vis their exclusive rights do not apply in two instances: works developed specially for digital distance education curriculums and second, as discussed below, copies or phonorecords of works not lawfully made. First, "*except with respect to a work produced or marketed primarily for performance or display as part of mediated instructional activities transmitted via digital networks*" the rights granted by section 110(2) do not apply.

In order to understand the sorts of works this proviso is attempting to exclude from the §110(2) educator privilege, the reader needs to first understand the concept of "mediated instructional activities," or MIA, that the TEACH Act creates. The term MIA is used twice, here in this opening "except" proviso and later in §110(2)(A) to indicate the sorts of material to which TEACH does indeed apply. As a result of the dual use of the phrase, once to include (the MIA "teaching activity" requirement of section 110(2)(A)) and second to exclude (the opening "except" proviso of section 110(2)) it might at first pass appear a confusing concept. Here is what I hope is a clarifying summary, putting it into more logical sequence, though not in the order presented in the statute, and without getting into specifics.

The Nature of an MIA Work

First, the definition of "mediated instructional activities," or MIA, discussed immediately below, itself provides some exclusion because the definition of what TEACH MIA includes naturally leaves other sorts of material excluded. This is a "supplemental material" exclusion. Now an educator can ascertain what MIA includes, and by definition what it excludes. In addition, the opening proviso of §110(2) will also carve out from the general rule of MIA inclusion a certain category of MIA *not* included because they are designed for use in digital distance education. (Understanding the operation of the opening "except" proviso of §110(2) is the immediate task as hand. But, of course, to understand that exclusion within the inclusion privilege, one must first understand the concept of MIA.)

The Nature of the Use of an MIA Work

Section 110(2)(A) indicates the sort of copyrighted uses to which TEACH MIA does in fact apply (see table 2.1). This is the MIA "teaching activity" requirement that links performance or display of copyrighted material to the curriculum. Works used for other purposes, outside the scope of MIA teaching, are thus also excluded from the §110(2) exemption.

The Conference Report explains the relationship between the two concepts of MIA (work and use):

> The limitation of the exemption to systematic "mediated instructional activities" in subparagraph (2)(A) of the amended exemption operates together with the exclusion in the opening clause of section 110(2) for works "produced or marketed primarily for performance or display as part of mediated instruction activities transmitted via digital networks" to place boundaries on the exemption. The former [TEACH section 110(2)(A)] relates to the nature of the exempt *activity*; the latter [opening "except" MIA proviso] limits the *relevant materials* by excluding those primarily produced or marketed for the exempt activity.[1]

TABLE 2.1
Comparison of Section 110(2)(A) Teaching Activity versus MIA

Section 110(2)(A) teaching activity requirements ("relates to the nature of the exempt activity")	Comment	Definition of MIA (three prongs) ("relates to [or limits] the relevant materials")
is made by	absent from	
at the direction of	broader than	controlled by
or under the actual supervision of an instructor	same as	or under the actual supervision of the instructor
as an integral part of	same as	as an integral part of
a class session (as defined by legislative history)	broader than	the class experience
offered as a regular part of the systematic mediated instructional activities of an	absent from, but included in the definition of MIA	
accredited nonprofit educational institution	absent from	
	added by the definition of MIA	and analogous to the type of performance or display that would take place in a live classroom setting

Look for more on why Congress would choose to exclude those materials "primarily produced or marketed for the exempt activity" toward the end of the MIA definition discussion.

The Three Ways for Works to Be Ineligible

1. Failing to Meet the Statutory Definition of Mediated Instructional Activities

The definition of MIA is also a part of the statute and appears as one of several definitional provisions following the operative provisions of §110(2).

In paragraph (2), the term "mediated instructional activities" with respect to the performance or display of a work by digital transmission under this section refers to activities that use such work as an integral part of the class experience, controlled by or under the actual supervision of the instructor and analogous to the type of performance or display that would take place in a live classroom setting. The term does not refer to activities that use, in 1 or more class sessions of a single course, such works as textbooks, course packs, or other material in any media, copies or phonorecords of which are typically purchased or acquired by the students in higher education for their independent use and retention or are typically purchased or acquired for elementary and secondary students for their possession and independent use.[2]

As a result of the above definition, there are three requirements that must be met before the performance or display of a copyright work by digital transmission can qualify for use under TEACH (i.e., before its use is considered part of MIA). If an educator is involved in a performance or display meeting the definition, then the materials performed or displayed in conjunction with that teaching are covered by the §110(2) exemption; that is, they can be used "by or in the course of a transmission." (Of course, there are many other requirements in TEACH, so do not stop after this discussion!) First, the teaching activity using the copyrighted material must be "an integral part of the class experience." Second, the use of the copyrighted material must be "controlled by or under the actual supervision of the instructor." Finally, the use of the copyrighted material must be "analogous to the type of performance or display that would take place in a live classroom setting." Other subsections of §110(2) and §112(f) both contain additional language that limits or restricts the amount of material in a distance education classroom to that which would be present in the live face-to-face classroom. A common theme throughout TEACH is to have distance education space mirror live classroom space, not exceed it in terms of the amount of copyrighted materials performed or displayed within its four walls, even if virtual.

Glance for a moment at §110(2)(A). There is also a multipronged approach present as well: instructor supervision, integral part, and again MIA. Though the language used in three prongs of the definition of MIA, above (integral part, instructor supervision, and analogous to), is not identical to the §110(2)(A) articulation, at least two of the concepts contain almost identical language and so the later discussion of the integral class and instructor supervision prongs especially (the analogous teaching prong less so) from the legislative history discussing §110(2)(A) is helpful here as well. First, the concept of "integral part" requires that "it be part of a class itself, rather than ancillary to it."[3] Second, under the instructor supervision prong, the

> ... performance or display may be initiated by the instructor. It may also be initiated by a person enrolled in the class as long as it is done either at the direction, or under the supervision, of the instructor. "Actual" supervision is intended to require that the instructor is, in fact, supervising the class activities, and that supervision is not in name only. It is not intended to require either constant, real-time supervision by the instructor or pre-approval by the instructor for the performance or display . . . and the concept of control and supervision is not intended to limit the qualification of such asynchronous activities for this exemption.[4]

The definition proceeds to indicate the sort of material that should *not* be considered MIA:

> The term does not refer to activities that use, in 1 or more class sessions of a single course, such works as textbooks, course packs, or other material in any media, copies or phonorecords of which are typically purchased or acquired by the students in higher education for their independent use and retention or are typically purchased or acquired for elementary and secondary students for their possession and independent use.

The use of the phrase "purchased or acquired" with respect to such items outside the MIA definition, "such works as textbooks, course packs, or other material in any media," is further explained by the legislative history: "The Committee notes that in many secondary and elementary school contexts, such copies of such materials are not purchased or acquired directly by students, but rather are provided for the students' independent use and possession (for the duration of the course) by the institution."[5] Based on the definition of MIA, these supplemental materials are *not part of the distance education classroom per se* and thus are not covered by the §110(2) privilege.

2. Meeting the Statutory Definition of MIA but "Produced or Marketed Primarily For"

For the second way for works to be ineligible for §110(2) transmissions, notice the opening proviso of the definition, "with respect to the performance or display of a work by *digital transmission* under this section." The Conference Report also points out a concern for works in digital form:

> The amended exemption is not intended to address other uses of copyrighted works in the course of digital distance education, including student use of supplemental or research materials *in digital form, such as electronic course-packs, e-reserves, and digital library resources.* Such activities do not involve uses analogous to the performance and displays currently addressed in section 110(2).[6]

These materials are not the target of actual teaching sessions for which §110(2) is designed, but represent materials students use in preparation for class or just might happen to "bring" into the classroom.

But does MIA refer only to materials used in digital transmissions? Perhaps, but the legislative history makes clear that TEACH applies to digital as well as analog, just as the Conference Report makes clear that "the term 'transmission' is intended to include transmissions by digital, as well as analog means."[7] Moreover, the very next comment in the Conference Report discussing the definition of MIA indicates that the concept applies across media:

> The "mediated instructional activity" requirement is thus intended to prevent the exemption provided by the TEACH Act from displacing textbooks, course packs or other material *in any media,* copies or phonorecords of which are typically purchased or acquired by students for their independent use and retention "in most post-secondary and some elementary and secondary contexts. . . ."[8]

In other words, MIA can mean digital as well as analog, though looking at the text of the statute alone might obscure this dual application.

Furthermore, the discussion in the Conference Report of the opening MIA proviso exception indicates that

> [t]he exclusion is not intended to apply generally to all educational material or to all materials having educational value. The exclusion [the opening "except" proviso] is limited to material whose primary market is "mediated instructional activities," i.e., materials performed or displayed as an integral part of the class experience, analogous to the type of performance or display that would take place in a live classroom setting. At the same time, the reference to "digital networks" is intended to limit the exclusion to materials whose primary market is the digital network environment, not instructional materials developed and marketed for use in the physical classroom.[9]

What is clear is that the opening "except" proviso excludes only those MIA "transmitted via digital networks," that are "produced or marketed for performance or display" for such purpose, and not MIA intended for the physical classroom and used by a distance educator in an analog transmission or MIA intended for the physical classroom that is converted to digital by a distance educator for digital use. What is excluded are those MIA products "produced or marketed primarily" for digital distance education. Furthermore, the use of MIA in § 110(2)(A) relates to the activities (teaching-learning) and thus must apply to both analog and digital MIA. This is logical as the opening MIA except proviso is an exclusion of the § 110(2) educator privilege and so is by design crafted narrowly, whereas the § 110(2)(A) is a general requirement of eligibility of the § 110(2) privilege and should be broader.

Confused? It appears that there are three categories of works. First, non-MIA works (like a textbook or course pack, whether analog or digital, that is excluded by the subsequent TEACH statutory definition of MIA and incorporated into § 110(2)(A)) cannot be used under § 110(2), as use would displace the need for purchase of such items by students.[10] Second, there are the precise MIA works for which the TEACH privilege was created, curricular materials that meet the definition of MIA—integral part of class experience, under control of instructor, and analogous to classroom settings—and these works, an atlas for example, can be used in exercise of a § 110(2) activity.

> One example of the interaction of the two provisions is the application of the exemption to textbooks. Pursuant to subparagraph (2)(A), which limits the exemption to "mediated instructional activities," the display of material from a textbook that would typically be purchased by students in the local classroom environment, in lieu of purchase by students, would not fall into the exemption. Conversely, because textbooks typically are not primarily produced or marketed for performance or display in a manner analogous to performances or display in the live classroom setting, they would not per se be excluded from the exemption under the exclusion in the opening clause. Thus an instructor would not be precluded from using a chart or table or other short excerpt from a textbook different from the one assigned for the course, or from emphasizing such an excerpt from the assigned textbook that had been purchased by the students.[11]

What is unfortunate about this example is the failure to assess the result if the instructor desired to use an entire textbook other than the one assigned; it can only be assumed that this would be excluded under the plain definition of MIA as well as other copyright principles such as fair use. By the same token, the use of a "chart or table or other short excerpt from a textbook different from the one assigned" one would expect to be a fair use[12]; thus, the comment adds or accomplishes little beyond what is already known of the general copyright law and its application to education.

Finally, there are works identified by the opening "except" proviso of §110(2): those MIA works "produced or marketed primarily for . . ." the distance classroom, in theory acceptable for use in §110(1) face-to-face teaching but excluded from the §110(2) uses by its opening "except" proviso. The last category might be a special multimedia product designed for use in conjunction with distance education, as an adjunct to a textbook (much like the workbook of old), or this might be some sort of digital tutorial or other study aid designed for students. The tutorial or study aid is not a "textbook, course packs or other material in any media . . . typically purchased or acquired by students" and so is not excluded by the definition of MIA. However, since in this case the item is *produced or marketed primarily for* the distance education environment (MIA "transmitted via digital networks"), the work is excluded by the opening "except" proviso of TEACH section 110(2).

The fact that a digital product might be adaptable to the distance education environment would not trigger the "except" proviso of the opening clause of §110(2), even if it were produced or marketed with that adaptability evident, because, according to the plain language of TEACH, the item must be "produced or marketed *primarily*" for that purpose, and not merely "possible for that purpose." Again, not all educational material is excluded (at the outset it would be excluded if it did not fall within the MIA concept, as discussed earlier), only that which meets the statutory definition of MIA and which is also designed as sold primarily for digital distance education and not distance education in general. But why did Congress exclude these materials when it would appear that they are so needed in distance education? Market factors again! As explained by the Conference Report:

> The exclusion for works "produced or marketed primarily for performance or display as part of mediated instructional activities transmitted via digital networks" is intended to prevent the exemption from undermining the primary market for (and, therefore, impairing the incentive to create, modify or distribute) those materials whose primary market would otherwise fall within the scope of the exemption . . . works produced or marketed primarily for activities covered by the exemption would be excluded from the exemption. The exclusion is not intended to apply generally to all educational materials or to all materials having educational value. . . . At the same time, the reference to "digital networks" is intended to limit the exclusion to materials whose primary market is the digital network environment, not instructional materials developed and marketed for use in the physical classroom.[13]

As a practical matter, these works might still be available for use in the distance education classroom but would likely be subject to the terms and conditions of a license.

3. Failing to Meet the "Lawfully Made" Requirement

A third category of excluded materials (the first are non-MIA—textbooks, course packs, etc.—excluded via the definition of MIA, and the second are works produced and marketed primarily for use in digital distance education), consists of "*a performance or display that is given by means of a copy of phonorecord that is not lawfully made and acquired under this title, and the transmitting government body or accredited nonprofit educational institution knew or had reason to know was not lawfully made and acquired.*" Requiring that materials performed or displayed be lawfully made and acquired is significant for several reasons. First, there was no such requirement in the pre-TEACH version of §110(2), either explicit in the text of the statute or implicit, as explained in the 1976 legislative history.

Second, the "lawfully made and acquired" requirement of §110(2) differs from the existing "lawfully made" requirement of §110(1),[14] as that proviso only applies "in the case of a motion picture or other audiovisual work, the performance, or the display of individual images, [of which] is given by means of a copy that was not lawfully made under this title, and that the person responsible for the performance knew or had reason to believe was not lawfully made."[15] The TEACH version applies to all categories of copyrighted material.[16]

Third, the "test" of unlawfulness goes both to the making of the work and its acquisition and links both to Title 17 of the United States Code (the copyright law), by means of the "under this title" language. However, Title 17 includes the anti-circumvention and anti-trafficking rules of §1201, so if an educator possessed a lawfully made copy of a DVD but, in performing its content for a distance education class, circumvented its (legitimate) access by his or her own ("hacking") efforts or used the fruits of someone else's labor (i.e., obtained the hack from a website—a prohibited trafficking—or some other means that violated the §1201 rules) then while the work would have been lawfully made (a purchased DVD), it would not have been lawfully acquired (its access required circumvention). Both conditions must be met: "the transmitting government body or accredited nonprofit educational institution must not have kn[o]w[n] or had reason to know [the work] was not lawfully made and acquired." As explained below, it is not circumvention of restricted use that is prohibited under §1201 but the circumvention of restricted access.

A Few Comments Regarding the Anti-Circumvention and Anti-Trafficking Rules   Circumventing an access control that a copyright owner places on his or her work violates §1201(a)(1). As discussed below, trafficking in either the anti-circumvention access or use "device" is also a violation. But what is an access or use control? It might be something as simple as technology that prohibits viewers from fast-forwarding past advertisements on a DVD (a use control),[17] from playing the DVD on a PC or platform other than a DVD player (an access control),[18] so-called technological handshake protocols[19] and geographic use restriction codes,[20] and even the authentication sequence that occurs between a printer and microchip contained on a toner cartridge.[21] These examples demonstrate the reach of the anti-circumvention and anti-trafficking rules and the controversy inherent in §1201.

For the §1201(a)(1) rules to apply, the access control must be effective in preventing unauthorized access,[22] though the control need not be 100 percent effective. In other words, simply because circumvention was possible does not mean the access control is not a "technological measure that effectively controls access to" copyrighted material and therefore not subject to the anti-circumvention rule of §1201(a)(1)(A). By the same token, Congress did not anticipate that attempts to remedy so-called playability problems should be viewed as an attempt at circumvention.[23] The access control must be put in place by the copyright owner or with his or her authorization. In other words, an educational institution or library that purchased an item from a retailer who placed such protection on the work without the approval of the copyright owner could circumvent the retailer's access control and not violate §1201. In addition, the technological access control must not degrade, corrupt, or distort the work; if it does, §1201 does not apply, as such is not an "effective" control.[24] The authorization and degradation conditions apply to both the §1201(a) anti-circumvention (§1201(a)(1)) and anti-trafficking rules (§1201(a)(2)) access rules.

Section 1201(a)(2) prohibits trafficking in the anti-circumvention access control. If a person writes a piece of code that, when combined with certain hardware, allows access to the information contained in a DVD or CD-ROM, and then the person shares that code with others, the person violates §1201(a)(2) for trafficking the access control.[25] This violation is true even if the DVD or CD-ROM was purchased from a legitimate source (i.e., it is a lawfully made copy) or if the eventual use one desires to make of the accessed work is a fair use or authorized under any of the other provisions of the copyright law. This is because separate liability still exists under §1201.[26] The fact that the range of fair uses available to the nonprofit library, archive, or educational institution is more limited because of the use and enforceability of the §1201 rules does not matter.

A second anti-trafficking rule prohibits the trafficking of technologies that circumvent use controls placed on protected works. This provision targets the manufacturers of so-called black box technologies that systematically remove use restrictions.[27] Section 1201(b) makes illegal the sale or distribution (trafficking) of a device that allows someone to use a copyrighted work in contravention of the protections placed by an owner. According to the House Report:

> This provision is not aimed at products that are capable of commercially significant noninfringing uses, such as consumer electronics, telecommunications, and computer products—including videocassette recorders, telecommunications switches, personal computers, and servers—used by business and consumers for perfectly legitimate purposes.[28]

Suppose a person markets a product called the "Disk Wizard." The product's only advertised use—to allow purchasers to circumvent use controls and convert and play any CD-ROM, videodisc, or DVD audiovisual programs on a personal computer—would likely violate §1201(b).[29] It might be designed to also circumvent access controls as well. If so, it would violate §1201(a)(1) circumvention and §1201(a)(2) trafficking rules.

How does §1201 litigation work in practice? Consider the following scenario:

> With respect to technological protective measures that control particular uses of a work once it has been lawfully accessed, there is no anti-circumvention rule. There is only an anti-trafficking rule. As a result, a user who, after gaining legitimate access to a protected work, employs a countermeasure to enjoy uses of that work for which he or she is unauthorized would not be liable. . . .[R]ather, the person who *provided* the countermeasure might be liable both for doing so and possibly for vicarious or contributory copyright infringement as well. (The user, of course, would still be liable for direct copyright infringement with respect to the unauthorized use.)[30]

According to the Dratler comment, assuming that the use itself does not violate the copyright law, it could nonetheless be an "unauthorized" access in anticipation of a later fair use. That is why Congress did not penalize the circumvention of use control, as it might be done by a fair user; it penalized only the trafficking of use control devices that allow use, fair or not, to occur.

In other words, one could circumvent a use control, but not the access control needed in order to use the protected work, because §1201(a)(1) prohibits the circumvention of access controls alone. One could circumvent a use control, but not traffic in the instrument of the use circumvention (prohibited by §1201(b)). Finally, you could not circumvent an access control (prohibited by §1201(a)) nor could you traffic in the circumventing access control because §1201(a)(2) prohibits this action.

The inescapable conclusion from the statutory language adopted by Congress and the legislative history discussed above is that Congress sought to ban all circumvention tools because most of the time those tools would be used to infringe a copyright. Thus, while it is not unlawful to circumvent for the purpose of engaging in fair use, it is unlawful to traffic in tools that allow fair use circumvention. That is part of the sacrifice Congress was willing to make in order to protect against unlawful piracy and promote the development of electronic commerce and the availability of copyrighted material on the Internet.[31] Let us return to the "lawfully made" requirement.

The TEACH "lawfully made" test is broad in focus. The target person or persons by which the "lawfully made and acquired" verification must be made is, in §110(1), only the "person responsible for the performance," i.e., the teacher, student, or guest lecturer.[32] In §110(2), however, it is the "accredited nonprofit educational institution" that is the focus of the inquiry.[33] Unlike the 110(1) "unlawfully made" copy proviso,[34] which is triggered when the "person responsible for the performance [i.e., the teacher or student or guest lecturer] knew or had reason to believe" the version of the work used was a copy that was unlawfully made, TEACH places the emphasis on the institution as a whole, with arguably the actual knowledge or suspicion ("had reason to believe") of every employee imputed upwards to its administrators and ultimately the institution.[35]

Obviously, an accredited nonprofit educational institution is a legal fiction; it cannot know or have reason to know anything. However, under the principle of respondeat superior in agency law and incorporated into the copyright law through the concept of vicarious copyright liability, any knowledge that employees possess, whether it be the instructor, distance education coordinator, or staff person, that a performance or display of a work is made from a copy of a work not lawfully made and acquired is imputed to the accredited nonprofit educational institution. As a result of this imputation, it could be said that if the "accredited nonprofit educational institution knew or had reason to know [the work] was not lawfully made and acquired," then the work cannot be used for §110(2) purposes. This arguably imposes a responsibility that is *institution-wide* and that extends to *all* TEACH 110(2) uses (performances and displays). Finally, the new "lawfully made" proviso is consistent with the compliance-oriented attitude that TEACH is attempting to create, with the task of promoting compliance falling upon the institution. In a reading of §110(2) from start to finish, this is the first statutory expression of that attitude. Under the principles of secondary liability, typically a third party such as a student would not be deemed to "know or have reason to know" anything. Thus it could be argued that, if a student knew the work was infringing, such knowledge would not in itself be imputed to the institution. However, if the student made a faculty member aware of the situation, the knowledge requirement might be met. In this small way, the §110(2) "lawfully made" proviso is somewhat more lenient than its §110(1) counterpart, which places the scienter on the person responsible for the performance, which could be a student.

Why the change? That TEACH adds a "lawfully made" requirement is arguably not an unreasonable expansion of that requirement to all categories of works, but why the shift in the mens rea inquiry from the knowledge of the person making the performance in §110(1) to the institution as whole in TEACH §110(2)? The 1976 legislative history offers little to explain the concern for audiovisual works alone that might shed light on the TEACH expansion, other than stating it is a problem, but why in 1976 audiovisual works posed a problem for infringement more than others sorts of works is unclear: "The final provision of clause (1) deals with the *special problem* of performances from unlawfully-made copies of motion pictures and other audiovisual works."[36] Perhaps it is logical that audiovisual works would be one of the most sought-after categories of works used in the traditional, physical classroom and that piracy (use of unlawfully made copies) could reach epic proportions if not restrained by an initial statutory prohibition. This attitude would also be consistent with a similar concern expressed by the 1976 Congress regarding piracy of audiovisual and §112.[37]

Distance education has progressed much since 1976—into the digital realm, of course, but also into new forms of analog transmission that make it much easier to access copyrighted works, both lawfully made and those that are not lawfully made: "As noted in the Register's Report, the purpose of the exclusion is to reduce the likelihood that an exemption intended to cover only the equivalent of traditional concepts of performance and display would result in the proliferation or exploitation of unauthorized copies."[38] The Conference Committee does not view this as an impediment to the acquisition of material for use in distance education, because the "educator would typically purchase, license, rent, make a fair-use copy, or otherwise lawfully acquire the copy to be used, and works not yet made available in the market (whether by distribution, performance or display) would, as a practical matter, be rendered ineligible for use under the exemption."[39]

These two "except" provisos, along with the incorporation of an MIA requirement in §110(2), indicate, then, that three categories of works are not covered by §110(2):

- First (nature of the work): online curricular materials embodied in the MIA exclusion (opening "except" proviso of §110(2)), those produced or marketed primarily for use in distance education;

- Second (nature of the "source"): suspect materials; that is, those that were not lawfully made and acquired, as expressed in the opening second "except" proviso of §110(2); and
- Third (nature of the use): reflected in the MIA requirement (§110(2)(A)) regarding supplemental materials such as electronic course packs, e-reserves, and digital library resources as well as textbooks, course packs, or other material in any media, because these materials, while educational in nature, do not relate to the actual use of copyrighted materials in the classroom (i.e., the activity of teaching).[40]

Notes

1. Conference Report, H. Rpt. No. 107-685, 107th Cong., 2d Sess. 229 (2002).
2. 17 U.S.C. 110.
3. Conference Report, H. Rpt. No. 107-685, 107th Cong., 2d Sess. 229 (2002) ("The performance or display must also be made as an integral part of a class session, so it must be part of a class itself, rather than ancillary to it."). Notice the MIA definition uses the phrase "integral part of the class *experience*" whereas section 110(2)(A) uses the phrase "integral part of *class session*" (first and second emphasis is added).
4. Conference Report, H. Rpt. No. 107-685, 107th Cong., 2d Sess. 228 (2002) ("First, the performance or display must be *made by, under the direction of, or under the actual supervision of an instructor.* Performance or display may be initiated by the instructor. It may also be initiated by a person enrolled in the class as long as it is done either *at the direction, or under the actual supervision, of the instructor.* 'Actual' supervision is intended to require that the instructor is, in fact, supervising the class activities, and that supervision is not in name only. It is not intended to require either constant, real-time supervision by the instructor or pre-approval by the instructor for the performance or display . . . and the concept of *control and supervision* is not intended to limit the qualification of such asynchronous activities for this exemption."). Notice that the definition of MIA uses the phrase "*controlled by or under the actual supervision of the instructor*" and eliminates the "made by, at the direction of," whereas §110(2)(A) uses the phrase "*made by, at the direction of,* or under the actual supervision of an instructor" (all emphasis added). This may appear odd, that a provision of a statute, §110(2)(A), at least partially defines itself with two identical terms. In other words, §110(2)(A) has the three-prong definition (integral class, instructor supervision, and MIA). When one looks to MIA to define the third §110(2)(A) prong, one finds three prongs, two of which are nearly identical; i.e., the integral part and instructor supervision. The only new concept is the "analogous to the type of performance or display that would take place in a live classroom setting" phrasing. This makes sense as the definition of MIA is used in conjunction with digital transmissions alone while the §110(2)(A) refers to all distance education activities, analog or digital.

5. Conference Report, H. Rpt. No. 107-685, 107th Cong., 2d Sess. 229 (2002).

6. Conference Report, H. Rpt. No. 107-685, 107th Cong., 2d Sess. 229 (2002) (first and second emphasis added).

7. Conference Report, H. Rpt. No. 107-685, 107th Cong., 2d Sess. 226 (2002).

8. Conference Report, H. Rpt. No. 107-685, 107th Cong., 2d Sess. 229 (2002) (emphasis added).

9. Conference Report, H. Rpt. No. 107-685, 107th Cong., 2d Sess. 227 (2002).

10. Conference Report, H. Rpt. No. 107-685, 107th Cong., 2d Sess. 229 (2002) ("The 'mediated instructional activity' requirement is thus intended to prevent the exemption provided by the TEACH Act from displacing *textbooks, course packs or other material in any media,* copies or phonorecords of which are typically purchased or acquired by students for their independent use and retention 'in most post-secondary and some elementary and secondary contents. . . .'") (emphasis added).

11. Conference Report, H. Rpt. No. 107-685, 107th Cong., 2d Sess. 229–230 (2002).

12. Reprinted in U.S. Copyright Office, Circular 21 Reproduction of Copyrighted Works by Educators and Librarians 10-11 (Washington, D.C.: U.S. Government Printing Office, no date).

13. Conference Report, H. Rpt. No. 107-685, 107th Cong., 2d Sess. 227 (2002).

14. Conference Report, H. Rpt. No. 107-685, 107th Cong., 2d Sess. 227 (2002) ("The exclusion of performances or displays 'given by means of a copy or phonorecord that is not lawfully made and acquired' under Title 17 is based on a similar exclusion in the current language of section 110(1) for the performance or display of an audiovisual work in the classroom.").

15. 17 U.S.C. 110(1).

16. Conference Report, H. Rpt. No. 107-685, 107th Cong., 2d Sess. 227 (2002) ("Unlike the provision in section 110(1), the exclusion here applies to the performance or display of any work.").

17. Exemption to Prohibition on Circumvention of Copyright Protection Systems for Access Control Technologies, Final Rule, 68 Federal Register 62011, 62015-62016 (October 31, 2003) (amending 37 C.F.R. §201.40) (proposed class 9: Audiovisual works released on DVD that contain access control measures that interfere with the ability to defeat technology that prevents users from skipping promotional materials.).

18. *Universal City Studios, Inc. v. Corley,* 273 F.3d 429 (2d Cir. 2001) (motion picture studios place CSS encryption technology on DVDs to prevent the unauthorized viewing and copying of motion pictures). "If a user runs the DeCSS program (for example, by clicking on the DeCSS icon on a Microsoft operating system platform) with a DVD in the computer's disk drive, DeCSS will decrypt the DVD's CSS protection, allowing the user to copy the DVD's files and place the copy on the user's hard drive." Id. at 437. "In considering the scope of First Amendment protection for a decryption program like DeCSS, we must recognize that the essential purpose of encryption code is to prevent unauthorized access. Id. at 452."

19. *Real Networks, Inc. v. Streambox, Inc.,* 2000 U.S. Dist. LEXIS 1889 (W.D. Wash. 2000) (preliminary injunction). ("In this way, the Streambox VCR acts like a black box which descrambles cable or satellite broadcasts so that [*12] viewers can watch pay

programming for free. Like the cable and satellite companies that scramble their video signals to control access to their programs, RealNetworks has employed technological measures to ensure that only users of the RealPlayer can access RealMedia content placed on a RealServer. RealNetworks has gone one step further than the cable and satellite companies, not only controlling access, but also allowing copyright owners to specify whether or not their works can be copied by end-users, even if access is permitted. The Streambox VCR circumvents both the access control and copy protection measures." Id. at *11–*12.)

20. *Sony Computer Entertainment America, Inc. v. Gamemasters, Inc.*, 87 F. Supp. 2d 976 (N.D. Cal. 1999). "Defendant concedes in its opposition papers that the Game Enhancer makes temporary modifications to the [PlayStation] computer program . . . changing these codes with the Game Enhancer does not alter the underlying software made by SONY. (Def. Opp. at 6). Based upon the declarations before this Court, the Game Enhancer's distinguishing feature appears to be its ability to allow consumers to play import or nonterritorial SCEA video games. As discussed above, SCEA specifically designed the PlayStation console to access only those games with data codes that match the geographical location of the game console itself. The Game Enhancer circumvents the mechanism on the PlayStation console that ensures the console operates only when encrypted data is read from an authorized CD-ROM. (Pltf's Reply at 7). Thus, at this stage, the Game Enhancer appears to be a device whose primary function is to circumvent a technological measure (or a protection afforded by a technological measure) that effectively controls access to a system protected by a registered copyright. . . . 17 U.S.C. at § 1201(a)(2)(A)." Id. at 987.

21. *Lexmark International, Inc. v. Static Control Components, Inc.*, 253 F. Supp. 2d 943 (E.D. Ky. 2003).

22. See 17 U.S.C. 1201(a)(3)(B).

23. Conference Report, H. Rpt. No. 105-796, 105th Cong., 2d Sess. 65 (1998) ("Steps taken by the makers or services of consumer electronics, telecommunications or computing products used for such authorized performances or displays solely to mitigate these adverse effects on product performance (whether or not taken in combination with other lawful product modifications) shall not be deemed a violation of sections 1201(a) or (b).").

24. H. R. Rep. No. 551 (Part 2), 105th Cong., 2d Sess. 40 (1998) ("[M]easures that cause noticeable and recurring adverse effects on the authorized display or performance of works should not be deemed to be effective.").

25. See *Universal City Studios, Inc. v. Corley*, 273 F.3d 429 (2d Cir. 2001) ("In November 1999, Corley posted a copy of the decryption computer program 'DeCSS' on his website http://www.2600.com. DeCSS is designed to circumvent 'CSS,' the encryption technology that motion picture studios place on DVDs to prevent the unauthorized viewing and copying of motion pictures. Corley also posted on his website links to other websites where DeCSS could be found." Id. at 435.).

26. See 17 U.S.C. 1203.

27. See *Real Networks, Inc. v. Streambox, Inc.*, 2000 U.S. Dist. LEXIS 1889 (W.D. Wash. 2000) (preliminary injunction) ("The only reason for the Streambox VCR to circumvent the Secret Handshake and interact with a RealServer is to allow an end-

user to access and make copies of content that a copyholder has placed on a RealServer in order to secure it against unauthorized copying. In this way, the Streambox VCR acts like a 'black box' which descrambles cable or satellite broadcasts so that viewers can watch pay programming for free." Finding of Fact 26, at *11. "[T]he Copy Switch is a 'technological measure' that effectively protects the right of a copyright owner to control the unauthorized copying of the work." Conclusion of law 8, Id., at *19.

28. H. R. Rep. No. 551 (Part 2), 105th Cong., 2d Sess. 39–40 (1998).

29. 17 U.S.C. (b)(1) (trafficking of the following "technology, product, service, device, component, or part thereof," is prohibited: "(A) is primarily designed or produced for the purpose of circumventing protection afforded by a technological measure that effectively protects a right of a copyright owner under this title in a work or a portion thereof; (B) has only limited commercially significant purpose or use other than to circumvent protection afforded by a technological measure that effectively protects a right of a copyright owner under this title in a work or a portion thereof; or (C) is marketed by that person or another acting in concert with that person with that person's knowledge for use in circumventing protection afforded by a technological measure that effectively protects a right of a copyright owner under this title in a work or a portion thereof.").

30. Jay Dratler Jr., Cyberlaw: Intellectual Property in the Digital Millennium §2.04, at 2-18–2-19 (2004) (footnotes omitted) (emphasis original).

31. *United Sates v. Elcom, Ltd.*, 203 F. Supp. 2d 1111, 1125 (N.D. Calif. 2002).

32. H. Rpt. No. 94-1476, 94th Cong. 2d Sess. 82 (1976), reprinted in 5 United States Code Congressional and Administrative News 5659, 5696 (1976) ("To come within clause (1), the performance or display must be 'by instructors or pupils,' thus ruling out performances by actors or singers, or instrumentalists brought in from outside the school to put on a program. However, the term 'instructors' would be broad enough to include guest lecturers if their instrumental activities remain confined to classroom situations.").

33. Conference Report, H. Rpt. No. 107-685, 107th Cong., 2d Sess. 227 (2002) ("But, as in section 110(1), the exclusion applies only where the transmitting body or institution 'knew or had reason to believe' that the copy or phonorecord was not lawfully made and acquired.").

34. Section 110(1) provides that the following are not infringing activities: the "performance or display of a work by instructors or pupils in the course of face-to-face teaching activities of a nonprofit educational institution, in a classroom, or similar place of instruction, *unless, in the case of a motion picture or other audiovisual work, the performance, or the display of individual images, is given by means of a copy that was not lawfully made under this title, and that the person responsible for the performance knew or had reason to believe was not lawfully made.*" 17 U.S.C. §110(1) (emphasis added).

35. These concepts are consistent with secondary liability in copyright law. Vicarious liability is based on the concept of respondent superior, where "an employer or principal [is] liable for the employee's or agent's wrongful acts committed within the scope of the employment or agency. *Black's Law Dictionary 1339*, 8th ed. (2004).

36. H. Rpt. No. 94-1476, 94th Cong., 2d Sess. 82 (1976), reprinted in 5 United States Code Congressional and Administrative News 5659, 5696 (1976) (emphasis added).

37. H. Rpt. No. 94-1476, 94th Cong., 2d Sess. 103 (1976), reprinted in 5 United States Code Congressional and Administrative News 5659, 5718 (1976) ("Section 112(b) represents a response to the arguments of instructional broadcasters and other educational groups for special recording privileges. Although it does not go as far as these groups requested . . . the ephemeral recordings made by an instructional broadcaster under subsection (b) must embody a performance or display that meets all of the qualifications for exemption under section 110(2). Another point stressed by the producers of educational films in this connection, however, was that ephemeral recordings made by instructional broadcasters are in fact audiovisual works that often compete for exactly the same market.").

38. Conference Report, H. Rpt. No. 107-685, 107th Cong., 2d Sess. 227–228 (2002), citing, U.S. Copyright Office, Report on Copyright and Digital Distance Education 159 (1999).

39. Conference Report, H. Rpt. No. 107-685, 107th Cong., 2d Sess. 228 (2002). The Register's Report observed: "The educator would typically purchase the copy to be used, providing some revenue to the copyright owner. In addition, works that had not yet been placed on the market, such as first-run movies, would as a practical matter be rendered ineligible, mitigating further any possible impact on sales to the public." U.S. Copyright Office, Report on Copyright and Digital Distance Education 160 (1999).

40. Conference Report, H. Rpt. No. 107-685, 107th Cong., 2d Sess. 229 (2002) ("The amended exemption is not intended to address other uses of copyrighted works in the course of digital distance education, including student use of *supplemental or research materials in digital form, such as electronic course-packs, e-reserves, and digital library resources.* Such activities do not involve uses analogous to the performance and displays currently addressed in section 110(2). The 'mediated instructional activity' requirement is thus intended to prevent the exemption provided by the TEACH Act from displacing *textbooks, course packs or other material in any media,* copies or phonorecords of which are typically purchased or acquired by students for their independent use and retention 'in most post-secondary and some elementary and secondary contents. . . .'") (emphasis added).

3

New Rights and Limitations Regarding Use of Copyrighted Material

Section 110(2) and Subsections (A), (B), and (C)

U NDER 110(2) AND SUBSECTIONS (A), (B), AND (C), TEACH establishes new rights and new limitations on the use of copyrighted material performed or displayed in the distance education environment.

Performances

Each of the next three clauses provides three pieces of information: the category or categories of copyrighted material (in copyright parlance, what works of authorship are governed by the §110(2) privilege granted educators), what specific uses may be made of the work (i.e., to what exclusive right or rights of the copyright owner do the §110(2) rights correlate), and any limitation on the amount or portion of the copyrighted work that may be used.

With respect to either nondramatic literary or nondramatic musical works, an educator may perform a work in either category in its entirety because the use of the work is provided in the statute without any qualifying language suggesting a limit on the amount of the work performed: "*the performance of a nondramatic literary or musical work.*" A nondramatic literary or nondramatic musical work would be a short story or a song, respectively, as opposed to a play (a dramatic literary work) or a musical or opera (a dramatic musical work). Since this language was first enacted by the 1976 Copyright Act and retained in the 2002 TEACH Act, examination of the 1976 legislative history for further elucidation is possible:

> The exemption for instructional broadcasting provided by section 110(2) would apply only to "performance of a nondramatic literary or musical work or display of a work." Thus, the copyright owner's permission would be required for the performance on educational television or radio of a dramatic work, of a dramatico-musical work such as an opera or musical comedy, or of a motion picture. . . . The clause is not intended to limit in any way the copyright owner's exclusive right to make dramatizations, adaptations, or other derivative works under section 106(2). Thus, for example, a performer could read a nondramatic literary work aloud under §110(2), but the copyright owner's permission would be required for him to act it out in dramatic form. [1]

The last sentence from the 1976 House Report is a valid statement of the law as a dramatic adaptation of a copyrighted work constitutes a work derivative of the orignal nondramatic literary work. The right to make derivative uses or versions of a work is an exclusive right of the copyright owner and not covered by the §110(2) performance and display privilege. Though in theory all performances of copyrighted material are derivative, the legislative history suggests that simple performance (read a work) does not impact the exclusive rights of the copyright owner; rather, a change of some form is necessary (act it out).

Looking at the 1976 legislative history, we can point out several other nuances. Notice the phrase "or display of a work." Under pre-TEACH law, an educator could display any work without limit to portion. TEACH, however, establishes a shifting portion limitation on displays of works in distance education, as discussed below. Second, in commenting about performance-right circumstances (i.e., when permission would be needed), the 1976 House Report includes the phrase "or of a motion picture." This is so because a motion picture—a category of audiovisual work—was not included in the pre-TEACH performance right; §110(2) at that time applied only to performances of a nondramatic literary or musical work. Third, the comment about preservation of a copyright owner's §106(2) right, the right to make derivative works, is still valid because, even under TEACH, §110(2) as revised grants only certain performance or display rights and says nothing about derivative rights. So a junior-high music teacher who would like to display the score of a version of Aaron Copland's *Fanfare for the Common Man* or Leonard Bernstein's *West Side Story* that he adapted for his young students would be displaying and performing a derivative work. One could argue that the making of such derivative work is a fair use, especially if such easier-to-play versions are not available in the market; if so, then this would represent a lawfully made copy, a critical criterion for a §110(2) use, as discussed in chapter 2. Circumstances could, of course, change, to make the creation of the adaptation an unfair use, if the teacher began commercial distribution of the score to other music teachers across the country.

There is no portion limitation on how much of a nondramatic literary or nondramatic musical work an educator may perform (see table 3.1). This remains unchanged by TEACH. Finally, the phrase "but the copyright owner's permission would be required for him to act it out in dramatic form" suggests that making a derivative use of a work—so a dramatization of the work is a derivative use of it—would require a license or other permission even though the purpose is educational. There is no suggestion in the legislative history that fair use might allow this use. Assuming this is still a valid statement of the law, once permission or license to make the derivative use is secured, § 110(2) would allow its transmission, as it would then be a lawfully made copy. However, it could be concluded that fair use might support the on-the-fly dramatization.

While an educator could display a nondramatic literary or nondramatic musical work, this would include exposition of the sheet music of the Copland or Bernstein score. But if an educator is thinking of reading a text or playing the score, then in copyright parlance one speaks of performing—that is, of a performance. Logic also supports the use of this distinction. So the music teacher might display the original Copland score to students and perform it for students as well. When a person attends a Gershwin evening of the local "pops" symphony, he or she expects to hear the music, not have the sheet music (the musical work) displayed but to have it performed. Obviously, some works might be able to be rendered only by display, such as a piece of fine art, likewise others, only by performance, such as an audiovisual work. An educator could of course display a nondramatic literary or nondramatic musical work, but reference would be to the text of the story or sheet music itself, the literary or the musical work. An educator performs a nondramatic literary or musical by reading or singing it. Since under TEACH display rights are subject to a possible portion limitation, as discussed below, there is a possible misalignment here: An educator could clearly perform the entire reading of the short story but would not necessarily be able to display a complete copy of the text by posting it on a course website (more on this issue later).

Before TEACH, the performance of a nondramatic literary or musical work was the only performance authorized by § 110(2); performance of other works required either a license or permission, or a turn to fair use to "justify" the performance—thus the need for reform. As the TEACH Conference Committee explained: "Unlike the current section 110(2) [i.e., pre-TEACH § 110(2)], which applies only to public performances of non-dramatic literary or musical works, the amendment would apply to public performances of any type of work, subject to certain exclusion set forth in section 110(2), as amended."[2] As the saying goes, the Congress giveth and the Congress taketh away. Let us look at the next use-portion clause and determine what the "certain exclusion" might be.

While it is true that "[t]he TEACH Act expands the scope of the section 110(2) exemption to apply to performances and displays of all categories of copyrighted works,"[3] the next clause limits the portion of the remaining categories of copyrighted works that can be performed or displayed. The performance of any other category of copyrighted work is limited to "*a reasonable and limited portion of any other work.*" But what is reasonable and limited? Here is an example of how the TEACH legislative history can be consulted, to help educators understand what Congress, or at least the Conference Committee, had in mind. "The performance of works other than non-dramatic literary or musical works is limited, however, to 'reasonable and limited portions' of *less than* the entire work."[4] The first sentence explaining the nature of the performance right applying to categories of works other than nondramatic literary or nondramatic musical works indicates that whatever the portion of the work performed that is reasonable and limited and allowed under §110(2), it is something "less than the entire work." This is a significant limitation, especially when compared to the rights of educators to perform any category of work and in its entirety under §110(1). Moreover, this limitation encompasses a category of copyrighted work that many educators view as an important building block of the curriculum: the audiovisual work, such as a VHS or DVD recording of a documentary or, where appropriate, theatrically released film.

If an educator is restricted to performing less than an entire work, what then is that acceptable portion under §110(2)? The statute indicates a "reasonable and limited portion." But how much is that? Again, the Conference Report is of some help: "What constitutes a 'reasonable and limited' portion should take into account both the nature of the market for that type of work and the pedagogical purposes of the performance."[5] These are two separate tests: a market test and a pedagogical purposes test. Determining what that reasonable and limited portion is takes into account both tests.

In considering the "nature of the market for that *type* of work," an educator should realize that here, as in a fair use analysis under §107,[6] some categories of works are more market-sensitive than others, such that the more an educator might perform of the work in a distance education environment, the greater the effect on the market—that is, a negative impact made upon the market for the work. While not explicit in either the statute or the legislative history, use of the word "market" implies economics, dollars and cents, and the positive or negative impact thereupon that a performance of it in the distance-classroom use can have. Furthermore, this is consistent with the concern expressed elsewhere

TABLE 3.1

Section 110(2), Limitations on Exclusive Rights: Exemption of Certain Performances and Displays

Exclusive Right of the Copyright Owner to which the Exemption Applies	Work of Authorship: Category of Copyrighted Material	Portion of the Work that May Be Performed or Displayed	Examples in the Classroom
Performance	Nondramatic literary works	No limitation on the portion (amount) of a work that can be performed	Broadcast ("transmission") of the reading of a short story or journal article
Performance	Nondramatic musical works	No limitation on the portion (amount) of a work that can be performed	Broadcast ("transmission") of the singing of a song or the humming of its melody
Performance	All other categories of works to which the performance right applies	The portion of a work that can be performed is limited to a "reasonable and limited" portion	Broadcast ("transmission") of any of the following works listed below:
	Dramatic literary		Acting out several scenes from *Our Town*
	Dramatic musical		Singing the opening number from the musical *Les Miserables*
	Pantomimes and choreographic works		Dancing a Fosse number from *Sweet Charity*
	Motion pictures		Playing the British Airbourne sequence from *The Longest Day*
	Other audiovisual works		Showing the "Jurassic" section from a film strip entitled "The End of Dinosaurs"
	Sound recordings		Playing a portion of a Pretenders song to complement a slide show, but only if the

(continued)

TABLE 3.1

Section 110(2), Limitations on Exclusive Rights: Exemption of Certain Performances and Displays (*continued*)

Exclusive Right of the Copyright Owner to which the Exemption Applies	Work of Authorship: Category of Copyrighted Material	Portion of the Work that May Be Performed or Displayed	Examples in the Classroom
			broadcast is by a digital audio transmission (otherwise no performance right in a sound recording exists)
	Derivative works		Reading a translation of a Pablo Neruda essay
Display	Any work to which the display right applies	"An amount comparable to that which is typically displayed in the course of a live classroom session"	Broadcast ("transmission") of any of the following works listed below: (assume the material is posted on the distance education course website then transmitted to students when accessed)
	Literary works, including computer programs		Posting a chart or table from an article on reserve, but not necessarily the entire article
	Musical works (nondramatic)		Posting a page of sheet music
	Dramatic works (including music)		Posting several scenes, but not necessarily the entire script
	Pantomimes and choreographic works		Posting the scripted score of a Broadway dance number
	Pictorial, graphic, and sculptural works		Posting a picture of a painting
	Architectural works		Posting a building design
	Derivative works		Posting an excerpt from the Neruda essay

in the TEACH legislative history,[7] and in other sections of the copyright law,[8] as to the negative impact on the market for a copyrighted work that results when a specific limitation on the exclusive rights of a copyright owner granted by the law is not carefully tailored.

Suppose an educator is teaching a literature class on "the myth and fable." Notice the phrase does not read the "nature of the market for that *particular* work"; rather, it reads the "nature of the market for that *type* of work." In other words, do not consider whether the market impact of performing a reasonable and limited portion of the 1930s black-and-white movie version of *Beauty and the Beast* would have more or less impact than a performance of the more recent animated Disney version of the same story. Rather, since both are audiovisual works, one might instead consider the market impact of performing (rendering a dramatic reading of) portions of the script to each adaptation of the story versus performing (playing a VHS or DVD of) a portion of the movie version of the story; that is, one might consider the market for the performance of a dramatic literary work versus the performance of an audiovisual work. If he or she read (performed) the entire sequence of scenes of Beauty's first several nights at the Beast's palace, or only showed (performed) a clip of the opening candelabra scene, an educator would likely not harm the market for either textual or visual rendering of the story (the screenplay or the movie, respectively) but might actually generate interest in the market for that type of work, for example, by piquing students' interest, prompting them to obtain and view the movie by renting it from a video store or purchasing a copy of it, thus having a positive market impact. By the same token, suppose the VHS or DVD is a documentary film. Showing a clip might not generate a market rush among students to obtain their own copy for viewing, but even if it did, it would be unlikely that the local video store would have the "Life Cycle of the Brown Tree Spore" in its inventory. But here is an important point to remember for future discussion of fair use in chapter 7: Fair use might not support a showing of that film in its entirety to a distance education class because the only market for this film is the educational market. The copyright owner might be able to demonstrate market harm through loss of performance license revenue, especially when the market is limited, thus the impact due to free-riding is more pronounced.

Is this too restrictive a requirement upon the educator? The Register's Report observed: "A teacher will rarely wish to devote a full class session to performing a movie or record; rather, the typical instructional use involves a segment or clip used to demonstrate or illustrate a point."[9] Perhaps an accurate statement pedagogically, that statement is quite out of touch with daily practice of most teachers, who routinely show an entire theatrical motion picture or other audiovisual program, such as a documentary film or instructional program. One obvious example of a complete viewing of a motion picture being necessary is in a film studies class. However, the case can also be made for limitations on audiovisual works designed specifically for education.[10] For example, in an astronomy class with a session on cosmology, having students view only the first four or five billion years of celestial history seems an odd imposition for the copyright law to make. Yet, even here the Register's Report suggested otherwise: "Under the proposed amendment, the law would permit a teacher in a music-appreciation course to play excerpts from sound recordings for the students, or the instructor in a film course to show clips demonstrating Hitchcock's directing style. (Students could then be referred to other sources in order to experience the entire work on their own.)."[11] Likewise, showing the entire Jean Cocteau or Disney movie would negatively impact the market for the work, as a student who had never watched a particular movie version of the story would not need to later rent or purchase it.[12] Unfortunately the whole-versus-part debate fails to recognize how these materials are used in the distance education classroom, as an instructor might not desire to take valuable synchronous class time streaming an entire audiovisual work, but he or she might like to have the entire work available to students as a part of asynchronous teaching exercises, reserving synchronous time for chat about either film.

The second test, requiring an accounting of the pedagogical purposes for the performance, asks whether the use of the copyrighted material is an effective teaching tool; that is, that the more of the work is performed, the more positive the pedagogical impact achieved. In its simplest expression, this purpose test asks whether a near complete ("less than the entire") performance of the copyrighted work, in the present example, of the movie version of *Beauty and the Beast*, is necessary. The statement of the Conference Report implies that a complete showing of an audiovisual work in a distance education classroom never satisfies a pedagogical purpose. While an educator might argue that what is reasonable and limited, applying the nature-of-the-market test and the pedagogical-purposes test, is in fact a performance of the entire work, recall the first sentence of the Conference Committee explanation does not anticipate this conclusion: It says, "'reasonable and limited portions' of *less than the entire work*." This is further supported by a second Conference Committee observation comparing the reformulated TEACH *display right* to this "reasonable and limited portion" performance right and observing that, for the display right, discussed below, a "display of the entire work could be appropriate and consistent with displays typically made in a live classroom setting."[13] The "appropriate and consistent" formulation allowing display of the "entire work" is not repeated with respect to a performance; rather, complete (entire work) performance is limited to nondramatic literary and nondramatic musical works.

If there can be variation as to the amount of a work performed and the impact on the *nature of the market* for that type of work, then there can also be variation as to the amount of a work performed and the impact or result of the *pedagogical purposes* achieved by the performance of that amount. Does an educator need to show every scene of interaction between Beauty and her sisters in *Beauty and the Beast* in order to demonstrate internal versus external beauty or the different nuances among the characters concerning how each covets versus how each loves, or would a few choice clips of dialog and interaction suffice? In the classroom of the twenty-first century, an odd series of results occurs if educators try to follow the law. Such elaborate tests are not a part of live, face-to-face teaching described in §110(1). In a hybrid class of both live and remote students, different sets of students would be able to view different amounts of the movie. Of course an easy solution is to obtain a license (contract) to perform (view live and transmit remote) the entire movie. But this option forces educators to obtain more and more of curricular content through license, which begs the question for another day: What, then, is the point of copyright?

Displays

Under the pre-TEACH §110(2) display right, there was no limitation on the portion of copyrighted works that could be displayed. However, TEACH, responding to the sensitivity of the new digital distance education environment, changes that. Recall that the pre-TEACH version of §110(2), enacted in 1976, envisioned distance education to consist of television, cable, or radio broadcasting. Revised §110(2) prepares educators for the opportunities of the digital age of distance education, but it also responds to potential threats of the digital age as well. By looking again at the legislative history, one can understand (though perhaps not agree with) the rationale of the Conference Committee, when it explains the limitation imposed by §110(2) on the display of copyrighted works in distance environments. The statutory text of the display limitation is as follows: "*or display of a work in an amount comparable to that which is typically displayed in the course of a live classroom session*." While an educator might at first blush be disappointed that he or she is limited in distance environments with respect to the portion of copyrighted material that can be displayed while not under the same restriction in §110(1) live face-to-face classroom scenarios, this limitation—unlike the second performance proviso ("reasonable and limited" versus "no limitation" in §110(1))—merely aligns the display of copyrighted material in remote instruction with that which occurs in live face-to-face teaching. In other words, an educator should not display more in a distance education setting, such as on a class website, than he or she would to students in a live class discussion of the same topic. However, if the educator would typically display the entire work in a face-to-face morning section of a class, the statute in theory allows that same amount, the entire work, to be displayed by the instructor in his or her distance education section scheduled for that afternoon. This makes sense, and, unlike the rules governing the performance of works other than nondramatic literary or nondramatic musical works discussed above, also accommodates the reality of twenty-first century education: An institution and its teachers may be engaged in simultaneous offering of both face-to-face and distance sections of the same course. Without the ability of a so-called portion "parity" between the on-campus and remote classrooms, teachers are forced to teach the same class two different ways. The other option is to treat all students the same, but that entails limiting the portion used with the on-campus students to that allowed for distance students for certain performances. This is a seemingly ludicrous though intended result of the statute and again underscores Congress's continued inability to match copyright law with current technological realities and teaching practicalities.

Why would an educator desire to display, scan, and load the entire content of copyrighted works onto a distance education website? There are, of course, numerous reasons, as use of an entire work can serve as the basis for instruction. For example, a map of the Ancient Mediterranean serves as the starting point for a course on Roman history; a Salinger letter to his editor regarding a draft of *Catcher in Rye* offers new dimension to students' understanding of the Holden Caulfield character; the original musical score of *Carousel* containing Oscar Hammerstein's stage notes handwritten in the margin allows students to chart the development of musical theater in America; reproducing early sketches of Jackson Pollack to compare with his later work helps students understand his influence on later artists; and so on. Arguably, these are all legitimate displays of entire copyrighted works and might parallel what one would display in the live face-to-face classroom. Furthermore, it is difficult to achieve maximum positive pedagogical impact from the display of half or some other less than whole portion of a map, sketch, or painting. On the other hand, displaying an entire article when the focus of the instruction-discussion centers on a chart or two or page or two alone would be unwarranted. First, it would *not* be comparable to an amount displayed in a live classroom. Second, the display of the entire article, when only a chart or page or two is needed, appears to place the article more in the realm of preparatory or assigned reading and, much like the text, course pack, or reserve item as discussed in chapter 2, is outside the scope of the TEACH display right.

Consider other works an educator might display, such as a periodical article, workbook, or textbook, and Congress's concern may become more palatable. Does an educator need to place an entire article or textbook on the course website (as opposed to the course e-reserve or virtual library)? As the legislative history points out, the concern is that educators will use the ease with which copyrighted material can be scanned, loaded, and stored on distance education websites to create scenarios in which more is loaded in distance (read "digital" here) education classroom spaces than would be brought into live classroom spaces or even displayed in traditional (read "pre-TEACH" here) distance education classroom spaces, such as television or radio broadcasts. As discussed later, TEACH is not about distance support material, such as the virtual library and its e-reserve, or the virtual bookstore with its e-reader and e-course packs.

TEACH is about and is only about what goes on in the classroom itself. The first comment from the Conference Report introduces this concept, which is revisited in the succeeding discussion:

> In addition, because "display" of certain types of works, such as literary works using an "e-book" reader, *could substitute for traditional purchases* of the work (e.g. a text book), the display exemption is limited to "an amount comparable to that which is typically displayed in the course of a live classroom setting." This limitation is a further implementation of the "mediated instructional activity" concept described below, and recognizes that a "display" may have a different meaning and impact in the digital environment than in the analog environment to which section 110(2) has previously applied.[14]

Notice once again the concern for crafting the TEACH § 110(2) right, the limitation on the exclusive rights of copyright owners that it grants to educators, in such a way that it not undermine the market for other educational products and services, in this case, the market for virtual library content such as e-books or e-course packs.

The concept of mediated instructional activity, MIA, also works to accomplish that link between material used (performed or displayed) in the classroom and the actual teaching in the classroom, not what students do at the library or at home in preparation for class. For example, reading the entire article would be preparation for a live chat in which the two charts would be displayed and discussed. If the focus of an entire class session is the presentation and critique, line by line, of a seminal article in a particular discipline and requires a distance educator to display the article in its entirety, such display would parallel an "amount comparable to that which is typically displayed in the course of a live classroom session." Typically, this is not the case with the use of most textual works, such as articles and books. More often, the instructor assigns an entire article or selected textbook chapters and then makes general comments or directs general discussion on the topic. Moreover, as the next Conference Committee comment indicates,

[t]he "limited portion" formulation used in conjunction with the performance right exemption is not used in connection with the display right exemption, because, for certain works, display of the entire work could be appropriate and consistent with displays typically made in a live classroom setting (e.g., short poems or essays, or images of pictorial, graphic, or sculptural works, etc.).[15]

In the seminal article presentation and critique example, the display of an entire article might well be appropriate under §110(2). A more typical use is suggested by a later comment discussing the concept of MIAs, "an instructor would not be precluded from using a chart or table or other short excerpt from a textbook different from the one assigned for the course, or from emphasizing such an excerpt from the assigned textbook that had been purchased by the students."[16] In this way the display proviso operates as a check on distance educators to think before they act (i.e., scan and load): Is the complete display of this work necessary to my teaching?

The display limitation also works in tandem with the revision TEACH brought to §112, the ephemeral recording section, discussed in chapter 6. Section 112 allows distance educators to reproduce, in some cases by digitalization, copyrighted material for use in distance education. This additional right to reproduce works is statutorily necessary as well, as §110 grants only rights of performance and display or, in §110(2), very limited transitory reproduction rights.[17] However, §112(f) limits the amount reproduced (scanned, then loaded) to an amount equal to a legitimate-use display or performance under §110(2).

Sound Recordings and Musical Works

Consideration of the Portion Limitation Mismatch

An example of a copyrighted musical work is the words and music to a song, fixed in a tangible form—that is, expressed in a piece of sheet music of a song. An example of a sound recording[18] would be the capturing of sounds on a recording, such as an LP, cassette, or CD. It need not capture music but could capture a dramatic reading of poetry, an instructional language session, or (more common) a book on tape. In the case of the dramatic reading recording or the more traditional music recording, that LP, cassette, or CD would actually consist of at least two copyrights, so to speak: one in the underlying work, the literary (poem) or musical work (song), and a second in the derivative work created by its recording—one copyright owned originally (there may have been an assignment of copyright to a publisher) by the poet and the other by the composer. As sound recordings often capture the performance of some other copyrighted work, a sound recording is often a derivative work, and since derivative works qualify for copyrighted protection, though permission would be required from the copyright owner of the poem or song, the performing artist also has a copyright interest in the recording. Of course, other copyrights may layer as well, for example, to Nelson Riddle, as the arranger (creator of a musical derivative work) of a Burt Bacharach and Hal David song (the composer and lyricist of the musical work) for an Andy Williams rendition (his derivative work, i.e., performance) of the song "Alfie."

The earlier discussion revealed a bit of a potential mismatch between displays and certain performances of copyrighted material in face-to-face (§110(1)) versus distance (§110(2)) "classrooms," for example, in a so-called hybrid course, where some students would be live, on campus, while others participate remotely, yet under the construction of the statute they would have different portions of works made available under §110. However, within §110(2) rests another possible mismatch (see table 3.2). In order to appreciate and understand the possible mismatch, one needs to understand the history and nature of the exclusive rights of copyright owners in sound recordings. Section 106(6) covers the performance of sound recordings and provides for the exclusive right by the copyright owner to "perform the copyrighted work publicly by means of a digital audio transmission."[19] For example, a CD of Sam Elliott or Kevin Costner reading a story about drovers on the Great Plains is a sound recording, and thus, by its nature, derivative of a literary work, that is, an original Louis L'Amour tale.

Under the 1976 Act there was no performance right in a sound recording. "Educators were therefore free to transmit performances of sound recordings to students without restriction (assuming that the use of any literary or musical work embodied in the sound recording was authorized by statute or license)."[20] And as discussed earlier, the performance of a nondramatic musical work or its display by or in the course of a transmission was in fact allowed under the 1976 version of §110(2). Without a performance right in the sound recording, if an instructor broadcast (transmitted) a playing of the recording of "Alfie" or the L'Amour narration, the only copyright at issue would have been the copyright underlying the sound recording, that of Bacharach and David, or literary work, that belonging to L'Amour. Since they were nondramatic musical or dramatic literary works, §110(2) authorized their pre-TEACH use.

Further, and as discussed above, the 2002 TEACH version of §110(2) also authorizes the performance of nondramatic literary and nondramatic musical works, the performance of a reasonable and limited portion of all other works, such as dramatic literary and dramatic musical works or sound recordings, and the display of musical works "in an amount comparable to that which is typically displayed in the course of a live classroom session" (in the example above, the instructor desires to display the Bacharach and David sheet music or L'Amour text as well as perform the sound recording of it). A sound recording would fall into the "the performance of a reasonable and limited portion of all other works" category, but, since there is no performance right in a sound recording, there is little concern regarding the portion limitation rules. But it is not that simple, as Congress amended the statute regarding the performance right and sound recordings sometime after the 1976 Copyright Act but before the passage of TEACH.

As Internet technologies emerged, Congress desired to prevent the development of digital delivery technologies from leading to widespread abuse and to grant copyright owners some control over the "ways in which their creative works are used"[21] (on the Internet). In response, Congress passed the Digital Performance Right in Sound Recordings Act (DPRSRA) in 1995.[22] Congress hoped that "[t]hese new technologies may also lead to new systems for the electronic distribution of phonorecords with the *authorization* of the affected copyright owners. Such systems could increase the selection of recordings available to consumers, and make it more convenient for consumers to acquire *authorized* phonorecords."[23] Here is the potential mismatch, and thus the potential problem: Section 110(2) addresses the performance and display of musical works, which would likely underlie any sound recording performed in the distance education classroom, unless of course the musical work is no longer protected by copyright. With a recent performance right granted to copyright owners in sound recordings under certain circumstances in DPRSRA (i.e., via digital audio transmission), without a coinciding performance right granted to educators for sound recordings in §110(2), the copyright owner's exclusive right in performances of sound recordings by means of a digital audio transmission remains unaffected (i.e., it is not limited by §110(2), other than by the default "performance of a reasonable and limited portion of all other works" proviso). As a result, an educator who desires to perform a CD in a Web-based (digital transmission) distance class might face the following: The CD consists of two copyrights, so to speak: one in the underlying musical work (words and music) and one in the sound recording (the performer), each governed by different portion limitation rules.

If the performance made by the educator is by means of a digital audio transmission, then the performance rights of two copyright owners are implicated: the owner of the musical work and the owner of the sound recording. Suppose the CD is of a song, that is, a nondramatic musical work. Recall that under the discussion of §110(2) discussed above we identified that there is no portion limitation on the amount of a nondramatic musical work that can be performed in a distance education classroom. However, the performance right granted to ed-

TABLE 3.2
The Potential Mismatch of Performance Rights in a Musical Work and a Sound Recording

Work of Authorship: Category of Copyrighted Material	Portion of the Work that May Be Performed	Authorization
Dramatic musical work	"reasonable and limited" ↓ NO MISMATCH ↑	Section 110(2)
Sound recording embodying the dramatic musical work or nondramatic musical work	"reasonable and limited" ↓ MISMATCH ↑	Section 110(2), if made by means of a digital audio transmission; if not by means of a digital audio transmission, there is no performance right
Nondramatic musical work	no limit, but because the sound recording embodies both the underlying copyright in the musical work and the performer's sound recording right and the two cannot practically be separated, the use of the musical work is limited to a "reasonable and limited" portion	Section 110(2)

ucators regarding the sound recording when performed by means of a digital audio transmission—a work whose performance falls into the "performance of a reasonable and limited portion of all other works" category—is limited. Thus we have the mismatch in the portion limitation of the two copyrights embodied in the same object, the CD. Because of this anomaly, there is an increased chance of infringement of the underlying protected elements when a performance of a sound recording is made in a digital environment, or at least the need to seek support for such uses in the concept of fair use or to secure permission or use rights by license.[24] Recourse to these options undermines the usefulness of the precise section of the copyright law designed to facilitate distance education. Of course the sound recording issue impacts most those educational entities that make extensive use of sound recordings in online course content.

However, and, as it turned out, in a twisted bit of clairvoyance in light of the Napster, Aimster, Grokster, etc., controversies, Congress observed that "certain types of subscription and interactive audio services might adversely affect sales of sound recordings and erode copyright owners' ability to control and be paid for use of their work."[25] Of course Congress was referring to more formal means of delivery such as pay-per-listen or audio-on-demand, but the attraction to consumers of online access systems is present in either formal or informal and illegal systems such as Napster or Aimster. As result of DPRSRA, there is now a performance right in sound recordings, but only when the performance is done by means of a digital audio transmission. Unfortunately, §110, enacted in 1976 (years before the addition of the digital audio transmission amendment), was not one of the sections amended by DPRSRA. "At that time, there was no discussion of whether sound recordings should be added to the coverage of section 110(2). This issue thus presents a new policy question that has not yet been considered."[26] In other words, the performance right granted to educators in the pre-TEACH §110(2) does not apply to sound recordings, but only to the underlying nondramatic literary and musical work on which sound recordings might be based.

> The failure to include sound recordings in the scope of current section 110(2) [pre-TEACH] *does* result in a discrepancy between a distance educator's ability to perform a nondramatic musical work and her ability to perform the sound recording in which it is embodied. In other words, the copyright owner of the music is essentially subsidizing some distance education activities, while the record producer remains free to charge for the same activities. One question is whether this makes sense, when typically a teacher will perform a musical work by playing a sound recording, rather than by a live performance [e.g., playing the song on the piano which would imply the musical work copyright alone, not the sound recording performance right.].[27]

If use of the sound recording is now subject to a performance right, then under TEACH the amount is limited to a reasonable and limited portion, with the result that the entire recording of the song could not be made available to distance education students.

Minimizing the Impact of the Performance "Digital Audio Transmission" Right in Sound Recordings

All is not lost, however, as §114 contains significant exceptions to the DPRSRA copyright owner's performance right and indicates that nonsubscription "broadcast" digital transmissions of sound recordings are exempted outright.[28] Furthermore, a large category of transmissions, "[n]onexempt, noninteractive subscription transmissions," are "eligible for statutory licensing,"[29] thus making them available for use by distance educators nonetheless, though at a set fee.

It could be argued that most "transmissions" that a school, college, or university would make are also not considered to be "broadcasts" for purposes of §114 (the section that elucidates the nature of the DPRSRA right), because qualifying broadcast transmissions pertain only to those transmissions "made by a terrestrial broadcast station licensed as such by the Federal Communications Commission."[30] As a result, while some of the activities of an educational institution (e.g., having a licensed broadcast station within its organizational structure, a possibility at many tertiary institutions) could conceivably qualify, most would not. If it did have a broadcast service to facilitate distance learning and it was nonsubscription, then the service would be exempted from the new DPRSRA performance right under §114(d)(1)(A). Moreover, if the transmission is a retransmission of a nonsubscription broadcast transmission, then §114(d)(1)(B)(iv) contains an exception for those circumstances where the "radio station's broadcast transmission is made by a noncommercial educational broadcast station. . . ." In those instances, "[d]istance education activities that entail digital 'broadcast transmissions' of sound recordings will not be subject to the section 106(6) performance right."[31]

To qualify as exempt transmissions and retransmissions under the §114(d)(1) broadcast transmission exception, the performance must be "other than as part of an interactive service." An interactive service is defined in §114(j)(7) as "one that enables a member of the public to receive a transmission or a program specially created for the recipient, or on request, a transmission of a particular sound recording, whether or not as part of a program, which is selected by or on behalf of the recipient." The definition goes on to indicate that the "ability of individuals to [make] request[s of] particular sound recordings" does not make the service an interactive one. There is a caveat to the "request line" exception of interactive service; the service must not "substantially consist of sound recordings that are performed within 1 hour of the request or at a time designated by either the transmitting entity or the individual making such request." This does not preclude the use of request lines, but a service whose broadcasts consisted completely of listener requests would trigger the "substantially consist of" rule and the service would indeed be an interactive service. According to the legislative history of the DPRSRA, "[t]he term 'interactive service' is intended to cover only services in which an individual can arrange for the transmission or retransmission of a specific sound recording to that person or another, individually."[32] However, a digital library of sound recordings that students could access at their discretion would appear to be an interactive service. Even a selection of those recordings placed on a course website, and used in class—this would qualify as an acceptable §110(2) use under TEACH, as opposed to an unacceptable or excluded use under TEACH, as would be the case with an audio e-reserve as

TEACH does not authorize the creation of e-reserve, textual or audio—might still be considered interactive for purposes of §114, and thus the performance right in a digital transmission of a sound recording would apply to the use.

Once the determination is made that the use is not interactive, then a digital transmission or retransmission will qualify for the (d)(1) exception and would not be covered by the performance right in digital audio transmission created by DPRSRA, if it is a "nonsubscription transmission" or is a retransmission of a "nonsubscription transmission," even if the retransmission itself is a subscription service.[33] Again, to be eligible under (d)(1), the service cannot be interactive. "The term 'interactive service' is intended to cover only services in which an individual can arrange for the transmission or retransmission of a specific sound recording to that person or another, individually."[34] According to the legislative history, the classic example is that of a "traditional radio or television station."[35]

The most significant impediment for any of the §114(d)(1) exemption applying to distance education scenarios is that it must be a nonsubscription transmission. While it might be tempting to hypothesize that most distance education transmission might be nonsubscription, a closer examination is necessary. "Certain distance education activities could entail subscription transmissions (transmissions that are controlled and limited to particular recipients, and for which payment is required)."[36] It would appear that a distance education Web class on music appreciation, for example, that has digital or digitized sound recordings available for students to access as part of the class, while not meeting the statutory definition of a broadcast, would nonetheless arguably be a subscription transmission. Section 114(j)(14) defines a subscription transmission as one that "is controlled and limited to particular recipients and for which consideration is required to be paid or otherwise given by or on behalf of the recipients to receive the transmission or a package of transmissions including the transmission." Would the password or other restrictive access mechanism employed by most distance education websites and which TEACH (as discussed below) requires be a situation where the transmission "is controlled and limited to particular recipients"? Would the payment of tuition fees or special distance education course surcharges meet the "or which consideration is required to be paid or otherwise given by or on behalf of the recipients" requirement? If the answer to both questions is in the affirmative, then the transmission could be considered a subscription service and not exempt under §114(d), and thus the performance right in the sound recording may operate to complicate the copyright considerations as suggested above.

Using the example of a digital audio service as part of a cable system, the legislative history observes that "[t]he payments required to satisfy the 'consideration' requirement might consist, for example, of an 'à la carte' fee for specific audio service, or of a fee for an overall package of services that includes the digital audio services (e.g., a cable system's tier of services for a fee)."[37] The scenario of parents paying for tuition might even be covered by the following concluding comment:

> The reference in the definition of payments "on behalf of" a recipient is intended to recognize that payments for a service may be made by one person on behalf of other people, such as a parent making payments for a child who lives away from home and receives the subscription service.[38]

Even if it is argued that the transmission would be a nonsubscription transmission, in either case under §114(d)(2)(C) an "eligible nonsubscription transmission or a subscription transmission not exempt under paragraph (1)" may not publish advance play lists. This might prevent an educator from providing a list of music selections to be covered during the semester and which class sessions each would be discussed in, because neither the eligible nonsubscription transmission nor a subscription transmission not exempt under paragraph (1) can "cause to be published, or induce or facilitate the publication, by means of an advance program schedule or prior announcement, the titles of the specific sound recordings to be transmitted, the phonorecord embodying such sound recordings, or, other than for illustrative purposes, the names of the featured recording artists. . . ."[39]

Second, subscription transmissions not exempt under (d)(1) (e.g., a nonbroadcast transmission), and eligible nonsubscription transmissions are eligible for statutory licensing under §114(d)(2). However, to be eligible for statutory licensing, the transmission cannot be part of an interactive service. Again, creating a mechanism whereby students can retrieve or call up songs would be interactive and not subject to statutory licensing, either. Moreover, the transmissions subject to the statutory license cannot exceed the "sound recording performance complement" as described in §114(j)(13) that places "limits on the number of selections a subscription transmission service can play from any one phonorecord or boxed set, or by the same featured recording artist."[40] In any given three-hour period, transmissions are limited to no more than three selections from any one phonorecord lawfully distributed for public performance or sale in the United States; in other words, no bootleg or self-made copies, even if fair use would apply to its recording. The three-song limit is reduced to two if the songs are transmitted consecutively. Up to four selections are allowed from any one recording artist or from a boxed set ("compilation"), but no more than three consecutively. Thus, even if the service was not interactive but the transmission content was decided upon by the instructor, these limits—while not imposing insurmountable rules on a distance education program in music and a given course within that program—might throw a wrench into a class period designed to compare various jazz trumpeters, for example, where transmissions of multiple songs by Chet Baker and Terrance Blanchard are expected within a single class session. The statute allows for situations where the selections transmitted are in excess of the numerical limits to nonetheless qualify, as long as the programming "was not willfully intended to avoid the numerical limitations prescribed."[41]

The Mismatch in Action: Final Thoughts

In face-to-face teaching there was never a problem with this jumble of multiple copyrights, because the §110(1) right allowed any category of copyrighted work to be performed or displayed and, likewise, any portion thereof. Second, no performance right was created by DPRSRA for face-to-face scenarios; the performance right in sound recordings created by DPRSRA applies only where the performance is made by means of a digital audio transmission.

Under the pre-TEACH formulation of §110(2), until 1995 this was not a problem, since there was no performance right whatsoever in sound recordings. Further, it could be argued that after 1995, when performance rights were created in sound recordings but only where the performance was rendered by means of a digital audio transmission, there was still little concern, because the pre-TEACH or old §110(2) was really about nondigital distance education broadcasting. If the DPRSRA performance right was "activated" by a pre-TEACH digital transmission, the limitation was perhaps less oppressive because the only performance right granted by pre-TEACH §110(2) was for nondramatic literary or nondramatic musical works. There was no performance privilege to perform sound recordings of any other category of works whatsoever. Perhaps that need never arose, or perhaps educational institutions licensed these performances or obtained permission, or perhaps the institution ignored these limitations.

However, with TEACH and its clear recognition and expansion of digital distance education transmissions, it is likely that an educator may wish to transmit a sound recording by means of digital audio transmission. The problem is that, in our poetry reading or musical sound recording example, there are two distinct copyrights at play (no pun intended), each with a different set of portion limitations. The "literary work" poem and "musical work" song can be performed without limit under §110(2), but the sound recording of each is limited to a reasonable and limited portion. According to the legislative history, as observed earlier, a reasonable and limited portion can never equal a performance of an entire work,[42] and so a mismatch occurs between the §110(2) performance of the underlying literary or musical work and the performance of the sound recording that embodies its derivative expression, at least when that sound recording is performed in a distance education encounter by means of a digital audio transmission.

Of course, the mismatch problem (underlying musical work versus digital transmission of the phonorecord that embodies its performance; i.e., the sound recording) is avoided altogether if the amount transmitted constitutes a reasonable and limited portion of the sound recording, in which case §110(2) would authorize use of the added performance right in the digital transmission of sound recordings under DPRSRA. Section 114(d)(3) provides for licenses of interactive services. However, given the realities of licensing costs, it would be unlikely that an educational institution would go through the cost and trouble of obtaining a license for its transmissions. As licensing markets for educational uses of copyrighted materials develop, the cost and effort of securing such rights should improve. Of course, fair use is always an option for instances beyond the §110(2) "reasonable and limited portion" limitation, but in those instances the use of a complete or substantial portion of the work may not result in a favorable result under a fair use analysis. The application of fair use in distance education is discussed in chapter 7. For now, let us return to §110(2), which by comparison to the complicated transmission and licensing provisions of §114 should appear simple.

Understanding the Concept of Instructional or "Teaching" Activity in Section 110(2)(A)

The next phrase, "*by or in the course of a transmission, if*," establishes that §110(2) concerns performances and displays in distance education settings. However, as the Conference Report makes clear, "the term 'transmission' is intended to include transmissions by digital, as well as analog means."[43] Odd models or hybrid models that combine analog and digital of distance education can both exist under a reformulated §110(2).

Subsections 110(2)(A) and (B) incorporate language from the pre-TEACH version of §110(2). For example, new §110(2)(A) expands the "systematic instructional activities" phrasing of pre-TEACH §110(2)(A), adding the "actual" instructor supervision and "integral part" language to an expanded concept of teaching activities as expressed by the new concept of "systematic *mediated* instructional activities." These concepts were covered earlier in the discussion of the opening clause exclusion regarding MIA. The concept advanced by §110(2) is that performances and displays must be made in conjunction with teaching-learning activities.

The language of pre-TEACH and post-TEACH §110(2)(B) is identical, but—par for the legislative drafting course—is not without its own little oddity of interpretation. In short, the TEACH language is used to prohibit the use of copyrighted material for background or entertainment, which the 2002 TEACH Conference Report claims already existed in the pre-TEACH version of §110. However, as far §110(1) is concerned, that restriction is forwarded in the legislative history of the 1976 Copyright Act explaining that the "teaching activities" language ("face-to-face *teaching activities* of a nonprofit educational institution") of §110(1) forbids "performances or displays, whatever their cultural value or intellectual appeal, that are given for the recreation or entertainment of any part of their audience."[44] The 1976 version of §110(2) used the phrasing "systematic instructional activities" to express the concept of teaching, but its legislative history contained no such exclusion for works of recreation or entertainment use. TEACH, of course, uses the updated "systematic mediated instructional activities" to express this concept in §110(2)(A), as discussed above. So far, so good; strange thing is, the teaching activities concept is represented statutorily in TEACH §110(2)(A), not §110(2)(B), yet the TEACH legislative history that also forbids entertainment performances and displays is contained in the discussion of §110(2)(B). According to the 2002 Conference Report, which refers to the Register's Report,[45] the §110(2)(B) language ("directly related and of material assistance to the teaching content of the transmission") contains a "test of relevance and materiality [that] connects the copyrighted work to the curriculum, and it means that the portion performed or displayed may not be performed or displayed for the mere entertainment of the students, or as unrelated background material."[46] In other words, according to the legislative history, the statutory language in the 1976 law that forbids recreational uses is different from language in TEACH that forbids the same sorts of performances and displays. Two different statutory phrasings are used to accomplish the same purpose, the "teaching activities" of §110(1), but with respect to §110(2) it is not the "systematic mediated instructional activities" of §110(2)(A), rather it is the §110(2)(B) ("directly related and of material assistance") language that does so. Stranger still is the fact that the precise statutory language that the Conference Report points to in support of the entertainment exclusion ("directly related and of material assistance to the teaching content of the transmission") existed in the 1976 version of §110(2), yet nothing in the legislative history discussing §110(2) expressed this exclusion at that time. The statutory language surely existed, but the interpretation was not explicit in the older legislative history. Moreover, the TEACH legislative history offers it explicitly but derives it from a source different from the near-identical language in §110(1), and made explicit in its 1976 legislative history.

While §110(2)(A) was presented earlier in the discussion of the MIA transmitted via digital networks, it is examined here in detail. Section 110(2)(A) requires that "*(A) the performance or display is made by, at the direction of, or under the actual supervision of an instructor.*" Under new subsection (2)(A), "the performance or display is made by, at the direction of, or under the actual supervision of an instructor," but this can include asynchronous "supervision." While the instructor must be exerting control—"the instructor is, in fact, supervising class activities, supervision is not in name or theory only"[47]—over the learning environment, "[i]t is not intended to require either constant, real-time supervision by the instructor or pre-approval by the instructor for the performance or display."[48]

TEACH requires that the performance or display be "an integral part of a class session." According to the legislative history "it must be part of a class itself, rather than ancillary to it."[49] The definition of "class session" is not defined by the §110(2)(A) legislative history but comes later in the Conference Report discussion of §110(2)(C)(ii)(aa), which clearly relates it back to the §110(2)(A) use in the second prong of the teaching activity requirement, that the performance or display be made "*as an integral part of a class session*":

> The requirement that technological measures be applied to limit retention for no longer than the "class session" refers back to the requirement that the performance be made as an "integral part of a class session." The duration of a "class session" in asynchronous distance education would generally be that period during which a student is logged on to the server of the institution or governmental body making the display or performance, but is likely to vary with the needs of the student and with the design of the particular course. It does not mean the duration of a particular course (i.e., a semester or term), but rather is intended to describe the equivalent of an actual face-to-face mediated class session (although it may be asynchronous and one student may remain online or retain access to the performance or display for longer than another student as needed to complete the class session).[50]

This represents a flexible definition of "class session," one that allows distance education to evolve and meet the 24/7 access of the modern distance education student. It must still be integral in terms of content, but it is less tied to temporal or location or structural designs; for example, the instructor and students logged on at the same time, with students collected in one place receiving the transmission during a set period during which the instructor lectures.

Here is the second time the term MIA is used in §110(2) to establish a general requirement for eligibility in subsection (2)(A): "*offered as a regular part of the systematic mediated instructional activities.*" Note that TEACH modifies the 1976 Copyright Act phrasing of §110(2)(A) in two ways. First TEACH inserts the word "mediated" into the phrase. Next, it replaces the "regular part of" wording with a more succinct "integral part of" clause. As discussed above, the general concept of systematic MIA is "intended to require the performance or display be analogous to the type of performance display that would take place in a live classroom setting."[51] The Conference Report comment recognizes that the MIA definition incorporates this precise limitation in its third prong: "and analogous to the type of performance or display that would take place in a live classroom setting." Finally, the reformulated teaching activities test of §110(2)(A) under TEACH requires that performance or display be "at the direction of, or under the actual supervision of an instructor."

Compare the *definition* of mediated instructional activities discussed earlier with the use of the term as part of the teaching activity requirements of §110(2)(A). First it must be "an integral part of the class session." The definition of MIA refers to "class experience." It could be argued that the §110(2)(A) "class session" is broader than the MIA "class experience," since several experiences can be part of a class session, especially considering the variable definition of class session, as discussed above. This would make sense in terms of statutory construction since MIA is a term with a precise definition that is then used in subsection 110(2)(A) as part of the broader teaching or instructional activities concept.

Second, §110(2)(A) requires that the performance or display be "made by, at the direction of, or under the actual supervision of an instructor." The MIA definition again uses similar language: "controlled by or under the actual supervision of the instructor." Here, it would appear as if the §110(2)(A) "made by, at the direction of" language is also broader than the MIA definition ("controlled by") because an instructor under §110(2)(A) could "direct" a student to make a performance or display of copyrighted material during a later asynchronous class session when the instructor might not necessarily be said to be controlling that performance or display. This makes sense, as the MIA class experience is narrower than the §110(2)(A) class session; there may be a class experience or two within a class session (as the MIA is contained within the §110(2)(A) activity), and so there must be more flexibility when looking at the supervision of individual class experiences within that session, and so it must include a performance or display of a work that is at least directed by the instructor, though it might not be "controlled by" or under the "actual supervision" of the instructor. The question is, Why would Congress include the term MIA in §110(2)(A), along with instructor supervision and integral class session requirements, then include those two requirements in the definition of MIA, which also includes a third "analogous to the type of performance or display" prong? One reason may be that the concept MIA is used twice, once to operate dependently as part of a so-called teaching activities subsection expressed in (2)(A), and second to operate independently as part of the MIA transmitted-via-digital-networks "except" proviso opening §110(2).

The Accreditation Requirement

The introductory paragraphs of §110(2) and §110(2)(A) use the phrase "accredited nonprofit educational institution" to indicate that a qualifying nonprofit educational institution must be accredited. The concluding phrase of §110(2)(A) reads: "*of a governmental body or an accredited nonprofit educational institution*." This is a new requirement. Pre-TEACH §110(1) and (2) both contained a "face-to-face teaching activities of a nonprofit educational institution" and a "regular part of the systematic instructional activities of . . . a nonprofit educational institution" phrase, respectively. The 1976 legislative history offers this brief comment in describing the §110(1) requirement: "Clause (1) makes clear that it applies only to the teaching activities 'of a nonprofit educational institution,' thus excluding from the exemption performances or displays in profit-making institutions such as dance studios and language schools."[52] The pre-TEACH law limited the educational entities able to use §110 to those that were nonprofit. TEACH now requires that the nonprofit organization be accredited as well. A provision defining "accreditation" follows the substantive provision of §110: "*For purposes of paragraph (2), accreditation—(A) shall be determined by a regional or national accrediting agency recognized by Council on Higher Education Accreditation or the United States Department of Education; and (B) with respect to an institution providing elementary and secondary education, shall be recognized by the applicable state certification or licensing procedures*." Notice that accreditation is not "defined in terms of particular courses or programs,"[53] such as a library school's accreditation by the American Library Association; rather, the focus is on the institution, and accreditation by the North Central Agency, for example.

Why the change? Why impose an additional qualification at the outset, one sure to eliminate some educational entities that are nonetheless nonprofit, though unaccredited, from the ability to use the privilege granted in §110? The Conference Report reiterates the Register's Report that "'nonprofit educational institutions' are no longer a closed and familiar group, and the ease with which anyone can transmit educational material over the Internet" requires placing some limitation on the type of entity that can avail itself of the TEACH §110(2) rights "in order to provide further assurances that the institution is a bona fide educational institution."[54] This limitation may work to prevent networks of typically nonaccredited home schools from participating in distance education under TEACH, because home school education networks operate under a variety of models, from informal virtual neighborhoods of parents and children to those operating under the oversight of a state education agency to outright for-profit entities.[55] Even though the Conference Report asserts it does not intend to discredit nonaccredited nonprofit institutions,[56] it may have that effect in practice.

Understanding the Limitation on Instructional Content in Section 110(2)(B)

TEACH leaves untouched the 1976 Copyright Act version of §110(2)(B): "*(B) the performance or display is directly related and of material assistance to the teaching content of the transmission.*" Yet the 1976 and the 2002 legislative histories appear to provide somewhat inconsistent explanations of the function of this identical clause. [57] While the 1976 legislative history does not provide much enlightenment, repeating the statutory construction, "Subclause (B) requires that the performance or display be directly related and of material assistance to the teaching content of the transmission,"[58] the 2002 TEACH legislative history is quite a different story.

Under TEACH §110(2)(B), the performance or display must also be "directly related and of material assistance to the teaching content" of the class; that is, it cannot be for recreation or entertainment. According to the Conference Report, which refers to the Register's Report,[59] and relating it to the statutory §110(2)(B) requirement, "this test of relevance and materiality connects the copyrighted work to the curriculum, and it means that the portion performed or displayed may not be performed or displayed for the mere entertainment of the students, or as unrelated background material."[60] Of course, §110(1) contained such a proscription, but TEACH now extends that to distance education transmissions as well. That's not too unsettling, notwithstanding the fact that unauthorized recreational performances under §110(1) have been the salvation of many K–12 teachers (i.e., showing a video as a reward or to keep the kids busy on a rainy afternoon or while grading papers); it is difficult to conceive of distance educators relying on this educational subterfuge to fill a session of instruction. What is unsettling is that, according to the legislative history, and as discussed earlier, TEACH uses different language to accomplish the prohibition than did the 1976 act. Further, the same statutory language in TEACH that now prohibits using performances or displays for "the mere entertainment of students, or as unrelated background material" also existed in the pre-TEACH law, yet no mention is made of it in the 1976 legislative history discussing the distance education requirements of §110(2). This anomaly was recounted earlier in detail.

While §110(1) per the 1976 legislative history forbids performances or displays "for the recreation or entertainment of any part of their audience,"

§110(2) per the 2002 legislative history forbids performances or displays "for mere entertainment of the students, or as unrelated background material." TEACH appears to add a second area of forbidden fruit: unrelated background material. In other words, even if the performance or display is not for mere entertainment alone, it might still be excluded under §110(2)(B) if it consists of unrelated background material. Unfortunately, no further explanation is provided by the legislative history.[61] Does this mean that related background material is acceptable but unrelated background material is not? Would the performance or display of material on the basic training of U.S. soldiers during World War II be acceptable "related background" material in a unit on D-Day in a U.S. history class, while the performance or display of material on hypothermia in the same unit and course would constitute unacceptable "unrelated background" material? Perhaps this is splitting too fine an interpretive proverbial hair, but if the goal is to give the legislative history substance, then there must be some material that is not necessarily used as entertainment but is nonetheless so tangential or peripheral that it is beyond the limit of acceptable relatedness or relevance. Of course, very related material may still in fact be excluded if performed or displayed for mere entertainment alone, such as making *Saving Private Ryan* available for students as a "reward" for doing such a good job on their D-Day assignments.

Identifying the Purpose and the Audience of a Section 110(2)(C) Transmission

Under the 1976 Copyright Act, the purpose of §110(2)(C) was to identify the purpose of the transmission. The statute accomplished this by indicating the acceptable persons to whom transmission could be made. Likewise the TEACH reformulation of §110(2)(C) accomplishes the same task but through the use of entirely different requirements. Why the change? The answer lies in the overall goal of TEACH, which is to offer a copyright law more in keeping with the realities of modern distance education and cure one of the major deficiencies in the pre-TEACH law. The 1976 view of distance education envisioned a distance education teaching and learning environment where students received instruction gathered together in the same physical class space, but at a location remote to the instructor.

Under the 1976 version of §110(2)(C)(iii), an acceptable transmission was one "made primarily for . . . reception by officers or employees of governmental bodies as a part of their official duties or employment." This language is repeated in TEACH §110(2)(C)(ii), requiring that "transmission is made solely for and . . . the reception of such transmission is limited to . . . officers or employees of governmental bodies as a part of their official duties or employment." However, the focus on the transmission for classroom use is not so much on the person under the 1976 law, but on its place: "primarily for reception in classrooms or similar places normally devoted to instruction" or, under old §110(2)(C)(i), to disabled students and others whose circumstances prevented them from "attendance in classrooms or similar places normally devoted to instruction" under §110(2)(C)(ii). Requiring the distance education students also to be relegated to the confines of the physical classroom proved a major impediment to the development of many modern distance education programs.

While the pre-TEACH concept of distance education focused upon the classroom as the locus of teaching—the students receiving the transmission needed to be gathered in "classrooms or similar places normally devoted to instruction" (think broadcast education here)—there could be some educational audience leakage in the sense that the transmission could reach others, as long as it was made primarily for students in some remote classroom. In fact the 1976 legislative history indicates that the "instructional transmission need only be made 'primarily' rather than 'solely' to the specified recipients to be exempt. Thus, the transmission could still be exempt even though it is capable of reception by the public at large."[62] The 1976 legislative history goes on to indicate that three factors should be considered when making the determination of "primarily for": subject matter, content, and time of its transmission.[63] For example, a broadcast on the local public television station of a show on U.S. history, consisting of a talking-head professor intercut with screens of PowerPoint type outline excerpts, shown at three in the afternoon or three in the morning, might be quite different from a captivating Ken Burn–style version of the same subject matter, broadcast during prime time.

The TEACH language allows for no such transmission audience leakage; rather, under subsection 110(2)(C) "*the transmission is made solely for*" students enrolled in the course, using the same exact "solely" language that the 1976 legislative history indicated was absent. Second, "*and to the extent technologically feasible, the reception of such transmission is limited to*" students enrolled in the course. Further, the shift between the pre-TEACH "where" (place of reception) to post-TEACH "who" (students officially enrolled) is also consistent with the emphasis in TEACH of placing a higher administrative burden on the institution to monitor or control the students to whom it transmits. One advantage, of course, is that by the plain language of the statute, TEACH transmissions can be made to offices, homes, cyber cafes, anywhere, as long as the new §110(2)(C) requirements are met; they no longer require that a physical classroom or similar place normally devoted to instruction be the target location of the transmission: "One of the great potential benefits of digital distance education is its ability to reach beyond the physical classroom, to provide quality educational experiences to all students of all income levels, in cities and rural settings, in schools and on campuses, in the workplaces, at home, and at times selected by students to meet their needs."[64] The two phrases in italics above work in tandem and require the institution to ask for whom the transmission is made (a sort of a who-do-you-want-to-receive-it test: "made solely for") and second inquire who is capable of receiving its transmission (a sort of a who-can-receive-it test: "reception of such transmission is limited to").

First, any transmission must be made *solely* for "*(i) students officially enrolled in the course for which the transmission is made; or (ii) officers or employees of governmental bodies as part of their official duties or employment.*" For example, the broadcast or Web-cast (transmission) of a performance or display of copyrighted material within a distance education class session must be made without any other intended audience in mind as to its content or structure. In other words, excluded would be content on general computer skills, made available on a college or university website as part of a general computer literacy or minimum skills student resources page that an instructor in an introductory library research skills class would like everyone to access and incorporate into a lesson plan. The transmission (performance or display) of any copyrighted material would *not* have been made solely for "(i) students officially enrolled in the course for which the transmission is made." Of course, if the institution had obtained the rights to perform or display the computer skills material in any fashion, the license might allow for such general use.

The use of the word "transmission" twice—"the *transmission* is made solely for . . . students officially enrolled in the course for which the *transmission* is made"—suggests that if the basic computer skills module were now placed onto a particular distance education course website, the transmission would appear to fulfill the §110(2)(C) "made solely for" requirement, as it is no longer made available for general campus student consumption. Even if the content also remained accessible on a general campus website as well as the distance education website, the latter would appear authorized under §110(2) because the transmission actually used in the distance education class ("transmission *is* made solely") was one that was made "solely for . . . students officially enrolled in the course for which the *transmission* is made."

TEACH requires that "to the extent technologically feasible, the reception of such transmission is limited to *(i) students officially enrolled in the course for which the transmission is made; or (ii) officers or employees of governmental bodies as part of their official duties or employment.*" This is not an absolute test but allows some technological leakage, as a result of a qualification on the reception limitation, the "to the extent technologically feasible" language. According to the

Conference Report: "This requirement is not intended to impose a general requirement of network security."[65] However, the institution must do something. While it does not require that the institution employ the use of technology to control copyright infringement or uses of copyrighted material beyond the confines of §110(2), it does at least require the institution to employ technology that regulates access to that content. In other words, making a performance or display of copyrighted material as part of a course through the institution's main website would not be acceptable, even though it was the institution's intent that it be *solely for* students officially enrolled in the course for which the transmission is made as opposed to the entire campus community, as in the case of material for use in a Sanskrit language course that would be of little use or interest to other students. As the Conference Report points out, "[r]ather, it is intended to require only that the students be identified, and the transmission should be technologically limited to such identified authorized recipients through systems such as password access or other similar measures."[66] This is nonetheless significant, as it signals an increased role for institutions that desire to use copyrighted material in furtherance of its educational mission and in conformity with §110(2). In return for that privilege of use, the institution is required to step forward and take an active role in compliance efforts, often through the use of technology. This is the first hint in TEACH that Congress views technology as the arbiter of the proper balance of rights between copyright owners and educational users. Technology is the key to limiting the exposure of copyrighted works to either unauthorized uses and, in this instance of the §110(2)(C) phrase, unauthorized users.

Must the system chosen by the institution be perfect? No, as the statute only requires that "to the extent technologically feasible" is "reception of such transmission [] limited to students officially enrolled in the course." Leakage (i.e., reception by persons other than "students officially enrolled in the course") is acceptable as long as the institution has attempted to limit ("to the extent technologically feasible") reception to "students officially enrolled in the course." It is less clear whether this "made solely for" proviso is intended to apply to the content of the program as well—for example, forbidding the broadcast of a *Frontline* or *Nova* episode that is of general educational value and appeal, in that it is not designed specifically for instructional activities. It seems more appropriate, given the nature of the second "technologically feasible" reception proviso, that the "made solely for" means that the intent must be that the transmission be "made solely for" students alone ("officially enrolled") and that the institution must make some good-faith effort to accomplish this using technology, but if the mechanism is not 100 percent successful, the broadcast is nonetheless permissible; i.e., use the *Frontline* or *Nova* episode, but do not make it available as a transmission of general interest to students beyond those "officially enrolled." Otherwise, it would appear that a large category of copyrighted materials of educational value would be excluded.

Does the new §110(2)(C) requirement that the transmission be made "solely for . . . students officially enrolled" mean that a traditional broadcast of an educational program over the local public television or cable network will not be allowed in the future? Yes and no. The "solely for" requirement applies only to the nature of the transmission and for whom it is made—"the transmission is made solely for . . . students officially enrolled." As the legislative history suggests, it is "intended to require only that the students be identified." However, the limitation on reception, the who-can-receive-it test, would appear to forbid such transmission from qualifying for the restructured §110(2) TEACH privilege. This would imply that a program shown on a general public television station would not qualify, because anyone within the local viewing audience could access it. The officially enrolled students would be among a sea of potential recipients and would not meet the requirement of the legislative history, that "transmission should be technologically limited to such identified authorized recipients." However, using the local cable channel to broadcast the program in conjunction with an access system that allowed a cable control box to block reception by general cable subscribers and allow reception by student viewers with the proper access code would appear to be the sort of mechanism the legislative history intended: the use of technology to limit reception to bona fide members of the class through the use of "systems such as password access or other similar measures." In this case, the cable broadcast would be made "solely for" students, even though nonstudents could, in theory, purchase access from the cable company if they so chose. Here, what limits reception is technology (by use of the cable station control box) and not network security, as would be the case if the educational entity were required to check the cable company subscriber list to ensure that it consists only of students registered for the course. This is consistent with the legislative history admonition that §110(2)(C) is "not intended to impose a general requirement of network security."

Rather than adding special rules for digital transmission (i.e., requiring increased technological measures for digital transmissions as TEACH establishes in §110(2)(D)(ii), for example, leaving traditional broadcasters without such requirements), the "solely for" and "reception of" provisos apply equally to any qualifying transmission. Even if the use of "systems such as password access or other similar measures" is simply not technologically feasible in that medium—a radio broadcast, for example—such transmission would arguably comply with the "reception of" proviso but fail to meet the "solely for" proviso. While the TEACH legislative history suggests that the §110(2)(C) requirement is "not intended to impose a general requirement of network security," the language of the statute suggests otherwise, unless of course one reads the "to the extent technologically feasible" condition as a modifying clause for both the "solely for" and "reception of" provisos ("the transmission is made solely for, and, *to the extent technologically feasible,* the reception of such transmission is limited to"). This seems unlikely. If it were Congress's intent, it could have restructured the modifying clause to either precede or follow the two provisos ("*to the extent technologically feasible* the transmission is made solely for, and, the reception of such transmission is limited to" or "the transmission is made solely for, and, the reception of such transmission is limited to, *to the extent technologically feasible*"). Further, the restructuring of §110(2)(C) by substituting "solely" for prior "primarily" appears to foreclose such possibilities, especially in light of the function of the word "primarily" in the 1976 Copyright Act as explained above in its legislative history quote.

Does this mean that traditional methods of educational broadcast are excluded from TEACH, at least when the broadcast of copyrighted material is contemplated? Yes. Otherwise, reading the statutory language to allow such transmission would appear to adopt the "primarily for" test of pre-TEACH §110(2) that considered the subject matter, content, and time of transmission. This would contradict the plain meaning of the word "solely" in the statute and its restructuring under TEACH. Like the 1976 law, which failed to anticipate any distance education technology other than traditional broadcast, the new law appears to err in the other direction, foreclosing most if not all traditional broadcasts. Whether this is the result of a drafting oversight or legislative design is difficult to determine. An easy solution is to admit that some mediums, like radio, simply do not allow for such controls. Of course, the statute may not all mean what it says, as courts are free to interpret the language otherwise and read a traditional broadcast audience exception in the statute, in the same way courts read a faculty exception into the work-for-hire statute, but its construction, even in light of its legislative history, appears hard to reconcile in this regard. This seems an odd result and a harsh one for traditional educational broadcasters. Perhaps over time, as satellite and the Internet transmissions replace broadcast transmissions, this additional anomaly will matter less.

Notes

1. H. Rpt. No. 94-1476, 94th Cong., 2d Sess. 82–83 (1976), reprinted in 5 United States Code Congressional and Administrative News 5659, 5696–5697 (1976).

2. Conference Report, H. Rpt. No. 107-685, 107th Cong., 2d Sess. 226-227 (2002).

3. Conference Report, H. Rpt. No. 107-685, 107th Cong., 2d Sess. 226 (2002).

4. Conference Report, H. Rpt. No. 107-685, 107th Cong., 2d Sess. 227 (2002) (emphasis added).

5. Conference Report, H. Rpt. No. 107-685, 107th Cong., 2d Sess. 227 (2002).

6. 17 U.S.C. §107(4). The fourth fair use factor considers the "effect of the use on potential market or value of the work."

7. Conference Report, H. Rpt. No. 107-685, 107th Cong., 2d Sess. 227 (2002) ("The exclusion for works 'produced or marketed primarily for performance or display as part of mediated instructional activities transmitted via digital networks' is intended to prevent the exemption from undermining the primary market for (and, therefore, impairing the incentive to create, modify or distribute) those materials whose primary market would otherwise fall within the scope of the exemption.").

8. See the discussion of the Software Rental Amendment Act of 1990 and the Digital Millennium Copyright Act of 1998. H.R. Rep. No. 101-735, 101st Cong., 2d Sess. 8 (1990) ("The Committee does not wish, however, to prohibit nonprofit lending by nonprofit libraries and nonprofit educational institutions. Such institutions serve a valuable public purpose by making computer software available to students who do not otherwise have access to it. At the same time, the Committee is aware that the same economic factors that lead to unauthorized copying in a commercial contest may lead library patrons also to engage in such conduct.").

9. U.S. Copyright Office, Report on Copyright and Digital Distance Education 158–159 (1999).

10. Laura N. Gasaway, Distance Learning and Copyright, 62 *Ohio State Law Journal* 783, 814 (2001) ("Many of these works are short, and their very nature makes them useless if less than the entire work is used. . . . The work was meant to be shown in its entirety to teach the content. Producers of educational videotapes traditionally have relied on sale of the works and not license fees for performance. . . .Thus, this restriction may not even aid the copyright holder's market, but it will seriously harm educational goals.").

11. U.S. Copyright Office, Report on Copyright and Digital Distance Education 159 (1999).

12. According to the Register's Report: "A 'limited' portion should be interpreted as the equivalent of a film clip, rather than a substantial part of the film. . . .This approach . . . would preserve the most significant primary markets, continuing the need for educators to license the use of an entire motion picture or sound recording. It would also remove most of the risk posed by downstream uses, since the availability of limited portions would not satisfy the public's interest in experiencing the work as a whole." U.S. Copyright Office, Report on Copyright and Digital Distance Education 158 (1999).

13. Conference Report, H. Rpt. No. 107-685, 107th Cong., 2d Sess. 227 (2002) (emphasis added) ("The 'limited portion' formulation used in conjunction with the performance right exemption is not used in connection with the display right exemption, because, for certain works, display of the entire work could be appropriate and consistent with displays typically made in a live classroom setting [e.g., an entire short poem or essay, or a complete image of a pictorial, graphic, or sculptural work, etc.]").

14. Conference Report, H. Rpt. No. 107-685, 107th Cong., 2d Sess. 227 (2002) (emphasis added).

15. Conference Report, H. Rpt. No. 107-685, 107th Cong., 2d Sess. 227 (2002).

16. Conference Report, H. Rpt. No. 107-685, 107th Cong., 2d Sess. 229–230 (2002).

17. Conference Report, H. Rpt. No. 107-685, 107th Cong., 2d Sess. 226 (2002) ("This section also clarifies that participants in authorized digital distance education transmission will not be liable for any infringement by reason of transient or temporary reproductions that may occur through the automatic technical process of

a digital transmission for the purpose of a performance or display permitted under the section.").

18. 17 U.S.C. 101 ("'Sound recordings' are works that result from the fixation of a series of musical, spoken, or other sounds, but not including the sounds accompanying a motion picture or other audiovisual work, regardless of the nature of the material objects, such as disks, tapes, or other phonorecords, in which they are embodied.").

19. 17 U.S.C. 106(6).

20. U.S. Copyright Office, Report on Copyright and Digital Distance Education 156 (1999).

21. S. Rep. No. 128, 104th Cong., 1st Sess. 14 (1995), reprinted in 1 United States Code Congressional and Administrative News 356, 357 (1995).

22. Pub. L. No. 104-39, 109 Stat. 336-44 (codified at 17 U.S.C. §§ 101, 106, 114, 115, 119, 801–803).

23. S. Rep. No. 128, 104th Cong., 1st Sess. 14 (1995), reprinted in 1 United States Code Congressional and Administrative News 356, 361 (1995) (emphasis added).

24. A sample provision for use in an institutional license is found in Appendix B, Model Distance Education Copyright Policy: *Use of Copyrighted Material in the Distance Education Classroom* Policy.

25. S. Rep. No. 128, 104th Cong., 1st Sess. 15 (1995), reprinted in 1 United States Code Congressional and Administrative News 356, 362 (1995).

26. U.S. Copyright Office, Report on Copyright and Digital Distance Education 156 (1999).

27. U.S. Copyright Office, Report on Copyright and Digital Distance Education 157 (1999) (emphasis added).

28. 17 U.S.C. 114(d)(1)(A).

29. S. Rep. No. 128, 104th Cong., 1st Sess. 16 (1995), reprinted in 1 United States Code Congressional and Administrative News 356, 363 (1995).

30. 17 U.S.C. 114(j)(3). See also S. Rep. No. 128, 104th Cong., 1st Sess. 19 (1995), reprinted in 1 United States Code Congressional and Administrative News 356, 366 (1995). ("Under this provision [section 114(d)(1)(A)], any transmission to members of the public that is neither a subscription transmission (as defined in section 114(j)(8)) nor part of an interactive service *is exempt* from the new digital performance right") (emphasis added).

31. U.S. Copyright Office, Report on Copyright and Digital Distance Education 96 (1999).

32. S. Rep. No. 128, 104th Cong., 1st Sess. 18 (1995), reprinted in 1 United States Code Congressional and Administrative News 356, 365 (1995).

33. S. Rep. No. 128, 104th Cong., 1st Sess. 19 (1995), reprinted in 1 United States Code Congressional and Administrative News 356, 366 (1995) ("In other words, retransmissions of broadcast stations' signals will be exempt even if the retransmission are themselves 'subscription' retransmissions under the Act.").

34. S. Rep. No. 128, 104th Cong., 1st Sess. 19 (1995), reprinted in 1 United States Code Congressional and Administrative News 356, 365 (1995).

35. S. Rep. No. 128, 104th Cong., 1st Sess. 19 (1995), reprinted in 1 United States Code Congressional and Administrative News 356, 365 (1995).

36. U.S. Copyright Office, Report on Copyright and Digital Distance Education 96 (1999) (citing 17 U.S.C. 114(j)).

37. S. Rep. No. 128, 104th Cong., 1st Sess. 36 (1995), reprinted in 1 United States Code Congressional and Administrative News 356, 383 (1995).

38. S. Rep. No. 128, 104th Cong., 1st Sess. 36 (1995), reprinted in 1 United States Code Congressional and Administrative News 356, 383 (1995).

39. 17 U.S.C. 114(d)(2)(C)(ii).

40. S. Rep. No. 128, 104th Cong., 1st Sess. 24 (1995), reprinted in 2 United States Code Congressional and Administrative News 356, 371 (1995).

41. 17 U.S.C. 114(j)(13). "It is not the intention of this legislation to impose liability where selections that are performed from separate phonorecords also may be incorporated on a different phonorecord or compilation, or also may appear on a different phonorecord under the name of another featured artist, in the absence of an intention by the performing entity to knowingly circumvent the numerical limits of the complement. An example of such a case is where the transmitting entity plays within a 3-hour period one selection from each of four phonorecords, which four selections also happen to be compiled on a soundtrack album. . . . However, where the transmitting entity willfully plays within a 3-hour period five selections of a single featured recording artist, regardless of whether they were played from several different phonorecords, and regardless of whether the transmitting entity knew that the transmission included more than three songs from a single album, the transmission does not come within the complement." S. Rep. No. 128, 104th Cong., 1st Sess. 35 (1995), reprinted in 1 United States Code Congressional and Administrative News 356, 382 (1995).

42. Conference Report, H. Rpt. No. 107-685, 107th Cong., 2d Sess. 227 (2002) ("The performance of works other than non-dramatic literary or musical works is limited, however, to 'reasonable and limited portions' of less than the entire work.").

43. Conference Report, H. Rpt. No. 107-685, 107th Cong., 2nd Sess. 226 (2002).

44. H. Rpt. No. 94-1476, 94th Cong., 2d Sess. 81 (1976), reprinted in 5 United States Code Congressional and Administrative News 5659, 5695 (1976).

45. U.S. Copyright Office, Report on Copyright and Digital Distance Education 80 (1999).

46. Conference Report, H. Rpt. No. 107-685, 107th Cong., 2d Sess. 230 (2002).

47. Conference Report, H. Rpt. No. 107-685, 107th Cong., 2d Sess. 228 (2002).

48. Conference Report, H. Rpt. No. 107-685, 107th Cong., 2d Sess. 228 (2002).

49. Conference Report, H. Rpt. No. 107-685, 107th Cong., 2d Sess. 229 (2002).

50. Conference Report, H. Rpt. No. 107-685, 107th Cong., 2d Sess. 231 (2002).

51. Conference Report, H. Rpt. No. 107-685, 107th Cong., 2d Sess. 229 (2002).

52. H. Rpt. No. 94-1476, 94th Cong., 2d Sess. 82 (1976), reprinted in 5 United States Code Congressional and Administrative News 5659, 5696 (1976).

53. Conference Report, H. Rpt. No. 107-685, 107th Cong., 2d Sess. 228 (2002) ("Accreditation is defined in section 1(b)(2) of the TEACH Act in terms of the qualifications

of the educational institution. It is not defined in terms of particular courses or programs.").

54. Conference Report, H. Rpt. No. 107-685, 107th Cong., 2d Sess. 228 (2002) (citing
U.S. Copyright Office, Report on Copyright and Digital Distance Education 159 (1999)).

55. Bonnie Rothman Morris, "Teach Your Children, Virtually: Home-Schooling
Families Have a New Option: A Public Education, Online," *New York Times*, May 29,
2003, at E1.

56. Conference Report, H. Rpt. No. 107-685, 107th Cong., 2d Sess. 228 (2002)
("Nor is it intended to limit or affect any other institutions or to imply that nonaccredited educational institutions are necessarily not bona fide.").

57. Conference Report, H. Rpt. No. 107-685, 107th Cong., 2d Sess. 230 (2002)
("The requirement of subparagraph (2)(B), that the performance or display must be
directly related and of material assistance to the teaching content of the transmission,
is found in current law, and had been retained in its current form.") (emphasis added).

58. H. Rpt. No. 94-1476, 94th Cong., 2d Sess. 83 (1976) reprinted in 5 United States
Code Congressional and Administrative News 5659, 5697 (1976).

59. U.S. Copyright Office, Report on Copyright and Digital Distance Education 80
(1999).

60. Conference Report, H. Rpt. No. 107-685, 107th Cong., 2d Sess. 230 (2002).

61. The Register's Report uses the additional concept of transitional material: "It is
important to note that the portion performed would have to be the subject of study
in the course, rather than mere entertainment for students, or unrelated background
or *transitional material*." U.S. Copyright Office, Report on Copyright and Digital
Distance Education 159 (1999) (emphasis added).

62. H. Rpt. No. 94-1476, 94th Cong., 2d Sess. 83 (1976) reprinted in 5 United States
Code Congressional and Administrative News 5659, 5697 (1976).

63. H. Rpt. No. 94-1476, 94th Cong., 2d Sess. 83 (1976) reprinted in 5 United States
Code Congressional and Administrative News 5659, 5697–5698 (1976).

64. Conference Report, H. Rpt. No. 107-685, 107th Cong., 2d Sess. 230 (2002).

65. Conference Report, H. Rpt. No. 107-685, 107th Cong., 2d Sess. 230 (2002).

66. Conference Report, H. Rpt. No. 107-685, 107th Cong., 2d Sess. 230 (2002).

4

New Responsibilities for the Institution
Section 110(2)(D)

THE MOST SIGNIFICANT SHIFT embodied in TEACH is the signal from Congress that intermediaries—in this instance, the instructor and his or her distance education support and computing staff and the institution—must now take an active part in copyright compliance strategies before the benefits of the §110 performance and display rights can accrue. Section 110(2)(D) presents two distinct sets of such compliance requirements. One set embodied in §110(2)(D)(i) applies to all qualifying transmissions, and a second set in §110(2)(D)(ii) applies in addition to digital transmissions. Why the dramatic shift? The section of the legislative history discussing §110(2)(D) is entitled "Additional safeguards to counteract new risks" and speaks of the increased danger of infringement in digital environments, yet it is clear that §110(2)(D)(i) applies to traditional broadcasts, nondigital transmission as well as digital transmissions. (It is §110(2)(D)(ii) that applies only to digital transmissions.) The threat of infringement is arguably greater in digital environments, in which perfect reproductions and instantaneous and widespread distribution are so easy to achieve (which is not to say that educators in digital settings have had any corner on the infringement market). The increased responsibility is the price all educators must pay, perhaps, for a past tendency of our human nature, in confronting the copyright law, to rationalize, "What's the harm?" Now, in response to Congress's expanded §110(2) use rights comes the answer:

[t]he digital transmission of works to students poses greater risks to copyright owners than transmissions through analog broadcasts. Digital technologies make possible the creation of multiple copies, and their rapid and widespread

dissemination around the world. Accordingly, the TEACH Act includes several safeguards not currently present in section 110(2).[1]

General Compliance Requirements of Section 110(2)(D)(i)

The initial set of compliance requirements includes three commands, embodied within the text of §110(2)(D)(i). First, the benefits of §110(2) are available only if "*the transmitting body or institution—(i) institutes policies regarding copyright.*" Second, the transmitting body or institution must ensure that it "*provides informational materials to faculty, students, and relevant staff members that accurately describe, and promote compliance with, the laws of the United States relating to copyright.*" Unfortunately, the legislative history does not provide any enlightening comment other than to repeat the statutory phrasing: "First, a transmitting body or institution seeking to invoke the exemption is required to institute policies regarding copyright and to provide information to faculty, students, and relevant staff members that accurately describe[s] and promote[s] compliance with copyright law."[2] Is a one-page copyright policy sufficient? Perhaps, but the clear use of the plural "policies" suggests that more effort than a one-pager is necessary. At least a series of one-page documents ("policies") is required. But how much is enough of the "informational materials"? Notice again the use of plural. The institution must provide "informational materials." Second, the policy and informational materials requirement is the responsibility of the institution, suggesting that it is not ad hoc but centralized, coordinated, and pervasive; that is, it occurs throughout the institution, and is part of its information infrastructure of policy formation, implementation, enforcement, and of training and assessment, as it must reach "faculty, students, and relevant staff members." Is a one-line comment in an employee handbook stating that "it is the policy of this institution not to infringe the copyrights of others" fulfilling the letter of the law? Is a one-page poster and one-page flyer sufficient "informational materials"? Frankly, these are the wrong questions to ask. Rather, the institution should be seeking as many ways, in the language of the Conference Report, "to promote an environment of compliance with the law, inform recipients of their responsibilities under copyright law, and decrease the likelihood of unintentional and uninformed acts of infringement."[3] Perhaps a better question to ask is, What will it take in our school district or on our campus to create an environment of compliance, recognizing that such compliance is built upon the incorporation of these attitudes into the infrastructure of the institution through policy adoption and implementation—and, more important—the assimilation through informational outreach of those attitudes into routine practice throughout the institution as well, resulting in a situation where the possibility of infringement is greatly reduced?

The statute requires that three groups be targeted: faculty, students, and relevant staff. Perhaps making the information part of an employee and student handbook would be a start. It should be apparent that there is an expectation of enforcement once a breech of any policy so conceived is discovered, so that the institution will respond as it normally would to violations of administrative policy by faculty, staff, and student. Without basic efforts of enforcement, the goal of an environment of compliance would be stifled. Also, a court would likely not look kindly upon a school, college, or university that attempted to fulfill the §110(2)(D)(i) requirement by writing policies on copyright but then looked the other way when infringement occurred, failing to enforce any of the policies that it did enact, adopt, institute, and so forth. In addition, an institution that might be tempted to embrace the minimum two or more one-page "policies" and single-poster "informational materials" approach would appear to be making a rather simplistic response, as if the copyright law were a menace that needed to be outwitted.

The content of the information, be it a poster or flyer, handout or brochure, or in-service or other training session, must do two things: first, describe ("accurately describes") the copyright law (i.e., explain it), and then "[promote] compliance" with it. This book began with a chapter describing the rights of copyright owners, then proceeded to the educator provisions of §110(1) and, of course, the new TEACH provisions. We're about half to two-thirds of the way through §110(2) and §112(f) of TEACH, not quite halfway through this book. It would be hard to conceive, with a straight legal face, of a scenario sufficient to promote an environment of compliance that consisted solely of a single 48-by-30-inch poster or a one-page flyer. Rather, it seems that copyright compliance is a process, part of ongoing risk management.

It should be noted that the first two compliance requirements of §110(2)(D) do not restrict the policies instituted or informational materials provided to those policies concerning distance education or §110(2) alone. Rather, the statute states that policies are instituted "regarding copyright" and informational materials are provided in order to describe and promote compliance with "the laws of the United States relating to copyright" and not that policies be instituted "regarding copyright relating to *distance education*" alone or informational materials are provided describing and promoting compliance with "the laws of the United States relating to *section 110(2) of the* copyright *law*." There appears to be no indication that the policy and informational materials requirement relates only to copyright issues in distance education; in fact, the plain language of the statute suggests just the opposite.

The final compliance proviso of §110(2)(D)(i) targets additional outreach to students. The institution must be sure that it "*provides notice to students that materials used in conjunction with the course may be subject to copyright protection*." The legislative history adds nothing, repeating verbatim the last proviso of §110(2)(D)(i).[4] The statute does not provide the form or content of the required copyright notice. It may be that, in time, the U.S. Copyright Office might issue a suggested form similar to the §108 notice required for interlibrary operations in libraries and archives[5] or that required for the circulation of software under §109.[6] Until then, a notice similar to the one below could be used by instructors to inform their distance education students, or perhaps all students; it incorporates language from the federal regulation.

All materials that under United States Copyright law would be considered the normal work product of the instructor, pursuant to the class or lecture note exception to the work-for-hire doctrine, are under the sole ownership of the instructor. This work product includes but is not limited to outlines, exercises, and discussion questions. See *Hays v. Sony Corp of America*, 847 F.2d 412 (7th Cir. 1988) and *Weinstein v. University of Illinois*, 811 F. 2d 1091 (7th Cir. 1987). Regarding websites, the instructor, the university, and the website designer share the copyright in the "look and feel" of the site. The underlying software that generates the website is also protected by copyright. Documents and other material appearing on the website or by link from the site may also be protected by copyright.

This site is maintained for educational purposes only. Your viewing of the material posted here does not imply any right to reproduce, to distribute, or to redisplay it other than for your own personal or educational noncommercial use. Links to other sites are provided for the convenience of the site user (staff or student) or visitor and do not imply any affiliation or endorsement of the other site owner or a guarantee of the quality or veracity of information contained on the linked site, nor should links be viewed as any form of implied license to use material found on the linked site in excess of fair use. As a student, your ability to post or link to copyrighted material is also governed by United States Copyright law. This instructor and/or other staff of the institution reserve the right to delete or disable your post or link or to deny access to any material if, in their judgment, the post or link would involve violation of copyright law. In addition, repeat instances requiring the institution to delete content or disable access may result in the denial of access to the institution's distance education networks or other information communication technologies.

Depending on the circumstances of the educational environment, the language regarding ownership of the copyrighted curricular materials could be modified to reflect the operation of the work-for-hire doctrine, which, as discussed in chapter 1, vests ownership of copyrighted materials created in the course of employment with the employer and not with the employee faculty member, or modified to reflect any other arrangement reflected in the policies and contracts of the particular institutional environment.

Common sense might dictate that such a notice should appear on the first page of the course syllabus or on the first page of an online Web course or at the beginning of an online broadcast. Notice the use of the article *the* before *course.* The statute does not use the phrase "a course." The notice provided to students should indicate "that [the] materials used in connection with *the* course may be subject to copyright protections." Does the use of word *the* imply that the notice requirement only applies to a §110(2) course—i.e., that the "transmitting body or institution [provide] notice to students that materials used in conjunction with *the course* may be subject to copyright protection"? "The course" then by definition becomes a distance education course, a course provided in conjunction with a §110(2) transmission.

On the other hand, does this proviso of §110(2)(D)(i) require that all syllabi or other documentation relating to course materials provided by the institution contain a copyright warning notice to the effect that materials associated with the class, whether it be material handed out, on e-reserve, or purchased from the bookstore (such as a textbook, workbook, or course pack), "may be subject to copyright protection"? The use of the article *the* might suggest a former interpretation. However, the latter notice-on-every-syllabi scenario or requiring other documentation (such as a slip containing such a notice inserted along with the return policy, for example, in every textbook, workbook, course pack, etc. purchased by students from the campus bookstore) or—as is the common practice at the K-12 level—handed out at the beginning of each school year, would be consistent with §110(2)(D) and its purpose of "promot[ing] an environment of compliance with the law, inform[ing] recipients of their responsibilities under copyright law, and decreas[ing] the likelihood of unintentional and uninformed acts of infringement." It is also consistent with the broader sweep of the other two provisos of §110(2)(D)(i), which relate to copyright policies and informational materials about copyright law, not just the copyright law regarding distance education. Moreover, such a practice would promote a more compliant school or campus environment and be consistent with a strategy of copyright risk management.

Specific Compliance Requirements of Section 110(2)(D)(ii)

Digital Transmissions

In addition to the §110(2)(D)(i) policies, informational materials, and notice requirements that apply to all distance education settings, §110(2)(D)(ii) contains a second set of compliance requirements that apply when the performance or display is by means of a digital transmission: "*(ii) in the case of digital transmissions.*" The subsection (ii) requirements signal Congress's concern, in spite of repeated statements to the contrary regarding the neutrality of the copyright as applied to technology, that digital is indeed different.[7] The significance is that, in the case of digital transmission, the institution must do more than adopt policies, distribute informational materials, and post notices; rather, the educational institution must employ technological measures to prevent users from abusing the rights of copyright owners. Technology is the bane of copyright owners, and Congress also views it as somewhat of a savior, perhaps, as well. This is a significant next step beyond the more passive strategies (policies, informational materials, and notices) of §110(2)(D)(i) requirements that place the responsibility of compliance with the user, be they faculty, student, or staff, and would at most trigger an after-the-fact response from the institution to remedy any circumstance of policy violation. In contrast, §110(2)(D)(ii) requires a proactive, before-the-fact plan. In short, §110(2)(D)(ii) requires that the institution, first, in order to avail itself of the benefits of the §110(2) performance and display privilege, employ technology to prevent certain retention and dissemination of copyrighted material (§110(2)(D)(ii)(I)). Second, and related, the institution must not interfere with any technological measure the copyright may have employed (§110(2)(D)(ii)(II)).

Technological Protection Measures

The institution may avail itself of the §110(2) rights only if it "*(I) applies technological measures that reasonably prevent*" retention or further dissemination of copyright material. The use of technology here serves as a requirement for eligibility.[8] First, it should be noticed that these two digital compliance requirements (prevention of retention and dissemination of §110(2)(D)(ii)(I)) are not absolutes, as the statute uses the phrase "reasonably prevent." "This requirement does not impose a duty to guarantee that retention and further dissemination will never occur."[9] Second, the required use of "technological measures" does not imply that constant real-time monitoring tactics are necessary.[10] The technology chosen need not be perfect, but it must at least do something to prevent further retention and dissemination; moreover, it must do it "reasonably" well. As the legislative history explains, "the 'reasonably prevent' standard should not be construed to imply perfect efficacy in stopping retention or further dissemination. The obligation to 'reasonably prevent' contemplates an *objectively reasonable standard* regarding the ability of a technological protection measure to achieve its purpose."[11] In other words, is the proactive plan and use of technology to achieve it by the institution reasonable under the circumstances? Notice that it is an objective standard of reasonableness, not a rationalized subjective standard. An institution that argues that it cannot afford to apply technological protection measures in the distance education setting when the institution apparently has the financial resources to mount a digital distance education program would likely not be making reasonable argument, at least not to a third party (the objective component) such as a federal judge. Moreover, this appears to be the sort of rationalization that can be so very dangerous in the copyright arena and which Congress through §110(2)(D)(i) and (ii) is trying to alter.

What sort of technologies are acceptable, that "reasonably prevent"? The Conference Report goes on to suggest the sort of objective and reasonable technological efforts that would satisfy the proviso.

> Examples of technological protection measures that exist today and would reasonably prevent retention and further dissemination, include measures used in connection with streaming to prevent the copying of streamed material, such as the RealPlayer "Secret Handshake/Copy Switch" technology discussed in *Real Networks v. Streambox*, 2000 WL 127311 [*Real Networks, Inc. v. Streambox, Inc.*, 2000 U.S. Dist. LEXIS 1889 (W.D. Wash. 2000) (preliminary injunction)], or digital rights management systems that limit access to or use of encrypted material downloaded onto a computer."[12]

RealPlayer is just an example, not a requirement. "It is not the Committee's intent, by noting the existence of the foregoing, to specify the use of any particular technology to comply with subparagraph (2)(D)(ii). Other technologies will certainly evolve."[13] The choice of particular technology is up to the institution. However, the incorporation of such technological measures is not a one-time action, as that would not be reasonable. As observed earlier, copyright compliance is a process. What is reasonable is that the institution, in the same way it might upgrade its course delivery software or switch to a better distance education mouse-trap, must also review and update its choice and array of technological protection measures. The Conference Report anticipates that monitoring (not of individuals but of the system) and maintenance on the part of the institution of its system or network reflect the natural technological evolution; it also recognizes the existence of the savvy and unfortunately hack-happy world of many students. A head-in-the-sand approach will not suffice:

> Further, it is possible that, as time passes, a technological protection measure may cease to reasonably prevent retention of the work in accessible form for longer than the class session and further dissemination of the work either due to the evolution of technology or to the widespread availability of a hack that can be readily used by the public. In those cases, a transmitting organization would be required to apply a different measure.[14]

Again, reasonableness is the charge of the day. Network and other distance education administrators need to be aware not only of advances in technology, which is likely, but also of the practices of students or other users of its distance education systems and network to counteract those advances.

At first glance these provisions—prevention of retention or further dissemination by recipients (students) in accessible form for longer than the class session—may appear harsh. However, the legislative history tempers this harshness by explanation of the intended meaning of "in accessible form" and "class session." Consider the first "retention" requirement of §110(2)(D)(ii)(I), that the institution employ the use of technological measures that reasonably prevent "*(aa) retention of the work in accessible form by recipients of the transmission from the transmitting body or institution for longer than the class session.*" The meaning of "class session," discussed earlier, is critical to understanding what the technological protection measures must do in order to comply with the statute. Recipients may not retain the work "in accessible form for longer than the class session," but how long is that? Recall the flexible concept of the class session:

> The requirement that technological measures be applied to limit retention for no longer than the "class session" refers back to the requirement that the performance be made as an "integral part of a class session." The duration of a "class session" in asynchronous distance education would generally be that period during which a student is logged on to the server of the institution or governmental body making the display or performance, but is likely to vary with the needs of the student and with the design of the particular course.[15]

So, apparently, as long as the "student is logged on to the server of the institution," he or she would be in a class session. Clever, no? But it is not that simple, as the concept is not without limit. The Conference Report continues with a prohibition: "It does not mean the duration of a particular course (i.e., a semester or term), but rather is intended to describe the equivalent of an actual face-to-face mediated class session (although it may be asynchronous and one student may remain online or retain access to the performance or display for longer than another student as needed to complete the class session)."[16] Furthermore, this requirement does not command that the institution remove the material from its server, only that access to it be time-sensitive, so at some point continued access to the material ceases.[17] In fact, as discussed in chapter 6, TEACH also amended §112, adding subsection 112(f), which facilitates copying and thus storage of copyrighted material intended for §110(2) performance or display.

So retention "for longer than the class session" does not occur just because the student is logged onto the site and accessing copyrighted material, as long as that access is for a period less than the entire course or semester, but how long can that be? A typical spring and fall college semester is three or four months or twelve to sixteen weeks in length. The legislative history suggests that the content could not be available the entire semester but only for the week or two the material is covered, with perhaps an additional week or two for those students working at a slower pace and then, say, another week or two during the midterm and final examination and review period. Unlike the "reasonable and limited" test of §110(2), the legislative history provides no list of factors to consider but prescribes a length in time that would mirror the "equivalent of an actual face-to-face mediated class session" and no longer than would be needed to "complete the class session."[18] "Flexibility" and "pedagogical goals" should work in tandem. Common sense is key, and again with deference to market factors, content should not be accessible for such a length of time ("remain in the possession of the recipient in a way") that it would "substitute for acquisition or for uses other than use in the particular class session."[19] This language suggests that erring on the side of caution is prudent. Recall that educational institutions should not place additional material online just because it is easy to do. As discussed earlier, the legislative history expressed this concern with respect to the display of material. Nor under §110(2)(D)(ii)(I) should materials be left on the course site because the distance education administrator is too lazy or preoccupied to remember to toggle off access to it by disabling a link from the course home page, for example. The implication is that §110(2)(D)(ii) creates vastly increased administrative cost for the institution engaged in the delivery of digital content in the distance education environment. Recall that focus of §110(2) is not on providing access to supplemental material, such as course readings, but only on providing access to that material used in actual instructional performances and displays. A need to have material remain accessible for a period of time longer than the actual instructional act might suggest, for purposes of a copyright audit, that the material is not the sort intended to be covered by §110(2). The following questions might be helpful: Is the material performed or displayed a part of actual instructional activity? How long does the material need to be available so the instructor and student can complete the teaching–learning cycle? What is a reasonable length of time by the end of which the student should have completed the learning objective, adjusting for different learning styles and paces and including review for tests or other forms of assessment?

The second major piece of this puzzle is that the retention "refers only to retention of a copy or phonorecord in the computer of the recipient of a transmission."[20] This explanation by the Conference Report suggests that retention of a copy that is printed out by the student or is downloaded onto a disk and held by the student for months after the class session and course have been completed, while by logic would be "longer than the class session," is still not technically a "retention," as it is *not* in the computer of the recipient, at least not according to the legislative history. The most that could be argued is that when the disk copy is accessed it is once again "in the computer of the recipient of a transmission."

The legislative history presents a definition of "in accessible form" that also is not apparent from a plain reading of the text of the statute.

> The reference to "accessible form" recognizes that certain technological protection measures that could be used to comply with subparagraph (2)(D)(ii) do not cause the destruction or prevent the making of a digital file; rather they work by encrypting the work and limiting access to the keys and the period in which such file may be accessed. On the other hand, an encrypted file would still be considered to be in "accessible form" if the [governmental] body or institution provides the recipient with a key for use beyond the class session.[21]

So the sorts of retentions that the technological measures must prevent are those that would occur from having continued and unencrypted access to copyrighted materials after the class session has ended, and not necessarily an unusable (in terms of technological protection measures) file copy of the work. As long as the file remains encrypted or otherwise unusable, it would still satisfy the proviso that it "reasonably prevent retention of the work in accessible form by recipients of the transmission from the transmitting body or institution for longer than the class session."

It would appear that there are several ways in which a student might have access to the work after the end of the class session, some of which might meet the requirements of §110(2)(D)(ii)(I), and some that might not. Consider the following examples. The work might still be accessible on the course website after the end of the "class session," either with or without the key; if a key is provided or the material is otherwise readable or usable, the requirement is not met. The student might have downloaded the work, either onto a disk or other external device such as a pen drive or onto the CPU hard drive or into account space on the school server, but in any case if that copy remains encrypted it is acceptable; the requirement is met. However, if the institution provided the key such that the student could combine the key with the file copy and access, view, use, etc. the work, this would not be acceptable. Finally, the student might have printed out a copy of the work while it was accessible and unencrypted during the class session. This also is acceptable.

In light of this discussion, the second technological measure can also be understood. That measure must also reasonably prevent the "*(bb) unauthorized further dissemination of the work in accessible form by such recipients to others.*"

Again, the discussion of what fulfills the "reasonably prevent" requirement also applies here as well. There is no requirement to ensure that dissemination "never occur" or that "perfect efficacy" is necessary. Like §110(2)(D)(ii)(I)(aa), the (bb) sub-clause also includes the "in accessible" proviso. As a result, the sort of further dissemination prohibited is one that is in accessible form; that is, one that is unencrypted. The technological measure need "not cause the destruction of the work or prevent the making of a digital file," as long as it remains unusable after the class session has ended or after it is disseminated. A system that keyed authorized access to a valid student password and IP authorization would ensure that, while an encrypted copy of the work might be disseminated by the student to another, that other student could not properly access the work now in his or her possession because it would not be in accessible form. The digital key would fail to access the work because the password and IP address would not match, for example.

Finally, these measures need not be designed to prevent access by certain persons, the "who," so to speak, as that is a topic of §110(2)(C). Rather, the §110(2)(D)(ii)(I) provisions are content-use provisions, in the sense that the requirements attempt to control downstream uses of copyrighted content.[22] This is an important distinction, underscored by the legislative history of §110(2)(C) as discussed earlier. For example, there need not be general network security or constant monitoring. In §110(2)(D)(ii), however, the more advanced and invasive technological measures described are only for use with digital transmissions dealing with post-class session retentions and disseminations, not pre-class session limitations of access under the "solely for" and "limited to" "officially enrolled students" provisos of §110(2)(C).

Interference with Technological Protection Measures

A final requirement of §110(2)(D)(ii) is found in §110(2)(D)(ii)(II), and requires that the transmitting body or institution "*(II) does not engage in conduct that could reasonably be expected to interfere with technological measures used by copyright owners to prevent such retention or unauthorized further dissemination.*" If the institution does engage is such conduct, it cannot avail itself of the §110(2) performance or display transmission right. Like the other compliance requirements of §110(2)(D), it serves as an eligibility door to the performance and display granting mechanism of §110. While this prohibition is not the equivalent of an anti-circumvention or anti-trafficking provision like §1201 as discussed in chapter 2, it does nonetheless prohibit the educational institution from engaging in certain kinds of behavior. Since the statute prohibits conduct that "could reasonably be *expected* to interfere" with technological measures used by copyright owners to prevent §110(2)(D)(ii)(I) retentions and disseminations, it would by logic also prohibit conduct that actually succeeds in interfering with those technological measures. But since the provision reaches even that conduct that one would reasonably expect to interfere (objective standard here also?) it might be argued that §110(2)(D)(ii)(II) is broader than §1201(a), which targets acts of actual circumvention. Although §1201 covers trafficking, while in theory §110(2)(D)(ii)(II) does not, it could be argued that trafficking conduct (posting the digital hack on a distance education course website for students to use) would also trigger the §110(2)(D)(ii)(II) proviso, as this would be conduct that one would reasonably expect to interfere with the protection measures used by the copyright owner.

Since these sorts of technological measures by nature apply only to copyrighted material in digital form, the proviso is placed with §110(2)(D)(ii) regarding those uses "in the case of digital transmissions." Unlike §1201, however, failure to meet this requirement does not create separate liability; rather, the provision operates only as an eligibility clause for the "acquisition of the §110(2) performance or display right."[23] However, as discussed below, such "interfering" conduct might also be a violation of the §1201 rules.

What are the sorts of protection measures that cannot be interfered with? The sorts that would be used by owners to "prevent such retention or unauthorized dissemination" under §110(2)(D)(ii)(I)(aa) and (bb). The legislative history quoted earlier offers two possibilities: "measures used in connection with streaming to prevent the copying of streamed material" or "digital rights management systems [that] limit access to or use of encrypted material downloaded onto a computer."[24] Notice that 110(2)(D)(ii)(I)(aa) and (bb) require the institution to use protection measures to assist copyright owners in preventing the sort of retentions and disseminations that might lead to infringement, whereas §110(2)(D)(ii)(II) requires that the institution not interfere with those measures already in place. In this way §110(2)(D)(ii)(I) and 110(2)(D)(ii)(II) complement each other to an extent and ensure that all copyrighted materials performed or displayed in the context of a §110(2)(D) digital transmission will be protected by technological measures, either by the copyright owner under 110(2)(D)(ii)(II), or, if none are present, by the institution under §110(2)(D)(ii)(I), at least as far as the targeted retention and dissemination requirement is concerned.

The likely sort of protection measures used by a copyright owner might be some sort of key encryption device that coordinates and limits the number of downloads that might be made of copyrighted material to the number of permissions the institution secured, perhaps further coordinated with the number of students enrolled in the course or the length of time an access code may function and allow use by students. A copyright owner might use a following technological measure such as RealPlayer or other streaming protection technology to prevent copying material streamed from a publisher's website. Likewise a copyright owner might use a digital rights management system that would limit downloading of encrypted copyrighted material to authorized recipient computers alone, whereby any dissemination by the recipient would be of an encrypted version such that any transfer would be unusable on the computer to which it was transferred.

Notice also that the prohibited interfering conduct applies only with respect to a particular transmission and not to the conduct of the wider institution. "As the context makes clear, this requirement refers to conduct that is taken in connection with the particular transmissions subject to the exemption, rather than to the broader activities of the transmitting body or institution generally."[25] As such an institution with a computer science or computer engineering department that specializes in encryption research would not trigger the 110(2)(D)(ii)(II) interference proscription when it stumbles upon a de-encryption technique and then proceeds to make others aware of it through normal channels of scholarly communication. However, if the institution then proceeded to use that decryption code in conjunction with a §110(2)(D) transmission that allowed the student recipients of the transmission to retain through downloading (contrary to "measures used in connection with streaming to prevent the copying of streamed material," from the legislative history "[e]xample[] of technological protection measures that exist"[26]) or to disseminate an unencrypted version of the work (contrary to "digital rights management systems that limit access to or use of encrypted material downloaded onto a computer," again from the legislative history, as an "[e]xample[] of technological protection measures that exist"[27]), this conduct "could reasonably be expected to interfere with the technological measures used by copyright owners to prevent such retention or unauthorized further dissemination" and the institution would trigger the "reasonably be expected to interfere" proviso and would not be able to avail itself of the privileges granted by §110(2). Of course, these or similar technological measures must have been imposed by the copyrighted owners on the copyrighted material, thus the significance of the "used by," not just created by.

In theory this language allows an institution to engage in decryption technology research that could later be used to circumvent a RealPlayer copy control but not eliminate its eligibility under §110(2). However, if it used that same decryption technology in a §110(2) transmission to interfere with a block a copyright owner did in fact place on a copyrighted work it made available for use in distance education, say in a stream from the copyright owner's website direct to students, then eligibility for transmissions by the institution under §110(2) would be lost. This is consistent with the legislative history comment: "Further, like the other provision under paragraph (2)(D)(ii), the requirement has no legal effect other than as a condition of eligibility for the exemption. Thus, it is not otherwise enforceable to preclude or prohibit conduct."[28] Moreover, it is consistent with the tandem or double-barrel approach of §110(2)(D)(ii)(I) and (II). Finally, it also consistent with the employ of §110(2) compliance requirements at the institutional level as a general prerequisite for §110(2) transmissions.

Of course, it can be said that the mere development of decryption technology would not violate the anti-circumvention and anti-trafficking rules of §1201, but the use of that decryption technology (circumvention) or dissemination of it (trafficking) might well violate the §1201 anti-circumvention and anti-trafficking rules, such as by posting it on the institution's website, for example.[29] On the other hand, development of such technology as well as its use or dissemination in contexts other than a particular §110(2) transmission would not violate the §110(2)(D)(ii)(II) proscription: "Nothing in section 110(2) should be construed to affect the application or interpretation of section 1201. Conversely, nothing in section 1201 should be construed to affect the application or interpretation of section 110(2)."[30] A §110(2)(D)(ii)(II) interference and the §1201 circumvention or trafficking event must each be assessed on its own merits. A particular course of conduct might trigger both, one, or neither set of rules. The distinction means that a §110(2)(D)(ii)(II) interference only forecloses the use of a §110(2) performance and display right, while a §1201 circumvention or trafficking violation is subject to separate penalty under Title 17. Thus, while a particular use or dissemination of a decryption code might well violate §1201, it would not trigger the §110(2)(D)(ii)(II) proviso unless it was used or disseminated in the specific context of distance education technological measures "that could reasonably be expected to interfere with technological measures used by copyright owners to prevent such retention or unauthorized further dissemination." By the same token, it would also appear that any use or dissemination of a §110(2)(D)(ii)(II) decryption code "hack" would necessarily violate §1201. However, not all "conduct that could reasonably be expected to interfere with technological measures used by copyright owners to prevent such retention or unauthorized further dissemination" would violate §1201. For example, posting a legitimate key, but one that the institution was supposed to withdraw from active use according to, say, a license agreement, would certainly not violate the §1201 anti-circumvention and anti-trafficking rules, but it certainly would be "conduct that could reasonably be expected to interfere with technological measures used by copyright owners to prevent such retention or unauthorized further dissemination,"[31] and thus would result in a loss of performance and display privileges under §110(2).

Protection against Making Transient Copies in Section 110(2), as Distinguished from Ephemeral Recordings under Section 112

Besides two provisions of §110(2) defining "mediated instructional activities" and "accreditation" appended at the conclusion of §110(2), a third and concluding provision contains an immunity statement for nonprofit educational institutions for the transient or temporary storage of copyrighted material in the course of an authorized transmission:

> *For purposes of paragraph (2), no governmental body or accredited nonprofit educational institution shall be liable for infringement by reason of the transient or temporary storage of material carried out through the automatic technical process of digital transmission of the performance or display of that material as authorized under paragraph (2). No such material stored on the system or network controlled or operated by the transmitting body or institution under this paragraph shall be maintained on such system or network in a manner ordinarily accessible to anyone other than anticipated recipients. No such copy shall be maintained on the system or network in a manner ordinarily accessible to such anticipated recipients for a longer period than is reasonably necessary to facilitate the transmission for which it was made.*

Examples might consist of a scenario where a copy of a work is made in the RAM of a computer in the instructor's office as he or she performs or displays the work and a second copy is made in the buffer file of the student receiving the §110(2) transmission. In either the case the copy is "transient or temporary." However, assuming the work performed or displayed is protected, a copy of a copyrighted work has been made. This provision gives immunity to the education institution. There are two requirements that must be met before the immunity operates. First, the only persons with access to the material should be enrolled students; that is, the "anticipated recipients." Second, the duration of the access of the anticipated recipients can be for a period no longer than the class session—a period no longer than "is reasonably necessary to facilitate the transmission for which it was made."

The purpose of the provision is to immunize the nonprofit educational institution against any potential liability for temporary or transient storage of material carried out through the automatic processes of making a §110(2) transmission. For example, additional copies of works may be created as material is accessed from storage on external or internal servers and loaded onto an institutional distance education server,[32] or a copy may be made in the hard drive or RAM of an instructor's or student's computer as part of the perception of a §110(2) transmission[33] or by a similar loading of material by instructors and students from their own computers onto the distance education servers of the educational institution.[34]

What about scenarios where a copy is made and retained to facilitate later transmission of that transient or temporary copy? It is not incidental "temporary or transient storage"; rather, it is of a more permanent nature, retained for a subsequent §110(2) use. Is the making of those copies authorized here? No, copies for storage for periods beyond transient or temporary are the purview of §112(f). Section 112(f) authorizes the institution to make so-called ephemeral copies of copyrighted materials as a precursor to a §110(2) transmission, as discussed in chapter 6. But what about those instances where an instructor or student loads material onto the course website beyond the control of the distance education administrative compliance structure? As a result of the inability to police the making of these transient or temporary copies, the provision "recognizes that transmitting organizations should not be responsible for copies or phonorecords made by third parties, beyond the control of the transmitting organizations."[35]

According to the statutory language of the provision, the immunity benefit targets the institution: "no . . . accredited non profit educational institution shall be liable for infringement." In the examples above, this would be for direct liability when others load transient or temporary materials onto its servers, computers, or other network facilities and copies are thus generated, or for secondary liability when it perpetuates the making of copies by the recipients of its transmissions when the materials are received and by automatic operation of the recipient's computer copies made in a RAM or on a hard drive.[36] The legislative history suggests that this immunity extends to the direct infringement that might conceivably occur by the recipient when a copy is made in his or her RAM or hard drive:

> The third paragraph added to the amended exemption by section 1(b)(2) of the TEACH Act is intended to make clear that *those authorized to participate* in digitally transmitted performances and displays as authorized under section 110(2) are *not liable for infringement* as a result of such *copies created as part of the automatic technical process of the transmission* if the requirements of that language are met."[37]

An officially enrolled student would be one of "those authorized to participate" as well as a more obvious group of "those authorized to participate," the instructional staff. Without any primary or direct infringement on the part of students with respect to transient or temporary copies, there can be no secondary liability (contributory or vicarious) on the part of the institution with respect to those copies, thus both groups are immunized.

Notes

1. Conference Report, H. Rpt. No. 107-685, 107th Cong., 2d Sess. 230 (2002).
2. Conference Report, H. Rpt. No. 107-685, 107th Cong., 2d Sess. 230 (2002).

3. Conference Report, H. Rpt. No. 107-685, 107th Cong., 2d Sess. 231 (2002).

4. Conference Report, H. Rpt. No. 107-685, 107th Cong., 2d Sess. 230 (2002) ("Further, the transmitting organization must provide notice to students that materials used in conjunction with the course may be subject to copyright protection.").

5. See 17 U.S.C. 108(f)(1) and 37 C.F.R. at §201.14 (Warnings of copyright for use by certain libraries and archives). 37 C.F.R. at §201.14 contains the text of the required notice, as follows:

> The copyright law of the United States (Title 17, United States Code) governs the making of photocopies or other reproductions of copyrighted material. Under certain conditions specified in the law, libraries and archives are authorized to furnish a photocopy or other reproduction. One of these specific conditions is that the photocopy or reproduction is not to be "used for any purpose other than private study, scholarship, or research." If a user makes a request for, or later uses, a photocopy or reproduction for purposes in excess of "fair use," that user may be liable for copyright infringement. This institution reserves the right to refuse to accept a copying order if, in its judgment, fulfillment of the order would involve violation of copyright law.

37 C.F.R. 201.14(b) provides that "[a] Display Warning of Copyright and an Order Warning of Copyright shall consist of a verbatim reproduction of the following notice, printed in such size and form and displayed in such manner as to comply with paragraph (c) of this section." 37 C.F.R. 201.14(c) provides for the "[f]orm and manner of use. (1) A Display Warning of Copyright shall be printed on heavy paper or other durable material in type at least 18 points in size, and shall be displayed prominently, in such manner and location as to be clearly visible, legible, and comprehensible to a casual observer within the immediate vicinity of the place where orders are accepted."

6. See 17 U.S.C. 109(b) and 37 C.F.R. 201.24 (Warning of copyright for software lending by nonprofit libraries). 37 C.F.R. 201.24(b) provides that "[a] Warning of Copyright for Software Rental shall consist of a verbatim reproduction of the following notice, printed in such size and form and affixed in such manner as to comply with paragraph (c) of this section." The text of the notice is as follows:

> Notice: Warning of Copyright Restrictions. The copyright law of the United States (Title 17, U.S. Code) governs the reproduction, distribution, adaptation, public performance, and public display of copyrighted material. Under certain conditions specified in law, nonprofit libraries are authorized to lend, lease, or rent copies of computer programs to patrons on a nonprofit basis and for nonprofit purposes. Any person who makes an unauthorized copy or adaptation of the computer program, or redistributes the loan copy, or publicly performs or displays the computer program, except as permitted by Title 17 of the U.S. Code, may be liable for copyright infringement. This institution reserves the right to refuse to fulfill a loan request if, in its judgment, fulfillment of the request would lead to violation of the copyright law.

7. See Tomas A. Lipinski, The Decreasing Impact of Technological Neutrality in Copyright Law and Its Impact on Institutional Users, 54 *Journal of the American Society for Information Science and Technology* 824 (2003).

8. Conference Report, H. Rpt. No. 107-685, 107th Cong., 2d Sess. 232 (2002) ("Paragraph (2)(D)(ii) provides, *as a condition of eligibility for the exemption,* that a transmitting body or institution apply technological measures that reasonably prevent both retention of the work in accessible form for longer than the class session and further dissemination of the work.").

9. Conference Report, H. Rpt. No. 107-685, 107th Cong., 2d Sess. 232 (2002).

10. Conference Report, H. Rpt. No. 107-685, 107th Cong., 2d Sess. 232 (2002) ("Nor does it imply that there is an obligation to monitor recipient conduct.").

11. Conference Report, H. Rpt. No. 107-685, 107th Cong., 2d Sess. 232 (2002) (emphasis added).

12. Conference Report, H. Rpt. No. 107-685, 107th Cong., 2d Sess. 232 (2002).

13. Conference Report, H. Rpt. No. 107-685, 107th Cong., 2d Sess. 232 (2002).

14. Conference Report, H. Rpt. No. 107-685, 107th Cong., 2d Sess. 232 (2002).

15. Conference Report, H. Rpt. No. 107-685, 107th Cong., 2d Sess. 231 (2002).

16. Conference Report, H. Rpt. No. 107-685, 107th Cong., 2d Sess. 231 (2002).

17. Conference Report, H. Rpt. No. 107-685, 107th Cong., 2d Sess. 231 (2002) ("The material to be performed or displayed may, under the amendments made by the Act to section 112 and with certain limitations set forth therein, remain on the server of the institution or government body for the duration of its use in one or more courses, and may be accessed by a student each time the student logs on to participate in the particular class session of the course in which the display or performance is made.") (emphasis added).

18. Conference Report, H. Rpt. No. 107-685, 107th Cong., 2d Sess. 231 (2002) ("It does not mean the duration of a particular course (i.e., a semester or term), but rather is intended to describe the equivalent of an actual single face-to-face mediated class session (although it may be asynchronous and one student may remain online or retain access to the performance or display for longer than another student as needed to complete the class session).").

19. Conference Report, H. Rpt. No. 107-685, 107th Cong., 2d Sess. 231 (2002) ("Although *flexibility* is necessary to accomplish the *pedagogical goals* of distance education, the Committee expects that a common sense construction will be applied so that a copy or phonorecord displayed or performed in the course of a distance education program would *not* remain in the possession of the recipient in a way that could *substitute for acquisition or for uses other than* use in the particular class session.") (emphasis added).

20. Conference Report, H. Rpt. No. 107-685, 107th Cong., 2d Sess. 231 (2002) ("Conversely, the technological protection measure in subparagraph (2)(D)(ii) refers only to retention of a copy or phonorecord in the computer of the recipient of a transmission.").

21. Conference Report, H. Rpt. No. 107-685, 107th Cong., 2d Sess. 232 (2002).

22. Conference Report, H. Rpt. No. 107-685, 107th Cong., 2d Sess. 231 (2002) ("Second, in the case of a digital transmission, the transmitting body or institution is required to apply technological measures to prevent (i) retention of the work in accessible form by recipients to which it sends the work for longer than the class session, and (ii) unauthorized further dissemination of the work in accessible form by such recipients. *Measures intended to limit access to authorized recipients* of transmissions

from the transmitting body or institution are not addressed in this subparagraph (2)(D). Rather, they are the subjects of subparagraph (2)(C).").

23. Conference Report, H. Rpt. No. 107-685, 107th Cong., 2d Sess. 232 (2002) ("Further, like the other provisions under paragraph (2)(D)(ii), the *requirement has no legal effect* other than as a condition of eligibility for the exemption. Thus, *it is not otherwise enforceable* to preclude or prohibit conduct.") (first and second emphasis added).

24. Conference Report, H. Rpt. No. 107-685, 107th Cong., 2d Sess. 232 (2002).

25. Conference Report, H. Rpt. No. 107-685, 107th Cong., 2d Sess. 231 (2002).

26. Conference Report, H. Rpt. No. 107-685, 107th Cong., 2d Sess. 232 (2002).

27. Conference Report, H. Rpt. No. 107-685, 107th Cong., 2d Sess. 232 (2002).

28. Conference Report, H. Rpt. No. 107-685, 107th Cong., 2d Sess. 231 (2002).

29. Such a posting of a decryption access code, in essence a hack, would violate the §1201 trafficking rules. See, e.g., *Universal City Studios v. Reimerdes*, 82 F. Supp. 2d 211 (S.D.N.Y. 2000); 111 F. Supp. 2d 294 (S.D.N.Y. 2000) (permanent injunction); aff'd sub. nom. *Universal City Studios, Inc. v. Corley*, 273 F.3d 429 (2d Cir. 2001); *321 Studios v. Metro Goldwyn Mayer Studios, Inc.*, 307 F. Supp. 2d 1085 (N.D. Cal. 2004) ("Therefore, as 321 markets its software for use in circumventing CSS, this Court finds that 321's DVD copying software is in violation of the marketing provisions of §§1201(a)(2) and (b)(1). Accordingly, this Court finds that 321's software is in violation of both §1201(a)(2) and §1201(b)(1), because it is both primarily designed and produced to circumvent CSS, and marketed to the public for use in circumventing CSS." Id. at 1099); *United States v. Elcom Ltd.*, 203 F. Supp. 2d 1111 (N.D. Cal. 2002) ("The indictment alleges that 'when an ebook purchased for viewing in the Adobe eBook Reader format was sold by the publisher or distributor, the publisher or distributor of the ebook could authorize or limit the purchaser's ability to copy, distribute, print, or have the text read audibly by the computer. Adobe designed the eBook Reader to permit the management of such digital rights so that in the ordinary course of its operation, the eBook Reader effectively permitted the publisher or distributor of the ebook to restrict or limit the exercise of certain copyright rights of an owner of the copyright for an ebook distributed in the eBook Reader format.' Indictment P1(g)." Id. at 1118); *Real Networks, Inc. v. Streambox, Inc.*, 2000 U.S. Dist. LEXIS 1889 (W.D. Wash. 2000) (preliminary injunction) ("Again, this argument fails to address the VCR's circumvention of the Secret Handshake, which is enough, by itself, to create liability under Section 1201(a)(2)" Id. at *24-*25) ("Given the circumvention capabilities of the Streambox VCR, Streambox violates the DMCA if the product or a part thereof: (i) is primarily designed to serve this function; (ii) has only limited commercially significant purposes beyond the circumvention; or (iii) is marketed as a means of circumvention. 17 U.S.C. §§1201(a)(2)(A-C), 1201(b) (b)(A-C). These three tests are disjunctive. Id. A product that meets only one of the three independent bases for liability is still prohibited. Here, the VCR meets at least the first two." Id. at *17).

30. Conference Report, H. Rpt. No. 107-685, 107th Cong., 2d Sess. 232 (2002).

31. "The reference to 'accessible form' recognizes that certain technological protection measures that could be used to comply with subparagraph (2)(D)(ii) do not cause the destruction or prevent the making of a digital file; rather they work by encrypting the work and limiting access to the keys and the period in which such file may be accessed. On the other hand, an encrypted file would still be considered to be in 'accessible form' *if the body*

or institution provides the recipient with a key for use beyond the class session." Conference Report, H. Rpt. No. 107-685, 107th Cong., 2d Sess. 232 (2002) (emphasis added).

32. Conference Report, H. Rpt. No. 107-685, 107th Cong., 2d Sess. 233 (2002) ("Organizations providing digital distance education will, in many cases, provide material from source servers that create additional temporary or transient copies or phonorecords of the material in storage known as 'caches' in other servers in order to facilitate the transmission.").

33. Conference Report, H. Rpt. No. 107-685, 107th Cong., 2d Sess. 233 (2002) ("Thus, by way of example, where content is protected by a digital rights management system, the recipient's browser may create a cache copy of an encrypted file on the recipient's hard disk, and another copy may be created in the recipient's random access memory at the time the content is perceived.").

34. Conference Report, H. Rpt. No. 107-685, 107th Cong., 2d Sess. 233 (2002) ("In addition, transient or temporary copies or phonorecords may occur in the transmission stream, or in the computer of the recipient of the transmission.").

35. Conference Report, H. Rpt. No. 107-685, 107th Cong., 2d Sess. 233 (2002).

36. *Intellectual Reserve, Inc. v. Utah Lighthouse Ministry, Inc.*, 75 F. Supp. 2d 1290 (Dist. Utah 1999). (No actual link, encouragement, and referral to a known site of infringing material is sufficient to establish liability for contributory infringement; court determined that visitors to the referred site engage in direct infringement when material at that site is copied onto their computers in RAM for viewing.)

37. Conference Report, H. Rpt. No. 107-685, 107th Cong., 2d Sess. 233 (2002) (emphasis added).

5

Summary of Part II

The Section 110(2) Requirements in a Nutshell

- There is no limitation on the portion of nondramatic literary or musical works that can be performed. (See discussion, pages 53–55.)
- The performance of all other works is limited to a reasonable and limited portion of the work. The amount is determined by considering a market test (for that type of work) and pedagogical purpose test, but in any case is less than the entire work. (See discussion, pages 56–61.)
- Display of all works is limited to an amount comparable to that which is typically displayed in the course of a live classroom session; it need not be less but it cannot be more, simply because the distance education environment makes it easy to present more materials online. (See discussion, pages 61–64.)
- Performance and display rights do not apply to works produced or marketed primarily for performance or display as part of mediated instructional activities transmitted via digital networks. In other words, instructional or curricular materials designed specifically for use in digital distance education are excluded. The market for these works is expected to develop through contract (license), not sales (copyright). (See discussion, pages 40–43.)
- The copy or phonorecord performed or displayed must be lawfully made and acquired under the copyright law. That means no bootleg or pirated copies or improper means of acquisition, for example, by a software hack that circumvents an access control under §1201. The transmitting school, college, or university must not know or have reason to believe the work

was not lawfully made and acquired, arguably establishing an institution-wide mens rea. (See discussion, pages 43–48.)

- Performance and display rights under §110(2) are available only to accredited nonprofit educational institutions. Definition of "accreditation" in the statute relates to institution, not a particular program. Accreditation must be by CHE- or DOE-certified entity for tertiary, by state educational agency for primary and secondary. (See discussion, pages 77–78.)

- The performance or display must be made by, at the direction of, or under the actual supervision of an instructor as an integral part of a class session offered as a regular part of systematic mediated instructional activities, but can be asynchronous as well as synchronous modes of instruction. (See discussion, pages 73–77.)

- The performance or display is directly related and of material assistance to the teaching content of the transmission. It cannot be for entertainment or supplied as unrelated background. (See discussion, pages 78–79.)

- The transmission is made solely for students officially enrolled in the course for which the transmission is made, incorporates the idea of the anytime, anywhere virtual classroom, but may exclude some forms of traditional network television or radio educational broadcasting. (See discussion, pages 79–81.)

- The reception of such transmission is limited, to the extent technologically feasible, to students officially enrolled in the course for which the transmission is made. There is no rule of general network security, but use of a password or similar measure is suggested. (See discussion, pages 81–84.)

- The school, college, university, or other educational entity must institute policies regarding copyright. (See discussion, pages 90–91.)

- The school, college, university, or other educational entity must provide informational materials to faculty, students, and relevant staff members that accurately describe, and promote compliance with, the laws of the United States relating to copyright. (See discussion, pages 90–91.)

- The school, college, university, or other educational entity must provide notice to students that materials used in connection with a distance education course may be subject to copyright protection. The use of such notices is recommended for all classes (place near beginning of course syllabus, outline, or reading list or use other mechanisms to alert students of the possible copyright protection in course content). (See discussion, pages 92–93.)

- If the performance or display is by means of a digital transmission, then the school, college, university, or other educational entity must apply technological measures that reasonably prevent retention of the work in accessible form by recipients of the transmission from the transmitting school, college, university, or other educational entity for longer than the class session. Flexible concept of class session allows for asynchronous but less than semester-long access. Concept of "in accessible form" is akin to a work in usable form; that is, an encrypted copy would not be "in accessible form." The technological measures need not be perfect, but efforts will judged under a reasonableness standard. (See discussion, pages 93–97.)

- If the performance or display is by means of a digital transmission, then the school, college, university, or other educational entity must apply technological measures that reasonably prevent unauthorized further dissemination of the work in accessible form by such recipients to others. Concept of "in accessible form" is akin to a work in usable form (e.g., an encrypted copy would not be "in accessible form"). The technological measures need not be perfect, but efforts will judged under a reasonableness standard. (See discussion, pages 97–99.)

- If the performance or display is by means of a digital transmission, then the school, college, university, or other educational entity must not engage in conduct that could reasonably be expected to interfere with technological measures used by copyright owners to prevent such retention or unauthorized further dissemination. This requirement creates no new liability. It is only a standard of eligibility for the §110(2) performance and display rights, though there may be alignment of conduct that renders a school, college, university, or other educational entity ineligible under §110(2)(D)(ii)(II) and also violates the §1201 anti-trafficking rules. (See discussion, pages 99–103.)

III

COMPLETING THE TEACH PUZZLE

6

The Ephemeral Recording
Privilege in Distance Education

The Old and the New

AFTER EXAMINING THE VARIOUS NEW RIGHTS as well as new responsibilities that educators have under TEACH and its reform of the copyright law, you, an educator at a qualifying school, college, university, or other educational entity, might desire to head over to the computer lab and begin designing online courses. However, an obvious question should immediately occur to you, if you have been following and understanding the copyright rights and copyright limitations–oriented structure of the copyright law. As you design the new online class that moments ago you were so excited about, you realize that to facilitate 24/7 ease of access (which the legislative history claims is brought to fruition in TEACH, in the reformed performance and display rights of §110(2)), you would like to store some copyrighted works on the institution's distance education servers for ready access, anytime, anywhere by students. Perhaps the material was found on the Web or on the institution's LAN, or perhaps you need to convert some print materials—say, a photograph or map, or a VHS tape (analog)—to store on the institution's distance education server or on your office computer workstations as well. Before you read further, if you have not seen the copyright problem, go back and read earlier discussions of exclusive rights in chapter 1 and the chapter 3 text discussing what new rights educators possess; that is, what limitations on the exclusive rights of copyright owners arise when you make use of copyrighted works in distance education.

When you paste copyrighted material from a website or the LAN, for example, onto a course website located on the institution's server, or download and store it anywhere else, for purposes of the copyright *a copy or phonorecord is created.* This implicates the exclusive right of copyright owners to reproduce their works. Likewise, when those print materials or VHS cassette recordings are converted and a digital version created, a copy or phonorecord also results. The revised §110(2) under TEACH does not offer any assistance. While §110(2) is certainly a "limitations on exclusive rights" provision, and under TEACH those rights are expanded considerably, the limitations on the exclusive rights provided by revised §110(2) limit only two specific exclusive rights of copyright owners: those of performance and display. Second, these copies would not be the sorts of copies made by the "transient or temporary storage of material carried out through the automatic technical process of a digital transmission" for which §110(2) now provides immunity; rather, these are long-term reproductions.

The Concept of Ephemeral Recordings

So the issue of making what might be called "preliminary" or "anticipatory" copies as a precursor to an authorized use under §110(2) is, according to the 1976 legislative history, a "problem of what are commonly called 'ephemeral recordings': copies or phonorecords of a work made for purposes of later transmission by a broadcasting organization legally entitled to transmit the work."[1] Fortunately, Congress had the foresight when it created TEACH to re-examine another section of the copyright law, one providing limitations on the exclusive reproduction rights of copyright owners. This section, §112, is known as the ephemeral recordings provision; that is, "Limitations on exclusive rights: Ephemeral recordings."

As the title implies, since reproducing is a necessary precursor to engaging in a permitted use under another provision of the copyright law, the recording is "ephemeral" in the sense that the copy so made is not itself the subject of use other than one connected to a specific and authorized use under the copyright law. Since its only purpose is to facilitate a use authorized elsewhere in the copyright law the use of which necessitates the making of a copy, it is ephemeral. But be careful: One could rationalize any number of initial copying activities in order to make a later potential "fair use" of it, like having to digitize that old import Violent Femmes EP, containing the only recording of their acoustic punk "classic" date song "Ugly," so you can later use a very small part of it in your PowerPoint presentation to a group of other educators at a conference or, in a more clandestine offering, make the entire song available to other acoustic punk aficionados. The former conference use would possibly be a fair use, but the latter music sharing—in light of the MP3[2] and P2P case law such as Napster,[3] Grokster,[4] Aimster[5] or "Next-ster" or whatever the name of the next generation of file-sharing software—is likely to be an unfair use.

An examination of §112 reveals that the privileged (limitation on copyright owner's exclusive rights) ephemeral recording (copying) right is statutorily dependent upon other specifically authorized "limitations on exclusive rights" provisions and not on a generalized concept of fair use. For example, §112(d)[6] authorizes ephemeral recordings for use in transmissions to the blind or handicapped in accordance with §110(8),[7] and §112(e)[8] authorizes the ephemeral recording of a sound recording used in transmissions in accordance with §114(d)(1)(C)(iv)[9] or under a statutory licensing under §114(f).[10] In other words, although one may believe that a subsequent use of copyrighted material would be acceptable under the law, and even if it is held to be so by a court (e.g., the use of the classic guitar riff from Roy Orbison's "Pretty Woman" by the rap group Two Live Crew was held to be a fair use by the Supreme Court),[11] §112 does not grant educators the right to make a recording of the song for some potential later distance education classroom use, even if it is a fair use unless that use is also authorized under some other operative statutorily dependent provision of the copyright law. In the case of distance education, the ephemeral recording rights granted under §112 are statutorily dependent upon §110(2).

The ephemeral recording right exists only when the use (performance or display) of the work is authorized under §110(2). This also means that making a copy of a work would, for a use authorized under §110(2), be acceptable (copying, then displaying several poems or short stories in a distance education American literature course), but using the copy to create a derivative work from it (copying, then dramatizing the short story for use in a drama class) would have to be justified under fair use or some provision of the copyright law, both as to the initial copying and storage and its subsequent iteration into a dramatic derivative work, as §110(2) rights do not apply to derivative works. Section 112 now offers educators the right to make a copy (ephemeral recording) of protected material, but the ephemeral recording rights are tied to very specific limitations of exclusive rights found elsewhere in the copyright law and linked by statutory reference in the various subsections of §112.[12]

Ephemeral Recordings under the 1976 Copyright Act

Even before TEACH, §112 recognized the "practical exigencies of [educational] broadcasting"[13] and offered an ephemeral recording right to distance educators, but, like much of the pre-TEACH distance education copyright law, it, too, upon review appeared stuck in time. Prior to TEACH, §112(b) allowed a qualifying §110(2) entity ("a governmental body or other nonprofit education organization entitled to transmit a performance or display of a work, under section 110(2) or under the limitations on exclusive rights in sound recordings specified by section 114(a)") to make "no more than thirty copies or phonorecords of a particular transmission program embodying the performance or display," provided that (1) "no further copies or phonorecords are reproduced from the copies or phonorecords made under this clause [i.e., ephemeral recordings under §112(b)]," and (2) all copies or phonorecords are "destroyed within seven years from the date the transmission program was first transmitted to the public."[14] The exception to this no-more-than-thirty copy/seven-year rule allowed the retention of one copy "preserved exclusively for archival purposes."[15]

Understanding this clause enacted in 1976 is important for several reasons. First, it remains in effect today. Since it was not amended by TEACH, it can still be used in conjunction with the new §112(f) ephemeral recording right that TEACH did create. Examining the nuances of an ephemeral recording right created several decades ago provides further understanding of the necessity of copyright reform, as well as the benefits and continued limitations of that reform. As the text quoted above indicates, §112(b) contains several limitations. First, the only performance or display that may be the subject of an ephemeral recording is one that is authorized under §110(2). Second, no further copies can be made of the "copies or phonorecords that are made under this clause." Third, while there is no limit on the number of times the ephemeral recording can be used (rebroadcast, for example) in an authorized performance or display under §110(2), under §112(b)(2) there is a time period within which those subsequent uses must be made: Except for the archival copy, "the copies or phonorecords [must be] destroyed within seven years from the date" of first transmission.

While §112(b) does not contain any language limiting what classroom use you can make of an ephemeral recording made under its provisions, the legislative history appears to add a use limitation akin to the familiar "teaching activities" limitation of §110(1) and §110(2): "Copies or phonorecords made for educational broadcast of a *general cultural nature*, or for transmission as part of an information storage and retrieval system would not be exempted from copyright protection under §112(b)."[16] Though using slightly different phrasing, the exclusion for works of "general cultural nature" appears consistent with the exclusion suggested by the 1976 and 2002 legislative history for performance and displays under §110(1) for works "whatever their cultural value or intellectual appeal, that are given for the recreation or entertainment of any part of their audience"[17] or, under §110(2), "for the mere entertainment of the students, or as unrelated background material,"[18] respectively. This §110(2) legislative history "exclusion" is of course that to which the §112(b) ephemeral recording right is statutorily linked, yet it does not include the concept of "cultural" performances or displays in its list of exclusions (entertainment and unrelated background). Perhaps that is why it is included in the §112(b) explanation, since the legislative intent (expressed in the legislative history) to exclude cultural works would surely by logic also intend to implicitly exclude even more tangential entertainment and unrelated background material uses. The problem with this explanation is that the §112(b) legislative history cannot be used to further embellish the nature of the §110(2) performance or display, because the former §112(b) legislative history ("general cultural nature") was written some twenty-five years before the quoted TEACH §110(2) legislative history ("entertainment or unrelated background"). However, as discussed in chapter 3, the later-in-time TEACH §110(2) legislative history indicates that indeed the 1976 version of §110(2) implicitly excluded those sorts of works as well.[19]

This limitation of the legislative history regarding subsequent uses of the ephemeral recording does not appear too restrictive, but other language in the legislative history is not so forgiving. The 1976 Copyright Act envisioned a scenario in which an educator might want to rebroadcast the teaching session he or she previously transmitted and so would like to make a copy of it; that is, make an ephemeral recording of the transmission. The right to do this is at the heart of the §112(b) recording privilege regarding the capture of a distance education teaching encounter that contained (§112(b) uses the term "embodying") the performance or display of the copyrighted material that the educator needed the §110(2) right to support in the first instance. In addition to exercising a retransmission right to use the performance or display now embodied as a recording of the distance education class session, an educator might desire to place several copies of the ephemeral recording (three of the statutorily allowed "no more than thirty") in the form of a DVD or videocassette on reserve at the library, in an e-reserve, or as part of a traditional reserve system, in order to facilitate students' review of course content. Yet the legislative history contains the following explanation of the §112(b) right: "to make no more than thirty copies or phonorecords *and to use the ephemeral recordings for transmitting purposes* for not more than seven years after the initial transmission."[20] Again, this is just legislative history and may reflect Congress's typically limited vision of how an educator or library supporting distance education in 1976 might desire to make the most effective use of the ephemeral recording it does make, and not other evolving options for use. In other words, the legislative history of §112(b) suggests the ephemeral recording could be used only in transmission or replay of the authorized §110(2) performance or display.

It could be argued that this limiting interpretation is consistent with the structure of §112, because the other ephemeral recording subsections specifically state the *uses* to which the ephemeral recording can be put,[21] while subsection (b) is silent as to any such command. Moreover, those uses when

stated are limited to either successive transmissions or, in only one other provision, subsection (d), to "archival preservation or security." Does the lack of
such restricting language imply statutory wiggle room, or is it another drafting oversight, with the legislative history of §112(b) and the remaining subsections reflecting the proper context (i.e., ephemeral recording for later
transmission; that is, replay or rebroadcast alone)?

On the other hand, is the lack of any directive regarding possible uses an
indication that there are indeed no such limitations? Support for this second
position might be found in comparison of the three clauses that allow
archival retention, in §112(b)(2), (d)(2), and (e)(1)(A) and (B). The clause
regarding the "archival purposes" is not linked to the word *use* or any similar
concept in §112(b) as it is subsection (d)(2) (i.e., "any such copy or
phonorecord *is used solely for* the transmissions authorized under section
110(8), *or for purposes of archival preservation or security*") but appears rather
in subsection (b)(2) regarding the length of time the ephemeral recordings
may be retained: "except for one copy or phonorecord that may be preserved
exclusively for archival purposes, the copies or phonorecords are destroyed
with seven years from the date the transmission program was first transmitted to the public."[22] Subsection (e)(1)(B) and (C) also contains an archive
provision tied to retention enunciation: "(B) The phonorecord is used solely
for the transmitting organization's own transmissions. . . . (C) Unless preserved exclusively for purposes of archival preservation, the phonorecord is
destroyed within 6 months from the date the sound recording was first transmitted to the public using the phonorecord." Certainly, the plain meaning
and language of the statute should govern, especially when examined with
similar provisions enacted at the same time. However, it is perhaps more tenuous to derive a privilege granted by statutory silence than it is to understand
a clear limitation of that privilege through use of the word "solely" in the actual text of the statute.

Nevertheless, other language in the 1976 legislative history also supports
a later use-in-transmission-only rule. Why allow thirty ("no more than
thirty") copies? According to the legislative history, multiple copies would
be used in subsequent §110(2) transmissions either by the recording institution or by other institutions with distance education programs with which
one of the thirty copies of the ephemeral recording was shared. An institution could transfer one of those authorized thirty copies to another institution for use in its own §110(2) performance or display: "exchanges of
recordings among instructional broadcasters are permitted. An organization
that has made copies or phonorecords under §110(2) (b) may use one of
them *for purposes of its own transmissions* that are exempted by §110(2), and
it *may also transfer* the other 29 copies to other instructional broadcasters *for*

use in the same way,"[23] that is, transmissions. As observed above, the legislative history also interprets §112(b) to exclude the use of ephemeral recordings "as part of an information storage and retrieval system," such as a library's e-reserve, where ephemeral recordings are called up by students accessing the bank of recorded lectures (class sessions) that might embody §110(2) performances and displays. This exclusion is also consistent with a view regarding subsequent uses, so prevalent in 1976 when §112(b) was enacted, that ephemeral recordings are limited to transmissions made in the context of synchronous teaching and are not the sort of asynchronous retrievals made by the learn-at-your-own-pace distance students of today, whereby access to the ephemeral recording is made from some sort of instructional jukebox of options. It could be argued that such a library of curricular recordings and any transmission from it would necessarily be made "as part of an information storage and retrieval system." Notwithstanding the "information storage and retrieval system" issue, it could also be argued that the stuck-in-time approach of the 1976 vision of distance education could still be interpreted to exclude all subsequent §110(2) transmissions except those that involve synchronous instruction. This view of a distance education transmission, while unarguably narrow, is nonetheless consistent with the rudimentary notion of distance education expressed elsewhere in the 1976 Copyright Act (e.g., the discussion of pre-TEACH §110(2) in chapter 1), and underscored again a vision of use for the ephemeral recording that remains linked to a subsequent §110(2) transmission (a class session replay) which, under its formulation in 1976, was tied to synchronous teacher-to-remote-classroom broadcasting. In light of this, it is unfortunate that TEACH did not also amend §112(b).

Depending on the content of some distance education encounters, neither §112(b) nor the revised §110(2) or the new §112(f) of TEACH may be needed. If the only content of the teaching encounter that is initially transmitted consists of noncopyrightable material or material in which the teacher or institution owns the copyright (e.g., all of the content is original material created by the instructor which, under the work-for-hire doctrine, is considered owned by the institution or where, by law or agreement, the copyright ownership rights belong to the instructor but nonexclusive rights to use the material in distance education have been granted to the institution), then there is no problem transmitting performances or displays of copyrighted material or making a copy of those transmissions. However, if that is not the case, then §110(2) allows for its initial performance or display and §112(b) allows for making a copy of it as it is being used; that is, "embodying the performance or display," capturing the entire class session for later replay or retransmission.

The Practical Impact of Linking the Ephemeral Recording Right to Section 110(2) Performances and Displays

The §112(b) right is limited, then, to the recording of the initial transmission for a subsequent §110(2) rebroadcast. There is no requirement that the ephemeral recording of the teaching encounter be in analog or digital, though it will most likely parallel the transmission in mode of format, though it need not. Embody the performance or display of copyrighted material in an analog transmission such as a television or local access cable broadcast and it is likely that the recording made of it—the ephemeral copy—is also analog. Likewise, embody the performance or display of copyrighted material in a digital transmission such as a Web cast and it is likely that the recording made of it—the ephemeral copy—is also digital. Of course, it is possible to conceive of a scenario in which the transmission of the teaching encounter occurs in analog vis-à-vis a broadcast, but its embodiment as an ephemeral recording is made in a digital format. Perhaps subsequent storage and manipulation issues suggest that digital is more effective for retention but for bandwidth reasons it is still rebroadcast in analog. In 1976, when the section was created, transmission and subsequent ephemeral recording would most likely both have been analog, but in 2005, both will most likely be in digital format. However, the text of §112(b) neither requires nor even suggests a preference for either format.[24]

What the law did in 1976 (actually the effective date of the 1976 Copyright Act was January 1, 1978), and continues to do in 2005 or any year thereafter until amended again, is tie any §112(b) ephemeral recording of a transmission to those performances or displays authorized under §110(2). The §112(b) right allows for the capturing "of a particular transmission program embodying *the* performance or display," that is, one made "under §110(2) or under the limitations on exclusive rights in sound recordings specified by §114(a)." Capturing a performance or display made outside of the defined §110(2) educator performance and display privilege is not allowed under §112(b). For example, you might read from a text during a distance education encounter and record that transmission under §112(b). Acceptable. An educator might show a very short video clip, a use not authorized under pre-TEACH §110(2), though arguably a fair use nonetheless. Acceptable? As discussed in chapter 3, this is now an acceptable distance education performance, although (as also discussed in chapter 3) performance of the entire video would not be an acceptable performance under current §110(2); therefore, an ephemeral recording of the class session that includes the performance of the entire video is not allowed, because use of the entire video is not allowed under §110(2). This is true even if fair use or license allows for its performance, as the language of §112(b) (or, as discussed below, §112(f)) links the ephemeral recording right to §110(2) performances or displays, not to a general requirement of lawfulness (lawful copy or phonorecord) but to a specific authorization vis-à-vis §110(2). Of course, the educational license could also allow for ephemeral recording rights as well as performance rights. In fact, it must in order for an ephemeral recording to be made, where performance or display is made under license, as ephemeral recording rights are tied to performance and displays authorized by statute, not those authorized by license.

Even in 2005 and beyond, an educator might desire to exercise ephemeral recording rights under §112(b) by recording the entire stream of a distance education class session. However, if that session included the performance of an entire video or more than a "reasonable and limited amount" (i.e., some amount greater than that which is acceptable under current §110(2)), then the ephemeral recording right of §112(b) would not allow for the capture of the stream ("cop[y] . . . of a particular transmission program embodying the performance"). The recording that §112(b) allows you to make is restricted to a copy or phonorecord of a particular transmission embodying the authorized §110(2) or 114(a) performance or display, as the case may be.

Arguably, the §110(2) rights are significantly expanded as a result of TEACH, but the discrepancy remains post-TEACH and may prove significant since more and more information is being acquired for use in the distance classroom through license, avoiding use of the §110(2) privilege. This is true because, as noted above, the §112 ephemeral recording rights are triggered when a performance or display is made by reference to specific sections of the copyright, like §110(2) *and not to* any other lawful use under the copyright law such as by license or fair use, unless, of course, the license also authorizes the recording. But it could be argued that having to continuously rely on fair use or favorable license terms and conditions as the rule, not the exception, instead of relying on §110(2) and §112(b) and (f), defeats the purpose of crafting specific statutory exemption for performance and display and ephemeral recording of copyrighted material by distance educators. Ephemeral recording rights for distance educators in §112(b) and as discussed below in §112(f) are linked to a §110(2) performance or display alone, or, in the case of §112(b), to §114(a) as well. Thus this mismatch of rights is also an issue in discussing the new ephemeral recording right created by TEACH in §112(f).

Under §112(b), as with the new §112(f) discussed below, any right to make an ephemeral recording is tied to a §110(2) performance or display right. In other words, the type and portion of a work an educator performs or displays in the distance classroom, for which the educator would also like to make an ephemeral recording, is limited to the type and portion allowed by §110(2). If §110(2) allows you to perform a "reasonable and limited portion" of an audiovisual work, then the amount of performance you could record under §112(b) is also by necessity limited to a "reasonable and limited portion," because the §112(b) recording merely captures the use (performance or display) of the material as part of a class session. This might seem obvious, or it might seem not troublesome, but what of a situation where you have a performance right to show an entire video, beyond the limitations of §110(2)? The educator would like to make a recording of the session for rebroadcast to use again or for purposes of review and evaluation (i.e., for archival purposes), under §112(b)(2). Section 112(b) would not support the making of the ephemeral recording because the performance or display is beyond that authorized in §110(2); rather, the right to perform the entire video resulted from the operation of the performance license, not from §110(2) privilege. Congress could have added "or any lawful purpose" to the §§110(2) and 114(a) reference in §112(b), but it did not. Drafting oversight again? One can only assume Congress was aware of this limitation when it drafted §112(b) in 1976, and in 2002 when it added §112(f), but it did not alter that limitation. Moreover, Congress included a similar §110(2)-dependent limitation in the new §112(f) construction.

As the use of licensed material increases in distance education, it underscores the need to ensure that the license or other permission mechanisms used to secure performance and display rights also allow for expanded ephemeral recording rights as well, either for rebroadcast or as an archive. Otherwise it is conceivable that, while the license terms and conditions would allow its use in a distance education encounter, they might not allow for recordings of the performance and display, either as described here under §112(b) or in the likely §112(f) scenario described next. It is imperative, then, that any license or other permission to use copyrighted material in a distance education environment also license or grant permission to reproduce the work in conjunction with and for a performance or display consistent with the performance or display for which the initial performance or display right or permission was sought as a precursor to a performance or display and for a potential replay of it as well, paralleling the §112(b) right discussed earlier and the new §112(f) right discussed below, as well as the ability to archive the work—again, in conjunction with and for a performance or display consistent with the performance or display for which the initial performance or display right or permission was sought.

The Rise of Digital Content in Distance Education and the Need for a New Ephemeral Recording Provision

Historically, the portion limitations of pre-TEACH §110(2) also limited the usefulness of §112(b). As a result, this provision was also locked in the time capsule of distance education as remote (read "television or radio") broadcasting. The 1976 legislative history makes the following connection: "§112(b) represents a response to the arguments of instructional broadcasters and other educational groups for special recording privileges. Although it does not go as far as these groups requested . . . the ephemeral recordings made by an instructional broadcaster under subsection (b) must embody a performance or display that meets all of the qualifications for exemption under §110(2)."[25] Factors were again at work in 1976 to force Congress to craft the §112(b) right so as not to undermine the market for such works.[26] The lesson here is that the §112 ephemeral recording right, both for existing subsection (b) and new post-TEACH subsection (f), is linked—perhaps *limited* is a better word—to that material, the use of which must be authorized under §110(2). As the 1976 legislative history observed, it is market concerns that often drive copyright policy making. Congress, always careful to preserve space for new markets to develop, linked the §112 ephemeral recording right to §110(2) in order to preserve that market space for copyright owners: "[A]nother point stressed by the producers of educational films in this connection, however, was that ephemeral recordings made by instructional broadcasters are in fact audiovisual works that often compete for exactly the same market."[27]

As discussed in great detail in chapter 3, TEACH expands the type and portions of works that could be used in a §110(2) performance or display. If the range of the §110(2) performance and display "space" is expanded under TEACH, and thus, by statutory connection the §112(b) ephemeral recording right "space" is also expanded, why the need to add new §112(f)? Section 112(b) can be viewed as an after-the-fact ephemeral recording provision. The answer lies in the timing and purpose of the ephemeral recording. A §110(2) performance or display must precede a §112(b) ephemeral recording: "Aside from phonorecords of copyrighted sound recordings [remember, there is no performance right in a sound recording unless rendered via a digital audio transmission, and at the writing of the 1976 legislative history there was no performance right in a sound recording whatsoever], the ephemeral recording made by an instructional broadcaster under subsection (b) *must embody a performance or display that meets all of the qualification for exemption under §110(2)*."[28] Once the performance or display is made under §110(2), §112(b) envisions that a copy or limited number of copies ("no more than thirty") would be made of the initial broadcast (embodying the §110(2) performance or display) for use in rebroadcasting the class session, either by the institution that made them or by other institutions for a similar purpose, and for a limited time period ("destroyed within seven years" except the archive copy). Thus the §112(b) right might be characterized as an after-the-class recording privilege.

As explained above, a before-the-class recording stored on the institution's server and retrieved as needed by the instructor or student for a §110(2) performance or display was excluded by §112(b).[29] There would seldom be a need to make a copy of the VHS tape for a "traditional" educational broadcast, as the instructor would just bring the tape in when ready to broadcast it live again. Of course, having a copy of the VHS tape, converted to digital, sitting on the institution's server and ready to transmit live, would have made the broadcast of it easier, but use of it in a pre-TEACH distance education classroom did not necessitate such conversion.

In contrast, for the new model of learn-as-you-go education to succeed, TEACH, by way of new §112(f), authorizes reproduction (i.e., loading a copy onto the institution's server[30] in order to facilitate access by students) as a precursor to an authorized TEACH §110(2) performance or display. New §112(f), added by TEACH, allows an educator to make an ephemeral before-the-fact recording of copyrighted content if, and only if, in a familiar (considering the preceding discussion) statutory construction, the subsequent transmission is a performance or display authorized under §110(2); that is, a revised post-TEACH version of §110(2). In the scenarios presented earlier, this sort of before-the-class sitting-on-the-server ephemeral recording is, by necessity, digital. Of course it could be argued that new §112(f) is not necessary, but that would mean that a Web-casting distance education instructor would have to bring the VHS tape into the distance education teaching lab, play (perform) it using VCR technology, and then use a digital Web-cam to capture the monitor screen as it played the tape—and then broadcast that "recording of a performance." Without a doubt a rather awkward and inefficient use of new technology (see table 6.1).

The statutory design of §112(f)(1) also suggests at first glance that the recording made be digital in form: "to make copies or phonorecords of a work *that is in digital form* and, solely to the extent permitted in paragraph (2), of a work *that is in analog form*."[31] The reference to "paragraph (2)" indicates the circumstances under which an analog-to-digital conversion copy can be made. Yet there is no actual restriction on the form of the copy, only its source. Section 112(f)(1) does not state "to make *digital* copies or phonorecords." However unlikely it be that an instructor would want to make an analog copy of a digital work, there is no language restricting that result as there is in §112(f)(2), where the only result of an analog source recording can be a conversion, an analog-to-digital copying. More important, and also in contrast to §112(f)(2), there is no portion limitation. A digital-to-digital or digital-to-analog ephemeral recording could be made of a work in its entirety, even though less than the entire work would be used in a subsequent §110(2) performance or display because its use in the distance education classroom was limited to a performance of a reasonable and limited portion or to an amount analogous to live classroom displays. Moreover, there is nothing in the statute that requires the subsequent §110(2) performance or display to also be digital. However unlikely it would be to broadcast by analog an ephemeral copy of a work that was stored in digital form under the §112(f)(1) right, it is not prohibited by statute; for example, an analog broadcast of a digital PowerPoint presentation that included the performance or display of copyrighted material would be allowed. Though the source of the ephemeral recording under §112(f)(1) must be digital, the §110(2) use that is made of it is not so limited: "to make copies or phonorecords of a work . . . *embodying the performance or display to be used* for making transmissions authorized under §110(2)." Like the other subsections of §112,[32] §112(f) uses the word "embodying," eliminating all doubt as to alternative uses for the digital copies made under §112(f). The ephemeral recording is made of the material embodying the performance or display that will later be used in a §110(2) teaching activity.

This before-the-fact copying allows distance education to offer an elasticized concept of the "teaching moment," as the interface of teacher and student ("learning moment") is no longer synchronous as it was in a §112(b) recording of that interface. The new concept of distance education bifurcates these real moments and makes them virtual, so to speak. "The benefit is likely to be particularly valuable for working adults. Asynchronous education also has the benefit of proceeding at the student's own pace, and freeing the instructor from the obligation to be in the classroom or on call at all hours of the day or night."[33] Sections 112(b) and 112(f) can be used in conjunction with a particular class session, even though §112(b) has limited application in digital distance education.[34] "Whether the delivery is asynchronous or synchronous, however, the process of transmitting content through the Internet involves a flourishing and proliferating sequence of reproductions."[35] An educator could make a before-the-fact digital-to-digital copy of a work or convert it (analog-to-digital, assuming §110(2) would authorize use in its entirety) for later use, storing it on the institution's server or on the instructor's laptop (using the new §112(f) right), and this is a before-the-class ephemeral recording. The educator could then perform the work as part of a PowerPoint presentation alongside the instructor's lecture or talking head commentary, then transmit (either traditional or digital broadcast) the lecture and PowerPoint material via the TEACH §110(2) right, making an analog or digital after-the-fact copy for backup (archive) or for rebroadcast later using the §112(b) right.

Understanding the New Ephemeral Recordings Right Created by Section 112(f)

In a slight shift of approach, but like the discussion of new §110(2), an examination of new §112(f), line-by-line or clause-by-clause, is suggested. Again, if the reader is not accustomed to reading statutes, especially statutes as textually rich as copyright provision, this is a good exercise.

New subsection (f)(1) begins "*Notwithstanding the provisions of § 106.*" This cues the reader to those exclusive rights listed in § 106 again, acknowledges that exclusive rights exist and does nothing to lessen their application to distance education, and moreover, indicates that any privilege to use the work in a particular way granted by the copyright law exists as a "limitation" on those rights. Think of this clause as a setup for the special use rights; that is, a limitation on an exclusive right, still a few clauses away, that this subsection grants to educators. This clause also indicates that, when all is said and done, one of the exclusive rights of the copyright owner, the right to reproduce the work, is limited by the ephemeral recording right, although the other exclusive rights enumerated in § 106 remain in full force, unless of course limited by other sections of the law, such as § 110(2) discussed in chapter 3.

The next clause can also be thought of more or less as a setup, but instead of preserving the operation of another section of the copyright law as did the opening clause for § 106, this clause indicates that another now familiar subsection of § 112, also granting an ephemeral recording right to distance educators, should also remain in unaffected: "*and without limiting the application of subsection (b).*" Because § 112(f) is new and moreover is in addition to an existing and unamended ephemeral recording provision of § 112 discussed above and also relating to distance education (i.e., § 112(b)), the second "setup" provision of § 112(f) indicates to the reader that the ephemeral recording right granted here, like the first "setup" provision regarding § 106, does nothing to impact that preexisting provision of the copyright law (i.e., those preexisting ephemeral recording rights in subsection (b) of § 112).

The Nature of the Section 112(f) Ephemeral Recording Right

As with other provisions of § 112,[36] the ephemeral recording right created by § 112(f)(1) is granted to an entity entitled by some other provision of the copyright law to transmit performances and/or displays of copyrighted material: "*it is not an infringement of copyright for a governmental body or other nonprofit educational institution entitled under § 110(2) to transmit a display or performance.*" This provision also indicates the legal result of the exercise of the ephemeral recording right; that is, it is *not an infringement*—a most important statement, because, without this right, the making of wholesale copies of protected material would surely violate the copyright owner's exclusive right of reproduction even if the performance or display of that recording might be authorized under § 110(2).

Here is the clause that indicates what right is granted: what activity will not be considered an infringement of copyright. A nonprofit accredited educational institution is given the right "*to make copies or phonorecords of a work.*" Observe also the use of plural, like § 112(b) with its no-more-than-thirty-copy rule; multiple copies are allowed by §112(f), but unlike §112(b), without limit. The legislative history recognizes that at times, in the course of distance education multiple copies are needed.[37] However, an educator should not go wild, as a successive clause controls the use to which these copies can be put. An educator must use a copy or three copies or thirty-three copies so made under §112(f) for §110(2) purposes (distance education teaching activity),[38] and must meet all the requirements of that section as discussed in the previous chapters. Section 112(f) is a before-the-fact copyright provision, and the eventual use of the recording is restricted by the portion limitation rules of §110(2); however, the amount that can be recorded in a §112(f)(2) before-the-fact recording is amount limited to that that can be later used in a §110(2) recording; this is in contrast to a §112(f)(1) before-the-fact digital (or even digital to analog) recording that is not necessarily so restricted.

The next (*"that is in digital form and"*) and succeeding clause can be viewed together. The statute is indicating that §112(f) views two likely scenarios of ephemeral recording: (1) a digital copy of a digital work and (2) a digital copy of an analog work. One could conceive of making an analog copy from a digital work under §112(f)(1) though one questions its usefulness in the distance education environment. But is this analog copy from a digital source prohibited by the statute? Observe that the use of the word "digital" in the statute modifies the source of the work, of which the educator is making copies or phonorecords. In the preceding clause it does not state, "to make *digital* copies or phonorecords of a work that is in digital form," but reads "to make copies or phonorecords of a work that is in digital form." While the statute does not specifically state that only digital copies may be made, those are the two likely scenarios that it presents. First, the legislative history uses the digital-to-digital and analog-to-digital examples in discussing the ability of educational institutions to load material onto its servers. The server example necessitates digital: "In order for asynchronous distance education to proceed, organizations providing distance education transmission must be able to load material that will be displayed or performed on their servers, for transmission at the request of students."[39] One can hypothesize that having an analog copy might be nice as well, but, while not prohibited outright, it appears inconsistent with the design of TEACH as suggested by its other clauses, discussed below.

The phrase *"solely to the extent permitted in paragraph (2), of work that is in analog form"* is the second mechanism by which the statute anticipates that ephemeral recordings will be made in anticipation of a bona fide teaching encounter; that is, a performance or display authorized under §110(2). This provision provides the other ephemeral recording scenario: digitalization of an analog copy. It also tells educators that the analog-to-digital ephemeral recording is governed by additional rules in paragraph (2) of §112(f).

TABLE 6.1
The Ephemeral Recording Right under Section 112(f)

Format of Source Material	Form of Recording	Portion of Source Material Recorded	Authorization
Digital	Digital	no limitation	§112(f)(1), and by legislative history institutional server example
Digital	Analog	no limitation	§112(f)(1)
Analog	Digital	an amount equal to that "authorized to be performed or displayed under §110(2)"	conversion authorized by §112(f)(2)
Analog	Analog	not allowed	while not prohibited per se, it is excluded, by statutory design, as analog recordings are allowed "solely to the extent permitted in paragraph (2)," and §112(f)(2) only authorizes "conversion of print or other analog versions"

As with the other ephemeral recording rights enunciated in §112, the right is linked to some other substantive use-rights provision (limitation of exclusive rights) of the copyright law. In distance education, that is, of course, §110(2). In contrast to §112(b), where the right granted is expressed as the ability "under §110(2) . . . to make no more than thirty copies or phonorecords of a particular transmission embodying the performance or display," §112(f) alters the clause, adding "to be used" to the statutory phrasing. This is an operative before-the-fact clause, with the "fact" being a subsequent §110(2) performance or display and the ephemeral recording coming as a precursor, before that performance or display. The link between "embodying the performance or display" and §110(2) transmission remains. However, §112(f) is the only precursor or before-the fact distance education ephemeral recording provision, thus it anticipates and authorizes an ephemeral recording in anticipation of an authorized use: "*embodying the performance or display* to be used *for making transmissions authorized under §110(2)*." In other words, you can make a copy of a work for future use as part of a performance or display authorized under §110(2).

General Requirements of Section 112(f):
Digital-to-Digital or Analog-to-Digital

Section 112(f) contains a number of general requirements applying to all works, those that are already in a digital format and those that must be converted. The first requirement is a retention and use rule governing the making of the ephemeral recording: "*if—(A) such copies or phonorecords are retained and used solely by the body or institution that made them.*" The legislative history adds little to an understanding of the clause, other than to reiterate that "[f]irst, they [the ephemeral recordings] may be retained and used solely by the government body or educational institution that made them."[40] This is an important clause nonetheless, as any retention and use of the ephemeral recording must be by the institution alone. It cannot transfer the ephemeral recording to another entity even if it would be for bona fide "transmissions authorized under §110(2)." This is in clear contrast to the legislative history explaining the "life-cycle" of a §112(b) ephemeral recording: "exchanges of recordings among instructional broadcasters are permitted. An organization that has made copies or phonorecords under subsection (b) may use one of them *for purposes of its own transmissions* that are exempted by section 110(2), and it *may also transfer* the other 29 copies to other instructional broadcasters *for use in the same way*."[41] Here, in contrast, the other institution must make its ephemeral recording of its own accord. The logic here is that trading in §112(f) ephemeral recordings (arguably in all likelihood, digital copies of phonorecords) in anticipation of even bona fide transmissions would pose too great a risk to the copyright owner, especially in light of recent file-sharing controversies demonstrating that possession of lawful copies can easily degenerate into the acquisition of unlawful copies.

The second general requirement is a downstream copying prohibition that requires that "*no further copies or phonorecords are reproduced from them, except as authorized under §110(2).*" Making multiple copies in anticipation of transmission embodying a §110(2) performance or display is of course acceptable, as discussed above. These are contemporaneous copies. Even the institution that retains and alone uses the ephemeral recordings authorized under §112(f) might still be tempted to make additional copies from these copies, for other arguably legal uses under the copyright law, such as for e-reserve. But since display or distribution of copyrighted material in an e-reserve is not an authorized §110(2) use (display) of that material nor is distribution even contemplated under any subsection of §110, those further copies could not be made. But what are the sorts of copies to which the "except as authorized under §110(2)" applies? Using a similar phrasing as §112(b)(1), the statute prohibits copies of copies, so to speak, and prevents the making of "*further copies or phonorecords* . . . except as authorized under §110(2)." As discussed at the end of chapter 4 and here below as well, the legislative history cues us to the possible "*except as authorized under §110(2)*" transitory copies that are automatically made during a bona fide §110(2) transmission.[42]

There is a general requirement that "*such copies or phonorecords are used solely for transmission authorized under §110(2)*." While any ephemeral recording made under §112(f) must be retained and used solely by the school, college, university, or other educational entity that made the copy or phonorecord, the school, college, university, or other educational entity may not also make another use of the ephemeral recording. It must retain and use the ephemeral recording itself (first clause of §112(f)(1)(A)) and it must control the copies made from the initial ephemeral recordings it does make (second clause of §112(f)(1)(A), no copies of copies, except qualifying "transient" copies). Finally, the institution can use the ephemeral recordings only for §110(2) transmissions of performances or displays, even if such use might be fair use or allowed by some other provision of the copyright law, such as lending under §109 or e-reserves, or by another right such as by contract (license), unless of course the license also recognizes the making of an ephemeral recording right. The legislative history adds little by way of explanation or example, reiterating the basic prohibition: "The authorized ephemeral recordings must be used solely for transmissions authorized under §110(2)."[43] Any use of an ephemeral recording made under §112(f) can only be for another §110(2) use.

As long as a qualifying educational institution follows rules linked to §110(2), a digital copy may be made from a digital version of the work and arguably an analog copy of a digital work as well, whatever its usefulness in distance education might be. If an institution desires to make a digital copy from an analog version (a conversion), then an additional set of rules applies.

Specific Requirements of Section 112(f): Analog-to-Digital

The second paragraph of §112(f) begins with an important statement, reading more like a policy statement than a substantive requirement or limitation: "*This subsection does not authorize the conversion of print or other analog versions of works into digital formats*." The policy statement is simple: §112(f) is not a digitalization provision in the same sense that §108(b) and (c) are.[44] "It should be emphasized that subsection 112(f)(2) does not provide any authorization to convert print materials or other analog versions of works into digital format except as permitted in §112(f)(2)."[45] Rather, the educator may digitize only after complying with the requirements of subsection 112(f)(2). Perhaps it is more a matter of perspective or attitude, and the legislative history provides an extended commentary as to the proper attitude:

The Register's Report notes the sensitivity of copyright owners to the digitalization of works that have not been digitized by the copyright owner. As a general matter, subsection 112(f) requires the use of works that are already in digital form.[46]

Digital copies of works can be pernicious. Once copyrighted works are in digital form, the ease with which one can abuse the copyright owner's exclusive rights creates great temptation to do so. As a result, copyright owners have expressed concern throughout the recent rounds of copyright reform expanding the "use" rights (limitations on exclusive rights of copyright owners) of nonprofit libraries and educational institutions, from the Software Rental Amendment Act of 1990[47] to the Digital Millennium Copyright Act in 1998.[48] Like the genie out of the proverbial bottle, once a work is digitized and made available on the Internet there is literally no stopping its exploitation. However, it is also clear that a readily available and usable digital copy may not be available. Rather than have the progress of distance education grind to a halt, Congress made provision for those circumstances when a preferred digital copy is simply not available. However, digitalization of a work in analog form must meet several requirements.

The second clause of paragraph (2) indicates that digitalization (analog-to-digital) is the exception to the general and preferred rule of digital-to-digital ephemeral recording: "*except that such conversion is permitted hereunder.*" However, when analog-to-digital is the only means of securing access to the work, then that digitalization is limited to the amount that will actually be used in a §110(2) performance or display: "*only with respect to the* amount *of such works authorized* to be *performed or displayed under section 110(2).*" This might be viewed as a portion limitation rule. As with the other provisions of §112, there is an alignment in §112(f) between the content of the ephemeral recording you make and the parameters of the use to be made of the work (i.e., performance and display under §110(2)). In other words, the extent of the ephemeral recording can be no larger than that which would be allowed by its eventual §110(2) use. In an effort to limit potential harm to copyright owners of digitalization, this §112(f)(2) clause limits the amount that may be digitized to that portion of the work that is acceptable for use under §110(2). Thus, even if an educator would like to digitize an entire audiovisual work, a VHS tape for example, so that it is easier to extract the "reasonable and limited" portion allowed to be performed under §110(2), he or she cannot do so, because only a "reasonable and limited" amount of the work can be performed under §110(2). So, too, a similar portion may be converted (analog-to-digital) as part of an ephemeral recording under §112(f)(2).

Notice that such an "amount" clause is missing from §112(b), the other section on ephemeral recording for distance education, as well as missing from §112(f)(1) ("of a work that is in digital form") as discussed earlier. While it is clear "that [any] such conversion is permitted hereunder, only with respect to the amount of such works authorized to be performed or displayed under §110(2)," thus linking the §112(f) ephemeral recording to an amount authorized under §110(2), such language is absent from §112(b). Does that mean the coordination of the recording amount between §112(b) and §110(2) need not be made? No, it does not, because that amount coordination is implicit in the operation of §112(b), as the ephemeral recording under §112(b) is made of an after-the-class teaching activity, the transmission of which the performance or display is a part. The after-the-fact recording ensures that a portion limitation is part and parcel of the operation of a §112(b) recording of an authorized performance or display under §110(2). Further, under §112(b), at least when it was enacted in 1976, there were no portions limitations in pre-TEACH §110(2). A reformulated §110(2) under TEACH introduces three categories of possible amounts: entire (performance of nondramatic literary and nondramatic musical works), reasonable and limited (all other works that are performed), and amount comparable to that which is typically displayed in the course of a live classroom session (displays). This trifurcation suggests a second reason why an explicit "amount" clause is needed in §112(f)(2): This provision is a before-the-fact recording. While there is no such portion limitation in a digital-to-digital recording or, arguably, digital-to-analog under §112(f)(1), though its use is still limited to a portion tied to the §110(2) authorized performance or display, the entire work is already in digital form so a specific limitation on the digital recording that resulted was less important. Congress was careful to craft a digitalization privilege that was not greater than necessary. Even though it might be more convenient to be able to convert more than the portion that the educator will eventually use in a §110(2) performance or display, that portion is all that is needed and, more to the point, it is all that is allowed under the statute.

The legislative history is not terribly helpful, restating the obvious language of the statute: "However, the Committee recognizes that some works may not be available for use in distance education, either because no digital version of the work is available to the institution, or because available digital versions are subjected to technological protection measures that prevent their use for the performances and displays authorized by §110(2)."[49] When one of two conditions exist, an analog-to-digital ephemeral recording can be made: "*if— (A) no digital version of the work is available to the institution; or (B) the digital version of the work that is available to the institution is subject to technological pro-*

tection measures that prevent its use for §110(2)." These two conditions appear straightforward. If there is no digital version available or the only digital version available is one that has a technological protection measure that prevents its use for a §110(2) use such that an educator would either be forced to forgo use of the material in the conduct of §110(2) activities or face the temptation to break through or hack around the technological protection measure, then he or she can convert an analog copy into a digital file.

In an illustrative example, suppose there were three qualifying educational institutions, School A, Technical College B, and University C. School A has a digital copy, Technical College B has a digital and an analog copy, and University C has only an analog copy. School A can make an ephemeral recording according to the requirements of §112(f)(1)—the retention and use rule and the no-further-copy rule of §112(f)(1)(A), and the use-for-§110(2)-transmission rule of §112(f)(1)(B). In a digital-to-digital or unlikely digital-to-analog ephemeral recording, there is no portion limitation rule and the entire work could be copied even if under a subsequent §110(2) transmission the rules of that section would limit the performance or display to something less than the entire work.

Technical College B, with both a digital and an analog copy, would use its digital copy as the source of its ephemeral recording and follow the same rules. It could not convert its analog copy to digital because that would violate the "conversion" rule of §112(f)(2)(A), which "prohibits the conversion of print or analog versions of works into digital formats" unless "no digital version of the work is available to the institution." That condition is not met, as indeed a "digital version of the work is available to the institution." Notwithstanding the discussion of the meaning of "available to the institution" below, surely a digital version of the work actually owned by Technical College B would trigger that proviso and eliminate the analog-to-digital conversion. Again, the concern of Congress was to protect against the proliferation of digital copies in the absence of an existing digital product market for that work, thus preserving the market for the digital version of the work. Institutions A and B have both already contributed to the revenue stream of the copyright owners by purchasing a digital version, institution B having done that twice, analog and digital. Moreover, the statute could be read to allow the ephemeral recording to be of the entire work, because, unlike the §112(b) provision that incorporates an after-the-fact recording of a §110(2) performance or display assuring that its portion limitations are also captured within the recording, the digital-to-digital before-the-fact recording need only be one "embodying the performance or display to be used for making transmissions authorized under §110(2)," with its later transmission limited to the amount authorized under §110(2).

University C has only an analog version, and it may convert (digitize) it, as long as the conditions of either of the two subprovisions of §112(f)(2) exist (no digital version of the work is available or the available digital version is subject to a technological protection measure). In either case, institution C may digitize only "the amount of such work authorized to be performed or displayed under §110(2)." The legislative history supports this significant limitation as well: "In those circumstances where no digital version is available to the institution or the digital version that is available is subject to technological protection measures that prevent its use for distance education under the exemption, §112(f)(2) authorizes the conversion from an analog version, *but only conversion of the portion or amount* of such works that are authorized to be performed or displayed under §110(2)."[50] As discussed earlier, the ephemeral recording under §112(f)(2), conversion of work from analog to digital form, has definite portion limitations associated with it.

Fair and Other Uses and the Sections 112 and 110(2) Misalignment Problem

Suppose an educator desired to convert an old beta tape to digital form. He or she could not convert the entire tape and then figure out what reasonable and limited portion is needed for class. The digitalization amount is limited to that which is authorized under §110(2), and since that is something less than an entire tape, digitalization rights are likewise limited. Even if the tape is to be used in one-quarter segments that eventually total the entire tape, the clear language of §112(f)(2) prohibits the educator from digitizing the entire tape. The ephemeral recording right is explicitly tied to the amount an educator can perform or display under §110(2). This is despite the legislative history, which makes clear that fair use can still apply in TEACH settings: "Fair use is a critical part of the distance education landscape. Not only instructional performances and displays, but also other educational uses of works, such as the provision of supplementary material or student downloading of course materials, will continue to be subject to the fair use doctrine."[51] In fact, the example used underscores just such an anomaly: "Fair use could apply as well to instructional transmissions not covered by the changes to §110(2) recommended above. Thus, for example, the performance of more than a limited portion of a dramatic work in a distance education program might qualify as fair use in appropriate circumstances."[52] The problem is, of course, that while using all or at least more than the amount authorized under §110(2) of the beta tape might be a fair use, the amount an educator can digitize under §112(f)(2) is still limited to the §110(2) portion. Fair use can apply to ephemeral recording just as easily or as stringently as it can to the performance and display of the material embodied by that recording. However, given the recent and limited observations some courts have been making regarding the right to cut and paste from digital works, as discussed in chapter 7, educators need to be aware of the drafting limitations of the statute, especially until the Supreme Court rules definitively on the matter.

It could be argued that if fair use would support the performance or display of an additional quarter of the tape, then fair use should also logically support the digitalization of the additional quarter as well. Perhaps it would, but perhaps not, for two reasons.

First, there are alternatives to digitizing the entire tape that still make it usable in distance education—clumsier, but still doable. As discussed earlier, Congress is careful to narrowly construct so-called digitalization rights whenever it amends the copyright law. As the Second Circuit observed in dicta, but as echoed by other courts, there is no fair use right to use material in the preferred format of the user-educator: "Fair use has *never been held* to be a guarantee of access to copyrighted material in order to *copy it by the fair user's preferred technique or in the format of the original.*"[53] Suppose an institution is mounting a full-fledged digital online education degree program, so having a digital copy of all classroom content would make things easier. More difficult but not impossible, educators could play the VHS tape on a regular TV monitor, then either record or stream the session with a digital Web camera. Ridiculous, you might think. In fact, these technologically Stone Age techniques are precisely the sorts of suggestions courts have recently been articulating as the limits of fair use in digital content such as DVD movies.

> One example is that of a school child who wishes to copy images from a DVD movie to insert into the student's documentary film. We know of *no authority for the proposition that fair use, as protected by the Copyright Act, much less the Constitution, guarantees copying by the optimum method or in the identical format of the original.* Although the Appellants insisted at oral argument that they should not be relegated to a "horse and buggy" technique in making fair use of DVD movies, the DMCA does not impose even an arguable limitation on the opportunity to make a *variety of traditional fair uses of DVD movies, such as commenting on their content, quoting excerpts from their screenplays, and even recording portions of the video images and sounds on film or tape by pointing a camera, a camcorder, or a microphone at a monitor as it displays the DVD movie.*[54]

Again, an option would be to license both the right to perform the entire video along with the right to make a complete digital copy of it.

Second, courts, like Congress, appear to have a heightened sensitivity when it comes to wholesale digital copying and distribution of copyrighted works.[55] Moreover, Congress is well aware of the potential for infringement by students at institutions of higher learning.[56] These trends suggest far less breathing room for fair use, especially regarding digital content, in educational settings.[57]

Determining When Digitalization Can Occur: The Meaning of "Available to the Institution"

The meaning given to the phrase "available to the institution" can have a significant impact on the range of circumstances in which a school, college, university, or other educational entity may exercise digitalization ephemeral recording rights under §112(f). Consider again the two circumstances, one of which must occur, before the ephemeral recording can take place: either "no digital version of the work *is available to the institution* or the digital version of the work that *is available to the institution* is subject to technological protection measures that prevent its use for §110(2)." Does "available to the institution" mean market availability, a concept more akin to obtainability, and, if so, would the institution be able to digitize only if that digital version of the work available for sale or from some other external source is subject to technological protection measures? If that digital version was available for purchase without such technological protection measures, the educational institution would have to acquire the work rather than convert. In the alternative, does it require only that the institution inquire whether a digital version already exists on campus or is otherwise accessible on-site from an online database, for example, or whether the digital version in its possession is now closed by the deactivation of a digital key (a technological protection measure that prevents its use for §110(2))? The implications and nuances of these alternative interpretations are discussed below (see table 6.2).

The legislative history is silent as to what the concept of "available to the institution" means. Two interpretations are possible—one narrow, the other broad. Does "available to the institution" mean a physical embodiment of a copyrighted work in analog form or digital version subject to technological protection measures that is actually owned by the institution, such as a videocassette (analog) or otherwise in the physical control or in the possession of the institution? In this narrow view, availability is synonymous with accessibility. Or, in the alternative, does it refer to any available version, such as a version available for purchase in the marketplace (as in the §108 requirement that a "reasonable effort" be made to "determine . . . that an unused replacement cannot be obtained at a fair price"[58]) or available through some other arrangement—interlibrary loan, for example? In this interpretation, availability is synonymous with obtainability. While it might appear a reasonable condition that the institution should make some effort beyond a mere campus check to see if a work is available, the problem, of course, is that if Congress had intended for a market check (obtainability) standard to be employed, it could have easily said so, as it did in the plain language of §§ 108(c) and 108(e).[59] Moreover, the § 108(c) and (e) clauses use the phrase "cannot be obtained." Although reading a market search into § 112(f)(2) is not precluded simply because the word "obtain" or the concept it represents is absent, when Congress has intended a market search in other provisions of the law, it has chosen that precise concept of "*obtain*ability."

Arguably using a broader view of "available to the institution" would mean that the institution would need to acquire (purchase) or at least make arrangements to borrow the work in its digital form, often at some or perhaps significant real or administrative cost, rather than convert an analog version. Using a broader view increases the burden on the institution and means that digitalization of an analog version cannot be made unless a digital version is not available at all or, according to TEACH § 112(f)(2)(B), it is available but subject to technological protection measures that prevent its use for TEACH § 110(2).

By the same token, reading a market availability test into the clause would be consistent with Congress's repeated attempt to preserve the market incentive to create and distribute copyrighted material into society. Unfortunately, this conclusion cannot be derived from the actual text of the statute. Under a narrow view, there is no incentive for a copyright owner to release a new version of his or her product, as there is no statutory requirement that the institution first make a check of the marketplace for the work and purchase a new digital copy of it. The market remains stuck in time, so to speak. On the other hand, if one reads "available to the institution" to mean obtainability, then the law encourages the copyright owner to make new digital versions of his or her work available. Of course obtainability might also mean by borrowing, which would do little to advance sales, but at least one other institution (the lending institution) would have made a prior purchase of a digital version of the work.

It would be useful to think through what Congress might be trying to accomplish here and determine whether one interpretation appears more likely than another in light of that. Apparently the incentive system should be structured with a view toward market development that increases access to new distance education products, while at the same time protecting copyright owners' rights. Generally, this would seem to imply a broad view of availability; i.e., the institution would need to make a market check before digitalization could occur and, if products are available in digital form, purchase them.

The commonsense use of the word "available" might suggest a narrow approach, as a work that would first need to be purchased would appear to be not available but obtainable. However, if "available" means only that the institution looks to its own resources, little is accomplished by the conditional language, because a school, college, university, or other educational entity could digitize the work if it had only an analog copy or a digital version that once was open but is now locked because the technological key access was not renewed. Not only would this appear to apply to a wide range of circumstances, it would provide little incentive to either buy a digital version or renew the key, not contributing much to the expansion of the digital distance education marketplace—a goal expressed repeatedly in the TEACH legislative history. In order to reduce the proliferation of self-made digital copies, §112(f)(2)(A) encourages official versions of works in digital form. Yet, under a narrow view, this clause provides no incentive to achieve its goal, as the institution with only an analog copy would of course digitize its own copy rather than buy a digital copy if it had the choice and one were "available." Of course this option yields a good result for the educator.

TABLE 6.2
Discerning the Meaning of "Available to the Institution" through Market Incentives

Statutory Condition	Narrow view: Internal search, digitalization can occur when . . . the version of the work owned by the institution is in analog form	Broad view: External (market) search, digitalization can occur when . . . no digital version of the work is available for acquisition in the marketplace or otherwise available from an external source, and the version owned by institution is in analog form
Section 112(f)(2)(A): "no digital version of the work is available to the institution"		
	Inquiry: "Do we own a copy?"	"Are we able to purchase a copy?"
Section 112(f)(2)(B): "the digital version of the work that is available to the institution is subject to technological protection measures that prevent its use for section 110(2)"	the version of the work owned by the institution is in digital form but the "key" has expired, thus the only available copy is one subject to a technological protection measure that prevents its use for section 110(2) performances or displays	the digital version of the work that is available for acquisition or otherwise available from an external source is protected by a "lock," a technological protection measure

From a copyright owner's perspective, concern over the digitalization of one's copyrighted products would suggest undertaking efforts to prevent the statutorily authorized digitalization rights of an educational institution from being triggered—unless, of course, as a copyright owner one does not mind if one's works proliferate digitally. As discussed earlier, Congress reminds us time and time again, however, that copyright owners tend not to take the latter view.

As a result, a narrow view of availability would also appear inconsistent with the fixation Congress appears to exhibit when it deals with digital copyright issues, especially within the rubric of the TEACH provisions. So, too, making that broader search requires a more participative response from the school, college, university, or other educational entity that only has an analog copy, and this also appears more consistent with the overall design of TEACH, though it does also appear to create some less than appealing choices for the copyright owner. For example, a copyright owner reluctant to release a digital version of his or her work into the marketplace for fear of increased ease of infringement who consequently presents only an analog version has just fulfilled §112(f)(2)(A), allowing digitalization when "no digital version of the work is available to the institution" even under a broad view of "available to." Likewise, a copyright owner who, upon release of a digital version of his or her work into the marketplace, desires to have some security upon it and thus places a technological protection measure on it, under 112(f)(2)(B) has just fulfilled the second condition for digitalization because "the [only] digital version of the work that is available to the institution is subject to technological protection measures that prevent its use for §110(2)"—an odd result, but perhaps one not foreseen by Congress.

This seems an odd incentive structure to create. In essence it creates a disincentive against the use of technological protection measures, found elsewhere in the copyright law (and also discussed in this book) and lauded as a necessary development in order to encourage the production and dissemination of new digital works by copyright owners while limiting the ability of copyright abusers to engage in unlawful reproductions and distributions. Two recent examples are the §1201 anti-circumvention and anti-trafficking rules and within TEACH itself such as §110(2)(D)(ii)(I) and (II) on the provision of digital distance education.[60]

Could one think of scenarios where an institution would have available a work that would in fact be subject to protection measures that prevent its use for §110(2)? Yes. Consider a situation where the digital work was acquired but the digital use or access key has expired, or there is a similar digital lockout, in the sense of the digital key, if the institution obtains a copy from another institution instead of from the copyright owner.

The incentive would work to some extent here because, at some earlier point in time, the institution would have purchased the work with its key, but has not renewed its key access. However, it still appears to be a disincentive to use protection measures because either the copyright owner's failure to offer unencrypted works or the institution's failure to renew its key access to the digital version triggers the §112(f)(2)(B) proviso: "the digital version of the work that is available to the institution is subject to technological protection measures that [do now in fact] prevent its use for §110(2)."

The safe conclusion: The institution must conduct a market check to see if a digital version is available. If only analog versions are owned or available as a form of acquisition, then digitalization may proceed. If the institution has acquired a digital version but somehow access to it is blocked for purposes of distance education, then a digital version can also be made. This result encourages the production and acquisition of digital products and leads owners to employ technological protection measures but offer affordable access to educational institutions.

The Original Section 112(b) Right and Using the "No Further Copy" Rule of Section 112(f)(1)(A) Together with the "Transitory or Temporary Storage Allowance" Rule in Section 110(2)

New §112(f) is an important provision for the educator for at least two reasons. First, it allows you to make a copy in anticipation of a later use. Second, when used in tandem with §110(2), it provides educators with a specific provision that limits three of the exclusive rights of the copyright owner: performance and display (both from §110) and reproduction (found in the ephemeral recording right of §112(b) and (f) and in §110).[61]

There is no limit on how long an educator may retain an ephemeral recording under §112(f). This should not pose a threat to copyright owners, as over time copyrighted content looses its instructional value, so the use of the made-before-the-fact ephemeral recording in a §110(2) performance or display will at some point naturally cease. If a recording of the transmission of the class session where the educator performed or displayed the work were made, this would be a §112(b) ephemeral recording subject to the seven-year rule under §112(f)(b)(2), though the institution could retain a permanent archive copy. Having this limitation is also logical because in the §112(b) ephemeral recording, the work is captured as part of an entire class session, as opposed to merely making a copy of the work by itself. The §112(b) ephemeral recording represents a class session complete with lecture and any copyrighted work performed or displayed vis-à-vis §110(2), whereas the §112(f) ephemeral recording of the work alone, detached from its class session, is a far less useful educational item—although, one could argue, far more dangerous to the copyright owner in terms of unlawful future uses by others. The §112(b) copy is part of a new audiovisual work capturing the entire teaching activity "that often compete[s] for exactly the same market"[62] (curricular materials) and thus its use over time is more properly limited.

The two sections can work in conjunction with each other, given the proper circumstances. For example, the digital copy created under §112(f) (a before-the-fact reproduction) and used in a bona fide (one that meets all the conditions of §110(2)) teaching encounter, can then be in essence copied again,[63] that is, recorded as an exercise of your §112(b) right to make an ephemeral recording (after-the-fact reproduction) of the transmission of that §110(2) teaching encounter. This after-the-fact capturing, in analog or digital, of the entire teaching session logically captures or includes (copies) any copyrighted material performed or displayed from a copyrighted work you had made a digital copy of under §112(f).

An educator could then use the recording, analog or digital, of your teaching session made under §112(b) in accordance with the conditions of that subsection (seven-year, no-more-than-thirty-copy rule and one-copy-archive rule). This would be in spite of the later §112(f)(1)(A) prohibition that no "further copies or phonorecords are produced from them [i.e., the copies or phonorecords made under the §112(f)(1) right], except as authorized under §110(2)."[64] This is so because it is necessary to give statutory value to the phrase "and without limiting the application of subsection (b)."

Another way to give significance to both provisions, the right to make an ephemeral recording of the teaching session that as a result also copies the §112(f) copy, in contradiction to the apparent §112(f)(1)(A) proviso against it, is that the §112(b) session recording does more than merely copy the §112(f) ephemeral recording: It copies the entire teaching session. In essence, the second §112(b) copy that is made is part of a bona fide transmission in the first instance under §110(2), and §112(b) merely gives us the right to make an ephemeral recording of it. Section 110(2) does not authorize the making of copies, as it is a performance-and-display provision. The "no further copies or phonorecords are reproduced *from* them" clause suggests not as much a prohibition on copying as it would if the phrase read "and no further copies or phonorecords are reproduced *of* them." The source activity is the performance or display undertaken in accordance with §110(2). The §112(b) copy of the entire teaching session that in result copies the work is an "of them" copy, not a prohibited "from them" copy under §112(f)(1)(A). Fulfilling the "except as authorized under §110(2)" language, the temporary or transient copies are indeed made "from them," the ephemeral recording.

Acceptable §110 transient copying is more a by-product of reproduction, whereas the §112(b) recording an educator would make is deliberate. Does it mean we could not make a §112(b) session recording if it also captured a §112(f) copy? An ephemeral recording under 112(b) is not a transitory copy for sure, so the legislative history would not appear to support use of §112(b) in conjunction with §112(f). However, by the same token, the session recording is not a copy of a §112(f) copy; it is, rather, a copy of a teaching encounter that embodies a §112(f) copy; that is, it is a copy made *of them* not *from them*. Conversely, the §110 transient or temporary storage copy *is* in fact a copy made *from them*, thus its specific exception is needed and referenced in §112(f)(1)(A).

The legislative history can also assist in interpreting the context of the (f)(1)(A) "no further copies" prohibition. The Conference Report explains it in this way, making reference to the sort of copies that would be allowed and that are indeed authorized by §110(2):

> No further copies or phonorecords may be made from them, except for copies or phonorecords that are authorized by subsection 110(2), such as the copies that fall within the scope of the third paragraph added to the amended exemption under §1(b)(2) of the TEACH Act.[65]

Looking back to §110(2) as amended by TEACH, and as discussed at the end of chapter 4, recall there are three paragraphs added at the end of the substantive provisions of §110 dealing with subsection (2). Two are definitional, covering mediated instructional activities and accreditation, and a third is an immunity provision of sorts:

> For purposes of paragraph (2), no governmental body or accredited nonprofit educational institution shall be liable for infringement by reason of the *transient or temporary storage of material carried out through the automatic technical process of digital transmission of the performance or display of that material as authorized under paragraph (2)*. No such material stored on the system or network controlled or operated by the transmitting body or institution under this paragraph shall be maintained on such system or network in a manner ordinarily accessible to anyone other than anticipated recipients. No such copy shall be maintained on the system or network in a manner ordinarily accessible to such anticipated recipients for a longer period than is reasonably necessary to facilitate the transmission for which it was made.[66]

In other words, the "except as authorized under §110(2)," copies that can be made from §112(f) digital ephemeral copies are those sorts of transitory copies made automatically as part of the §110(2) teaching encounter—for example, those temporary copies created in the RAM of a computer in conjunction with the performance or display of copyrighted materials viewed on a computer's screen. By design these *transient or temporary storage* copies would likely be made of material the source of which is a §112(f) ephemeral recording sitting on the server of a school, college, university, or other educational entity. It would be a "copy[] or phonorecord . . . reproduced *from* them" in violation of the §112(f)(1)(A) proviso, thus the "except as authorized under §110(2)" clause is needed in order to allow the transient or temporary storage copies to be later made from the ephemeral recording.

Moreover, there is nothing that prohibits the interaction and conjunctive use of both §112 subsections, (b) and (f), should the proper circumstances apply. If it was intended that §112(b) not be used with §112(f), a more precise statement could have been made to that effect. More to the point, all that does exist is a clear statement that §112(f) should operate "without limiting the application of subsection (b)" and a second clear statement in the transitory or temporary copying provision of §110 that such copying from §112(f) copies should not constitute infringement. The copying space in between those two appears rather gray, to say the least. Of course, Congress might simply not have thought of all the permutations of distance education.

The Section 112(b) and (d) Requirements in a Nutshell

- A nonprofit organization entitled to transmit a performance or display of a work, under §110(2) may make no more than thirty copies of the transmission, capturing ("embodying") the performance. (See discussion pages 117–119.)
- Copies made under §112(b) of the "transmission program embodying the performance or display" must be destroyed within seven years from the date of first transmission. One copy can be kept for archival purposes. (See discussion pages 117–119.)
- While a copy of the "transmission program embodying the performance or display" may be rebroadcast and may also be transferred to another institution for use in its broadcast, additional copies may not be reproduced from the original group of copies (i.e., no copies of copies). (See discussion pages 119–121.)
- In addition to §112(f), §112(b) remains a valid provision of the ephemeral recording section and both sections can apply to the same teaching activity. (See discussion pages 142–145.)
- A "before-the-fact" ephemeral recording can be made of the copyrighted material performed or displayed in a §110(2) transmission. The amount or portion of a digital-to-digital or, arguably, digital-to-analog copy is not necessarily limited to §110(2) limits, though its subsequent use is. The amount or portion of an analog-to-digital copy is limited both as to its ephemeral recording and its subsequent use in a transmission by the §110(2) limits. There is no statutory language authorizing an analog-to-analog ephemeral recording, and since §112 is in the nature of a privilege,

a limitation on the copyright owner's exclusive right is by operation prohibited. (See discussion pages 126–131.)

- The ephemeral recording must be retained and used solely by the school,
college, university, or other educational entity that made it. Any use of it
must be for a transmission authorized by §110(2), and it cannot serve as
the source of further copies except as described in §110(2) as one in transient or temporary storage. (See discussion pages 131–132.)
- An analog-to-digital ("conversion") ephemeral recording can be made
only if one of two conditions or circumstances exist, either (1) no digital
version of the work is available to the institution or (2) the digital version
of the work that is available to the institution is subject to technological
protection measures that prevent its use for §110(2). An unresolved issue
remains regarding whether "available to the institution" refers to marketplace or sources external to the school, college, university, or other educational entity, but such interpretation, though not explicit in the text, is
consistent with other sections of the copyright law and on balance pre-
serves the market incentives and concerns expressed in the TEACH legislative history. (See discussion pages 132–136.)

Notes

1. H. Rpt. No. 94-1476, 94th Cong., 2d Sess. 101 (1976), reprinted in 5 United States
Code Congressional and Administrative News 5659, 5716 (1976).

2. *UMG Recordings v. MP3.com, Inc.*, 92 F. Supp. 2d 349 (S.D.N.Y. 2000).

3. *A&M Records, Inc. v. Napster, Inc.*, 239 F. 3d 1004 (9th Cir. 2001). ("We find no
error in the district court's determination that plaintiffs will likely succeed in establishing that Napster users do not have a fair use defense." Id. at 1019.).

4. *Metro-Goldwyn Studios, Inc. v Grokster, Ltd.*, 259 F. Supp. 2d 1029 (C.D. Calif. 2003)
P2P sharing software distributors Grokster and StreamCast not liable for contributory
(factors regarding technical assistance rendered: timing, i.e., post-infringement, routine,
nonspecific) or for vicarious liability (factors: no right to terminate, did not promote
uses, no control over access, no ability to patrol or police), district court distinguished
the circumstances of the distribution from those of Napster (more akin to premise liability, i.e., use of its system). aff'd _F/3d_, 2004 WL 1853717 (9th Cir. 2004).

5. *In Re Aimster Copyright Litigation*, 334 643(7th Cir. 2003) (grant of preliminary
injunction to shut down Aimster upheld) ("Teenagers and young adults who have access to the Internet like to swap computer files containing popular music. If the music
is copyrighted, such swapping, which involves making and transmitting a digital copy
of the music, infringes copyright. The swappers, who are ignorant or more commonly
disdainful of copyright and in any event discount the likelihood of being sued or prosecuted for copyright infringement, are the direct infringers. But firms that facilitate
their infringement, even if they are not themselves infringers because they are not mak-

ing copies of the music that is shared, may be liable to the copyright owners as contributory infringers." Id. 645.).

6. The text of 17 U.S.C. 112(d) is as follows: "(d) Notwithstanding the provisions of § 106, it is not an infringement of copyright for a governmental body or other nonprofit organization entitled to transmit a performance of a work under § 110(8) to make no more than ten copies or phonorecords embodying the performance, or to permit the use of any such copy or phonorecord by any governmental body or nonprofit organization entitled to transmit a performance of a work under § 110(8), if— (1) any such copy or phonorecord is retained and used solely by the organization that made it, or by a governmental body or nonprofit organization entitled to transmit a performance of a work under § 110(8), and no further copies or phonorecords are reproduced from it; and (2) any such copy or phonorecord is used solely for transmissions authorized under § 110(8), or for purposes of archival preservation or security; and (3) the governmental body or nonprofit organization permitting any use of any such copy or phonorecord by any governmental body or nonprofit organization under this subsection does not make any charge for such use."

7. The text of 17 U.S.C. 110(8) is as follows: "(8) performance of a nondramatic literary work, by or in the course of a transmission specifically designed for and primarily directed to blind or other handicapped persons who are unable to read normal printed material as a result of their handicap, or deaf or other handicapped persons who are unable to hear the aural signals accompanying a transmission of visual signals, if the performance is made without any purpose of direct or indirect commercial advantage and its transmission is made through the facilities of: (i) a governmental body; or (ii) a noncommercial educational broadcast station (as defined in § 397 of title 47); or (iii) a radio subcarrier authorization (as defined in 47 C.F.R. §§ 73.293-73.295 and 73.593-73.595); or (iv) a cable system (as defined in § 111(f))."

8. 17 U.S.C. 112(e) governs the granting of statutory licenses.

9. The text of 17 U.S.C. 114(d)(1)(C)(iv) is as follows: "(d) Limitations on exclusive right. Notwithstanding the provisions of § 106(6)—(1) Exempt transmissions and retransmissions. The performance of a sound recording publicly by means of a digital audio transmission, other than as a part of an interactive service, is not an infringement of § 106(6) if the performance is part of . . . (C) a transmission that comes within any of the following categories . . . (iv) a transmission to a business establishment for use in the ordinary course of its business: Provided, That the business recipient does not retransmit the transmission outside of its premises or the immediately surrounding vicinity, and that the transmission does not exceed the sound recording performance complement. Nothing in this clause shall limit the scope of the exemption in clause (ii)."

10. 17 U.S.C. 114(f) governs licenses for certain nonexempt transmissions.

11. *Campbell v. Acuff-Rose Music, Inc.*, 510 U.S. 569 (1994).

12. H. Rpt. No. 94-1476, 94th Cong., 2d Sess. 101 (1976), reprinted in 5 United States Code Congressional and Administrative News 5659, 5716 (1976) ("In other words, where a broadcaster has the privilege of performing or displaying a work either because he is licensed or because the performance or display is exempted under the statute. . . . The need for a limited exemption in these cases because of the practical exigencies of broadcasting has been generally recognized.").

13. H. Rpt. No. 94-1476, 94th Cong., 2d Sess. 101 (1976), reprinted in 5 United States Code Congressional and Administrative News 5659, 5716 (1976).

14. 17 U.S.C. 112(b): "Notwithstanding the provisions of section 106, it is not an infringement of copyright for a governmental body or other nonprofit organization entitled to transmit a performance or display of a work, under section 110(2) or under the limitations on exclusive rights in sound recordings specified by section 114(a), to make no more than thirty copies or phonorecords of a particular transmission program embodying the performance or display, if—(1) no further copies or phonorecords are reproduced from the copies or phonorecords made under this clause; and (2) except for one copy or phonorecord that may be preserved exclusively for archival purposes, the copies or phonorecords are destroyed within seven years from the date the transmission program was first transmitted to the public."

15. 17 U.S.C. 112(b)(2).

16. H. Rpt. No. 94-1476, 94th Cong., 2d Sess. 103 (1976), reprinted in 5 United States Code Congressional and Administrative News 5659, 5718 (1976) (emphasis added).

17. H. Rpt. No. 94-1476, 94th Cong., 2d Sess. 103 (1976), reprinted in 5 United States Code Congressional and Administrative News 5659, 5718 (1976).

18. Conference Report, H. Rpt. No. 107-685, 107th Cong., 2d Sess. 230 (2002).

19. Conference Report, H. Rpt. No. 107-685, 107th Cong., 2d Sess. 230 (2002) ("The requirement of subparagraph (2)(B), that the performance or display must be directly related and of material assistance to the teaching content of the transmission, is found in current law and has been retained in its current form.").

20. H. Rpt. No. 94-1476, 94th Cong., 2d Sess. 81 (1976), reprinted in 5 United States Code Congressional and Administrative News 5659, 5795 (1976).

21. Subsection (a)(1)(B) states that the "copy or phonorecord *is used solely for* the transmitting organization's own transmissions." (emphasis added). Subsection (c)(2) states that "none of such copies or phonorecords *is used for any performance other than* a single transmission to the public by a transmitting organization entitled to transmit." (emphasis added). Subsection (d)(2) states that "any such copy or phonorecord *is used solely for* the transmissions authorized under §110(8), or for purposes of archival preservation or security." Subsection (e)(1)(B) states that the "phonorecord *is used solely for* the transmitting organization's own transmissions originating in the United States." (emphasis added).

22. 17 U.S.C. 112(b). Subsection 112(a)(1)(C) contains a similar retention timeline: "unless preserved exclusively for archival purposes, the copy or phonorecord is destroyed within six months from the date the transmission program was first transmitted to the public." Another provision of §112(a)(1) contains the "used solely for" transmission limitation §112(a)(1)(B)(B).

23. H. Rpt. No. 94-1476, 94th Cong., 2d Sess. 104 (1976), reprinted in 5 United States Code Congressional and Administrative News 5659, 5719 (1976) (first, second, and third emphasis added).

24. This lack of format specificity is consistent with the historical tenet underlying copyright, that copyright law should express a neutral position toward any technology that is used to embody a protected work or facilitate the use of such work. See Tomas

A. Lipinski, The Decreasing Impact of Technological Neutrality in Copyright Law and Its Impact on Institutional Users, 54 *Journal of the American Society for Information Science and Technology* 824 (2003).

25. H. Rpt. No. 94-1476, 94th Cong., 2d Sess. 103 (1976), reprinted in 5 United States Code Congressional and Administrative News 5659, 5718 (1976).

26. H. Rpt. No. 94-1476, 94th Cong., 2d Sess. 103 (1976), reprinted in 5 United States Code Congressional and Administrative News 5659, 5718 (1976) ("They [producers of educational films] argued that it is unfair to allow instructional broadcasters to reproduce multiple copies of films and tapes, and to exchange them with other broadcasters, without paying any copyright royalties, thereby directly *injuring the market of producers of audiovisual works* who now pay substantial fees to authors for the same uses. These arguments are persuasive and justify the placing of reasonable limits on the recording privilege.") (emphasis added).

27. H. Rpt. No. 94-1476, 94th Cong., 2d Sess. 103 (1976), reprinted in 5 United States Code Congressional and Administrative News 5659, 5718 (1976).

28. H. Rpt. No. 94-1476, 94th Cong., 2d Sess. 103 (1976), reprinted in 5 United States Code Congressional and Administrative News 5659, 5718 (1976) (emphasis added).

29. H. Rpt. No. 94-1476, 94th Cong., 2d Sess. 101 (1976), reprinted in 5 United States Code Congressional and Administrative News 5659, 5716 (1976) ("Copies or phonorecords made for educational broadcasts of a general cultural nature, *or for transmission as part of an information storage and retrieval system*, would not be exempted from copyright protection under section 112(b).") (emphasis added).

30. Conference Report, H. Rpt. No. 107-685, 107th Cong., 2d Sess. 234 (2002) ("In order for asynchronous distance education to proceed, organizations providing distance education transmission must be able to *load material that will be displayed or performed on their servers*, for transmission at the request of students. The TEACH Act's amendment to section 112 makes that possible." (emphasis added)).

31. 17 U.S.C. 112(f)(1) (first and second emphasis added). Congress's purpose is expressed in the Conference Report: "One way in which *digitally transmitted distance education* will expand America's educational capacity and effectiveness is through the use of asynchronous education, where students can take a class when it is convenient for them, not a specific hour designed by the body or institution." Conference Report, H. Rpt. No. 107-685, 107th Cong., 2d Sess. 233 (2002) (emphasis added).

32. Subsection (a)(1) states "to make no more than one copy or phonorecord of a particular transmission program *embodying* the performance or display, if . . ." (emphasis added). Section (c) states "to make for distribution no more than one copy or phonorecord, for each transmitting organization specified in clause (2) of this subsection, of a particular transmission program *embodying* a performance of a nondramatic musical work of a religious nature, or of a sound recording of such a musical work if, . . ."(emphasis added). Subsection (d) states "to make no more than ten copies or phonorecord *embodying* the performance. . . ." (emphasis added).

33. Conference Report, H. Rpt. No. 107-685, 107th Cong., 2d Sess. 233–234 (2002).

34. U.S. Copyright Office, Report on Copyright and Digital Distance Education 95 (1999) ("Section 112(b) has only a limited applicability to digital distance education

transmissions. It would permit, for example, the reproduction, and retention for seven years, of thirty copies of a digital broadcast of a transmission program authorized by section 110(2).").

35. Kenneth D. Crews, Distance Education and Copyright Law: The Limits and Meaning of Copyright Policy, 27 *Journal of College and University Law* 15, 29 (2000).

36. Subsection (a)(1) applies to "a transmitting organization entitled to transmit to the public a performance or display of a work, under a license or statutory license under section 114(f). . . ." Subsection (b) applies to "a governmental body or other nonprofit organization entitled to transmit a performance or display of a work, under section 110(2) or under the limitation on exclusive rights in sound recordings specified by section 114(a). . . ." Subsection (d) applies to "a governmental body or other nonprofit organization entitled to transmit a performance of a work under section 110(8). . . ." Subsection (e) applies to "a transmitting organization entitled to transmit to the public a performance of sound recording under the limitation on exclusive rights specified by section 114(d)(1)(C)(iv). . . ."

37. Conference Report, H. Rpt. No. 107-685, 107th Cong., 2d Sess. 234 (2002) ("The subsection recognizes that it is often necessary to make more than one ephemeral recording in order to efficiently carry out digital transmissions, and authorizes the making of such copies or phonorecords.").

38. Conference Report, H. Rpt. No. 107-685, 107th Cong., 2d Sess. 234 (2002) ("Under new subsection 112(f)(1), transmitting organization authorized to transmit performances or displays under section 110(2) may load on their servers copies or phonorecords of the performance or display authorized to be transmitted under section 110(2) *to be used for making such transmissions.*") (emphasis added).

39. Conference Report, H. Rpt. No. 107-685, 107th Cong., 2d Sess. 234 (2002) (emphasis added).

40. Conference Report, H. Rpt. No. 107-685, 107th Cong., 2d Sess. 234 (2002).

41. H. Rpt. No. 94-1476, 94th Cong., 2d Sess. 104 (1976), reprinted in 5 United States Code Congressional and Administrative News 5659, 5719 (1976) (first, second, and third emphasis original).

42. "No further copies or phonorecords may be made from them, except for copies or phonorecords that are authorized by subsection 110(2), such as the copies that fall within the scope of the third paragraph added to the amended exemption under section 1(b)(2) of the TEACH Act." Conference Report, H. Rpt. No. 107-685, 107th Cong., 2d Sess. 234 (2002) (The third paragraph refers to the transient and temporary copying proviso; the first and second paragraphs define *MIA* and *accredited,* respectively.).

43. Conference Report, H. Rpt. No. 107-685, 107th Cong., 2d Sess. 234 (2002).

44. Section 108(b) states that "[t]he rights of reproduction and distribution under this section apply to three copies or phonorecords of an unpublished work duplicated solely for purposes of preservation and security or for deposit for research use in another library or archives of the type described by Clause (2) of subsection (a), if—(1) the copy or phonorecord reproduced is currently in the collections of the library or archives; and (2) any such copy or phonorecord that is reproduced in *digital format* is not otherwise distributed in that format and is not made available to the public in that format outside the premises of the library or archives" (emphasis added). Section

108(c) states that "[t]he right of reproduction under this section applies to three copies or phonorecords of a published work duplicated solely for the purpose of replacement of a copy or phonorecord that is damaged, deteriorating, lost, or stolen, or if the existing format in which the work is stored has become obsolete, if—(1) the library or archives has, after a reasonable effort, determined that an unused replacement cannot be obtained at a fair price; and (2) any such copy or phonorecord that is reproduced in *digital format* is not made available to the public in that format outside the premises of the library or archives in lawful possession of such copy" (emphasis added). Both sections allow for the digitalization of copyrighted works, subject to certain conditions of course, but the statutory language is clear in its grant of digitalization rights to qualifying nonprofit libraries and archives.

45. Conference Report, H. Rpt. No. 107-685, 107th Cong., 2d Sess. 234 (2002).

46. Conference Report, H. Rpt. No. 107-685, 107th Cong., 2d Sess. 234 (2002).

47. Pub. L. No. 101-650 (Title VIII), 104 Stat. 5134 (1990). Congress was aware that by allowing libraries to purchase and circulate software programs to patrons it might exacerbate the problem of software piracy. Rather than preventing the use of software by patrons outside of the library altogether, the 1990 law required libraries to attach a warning to the circulating software in its collection. The U.S. Copyright Office promulgated regulations prescribing the language of the notice that must appear on "the [software] packaging, which is lent by a nonprofit library for nonprofit purposes." 37 C.F.R. §201.24 (2000) (warning of copyright for software lending by nonprofit libraries). 37 C.F.R. §201.24(b) provides that "[a] Warning of Copyright for Software Rental shall consist of a verbatim reproduction of the following notice, printed in such size and form and affixed in such manner as to comply with paragraph (c) of this section." The text of the notice is as follows: "Notice: Warning of Copyright Restrictions. The copyright law of the United States (Title 17, U.S. Code) governs the reproduction, distribution, adaptation, public performance, and public display of copyrighted material. Under certain conditions specified in law, nonprofit libraries are authorized to lend, lease, or rent copies of computer programs to patrons on a nonprofit basis and for nonprofit purposes. Any person who makes an unauthorized copy or adaptation of the computer program, or redistributes the loan copy, or publicly performs or displays the computer program, except as permitted by Title 17 of the U.S. Code, may be liable for copyright infringement. This institution reserves the right to refuse to fulfill a loan request if, in its judgment, fulfillment of the request would lead to violation of the copyright law." Congress was concerned that libraries might become hotbeds of copyright infringement. To balance the rights of owners and users, Congress required that libraries remind patrons of their obligation to honor the copyright of others, such as software and phonorecord owners. In explaining the new §109(b)(2)(A) requirement, the House Report offered the following: "The Committee does not wish, however, to prohibit nonprofit lending by nonprofit libraries and nonprofit educational institutions. Such institutions serve a valuable public purpose by making computer software available to students who do not otherwise have access to it. At the same time, the Committee is aware that the *same economic factors that lead to unauthorized copying* in a commercial contest *may lead library patrons also to engage in such conduct*." H.R. Rep. No. 101-735, 101st Cong., 2d Sess. 8 (1990) (first and second emphasis added).

48. Pub. L. No. 105-304, 112 Stat. 2869 (1998) (Digital Millennium Copyright Act or DMCA). For example, in providing qualifying libraries and archives the right to digitalize unpublished works for purposes of "preservation and security" in §108(b) and if a published work is "damaged, deteriorating, lost, or stolen, or if the existing format in which the work is stored has become obsolete" in §108(c), Congress also limited the use of that digital copy to in-house use only, as both §108(b) and (c) contain the proviso: "is not made available to the public in that format outside the premises of the library or archives in lawful possession of such copy." Congress explained its rationale and concern, as the DMCA Senate Report cautioned: "This proviso is necessary to ensure that the amendment strikes the appropriate balance, permitting the use of digital technology by libraries and archives while guarding against the potential harm to the copyright owners' market from patrons obtaining unlimited access to digital copies from any location." S. Rep. 105-190, 105th Cong., 2d Sess. 61–62 (1998). The DMCA Senate Report trod carefully into the digital age, unwilling to endorse the concept of the digital library and drawing a distinction between traditional and virtual libraries, in spite of developments within the library and archive community to move precisely in the direction of the transparency of information and library and archive services: "Although online interactive digital networks have since given birth to online digital 'libraries' and 'archives' that exist only in the virtual (rather than physical) sense on Web sites, bulletin boards and home pages across the Internet, it is not the Committee's intent that section 108 as revised apply to such collections of information. . . . The extension of the application of section 108 to all such sites is tantamount to creating an exception to the exclusive rights of copyright holders that would permit any person who has an online Web site, bulletin boards, or a home page to freely reproduce and distribute copyrighted works. Such an exemption would *swallow the general rule and severely impair the copyright owner's right and ability to commercially exploit their copyrighted works.*" S. Rep. 105-190, 105th Cong., 2d Sess. 62 (1998) (emphasis added). As with TEACH, the DMCA Congress did not trust human nature or technologies to control infringing events once material is digitally available beyond the confines of the library or archives or, in a similar concern of TEACH, beyond the doors of the educational institution.

49. Conference Report, H. Rpt. No. 107-685, 107th Cong., 2d Sess. 234 (2002).

50. Conference Report, H. Rpt. No. 107-685, 107th Cong., 2d Sess. 234 (2002) (emphasis added).

51. U.S. Copyright Office, Report on Copyright and Digital Distance Education 161–162 (1999), as quoted, in Conference Report, H. Rpt. No. 107-685, 107th Cong., 2d Sess. 235 (2002).

52. U.S. Copyright Office, Report on Copyright and Digital Distance Education 161–162 (1999), as quoted, in Conference Report, H. Rpt. No. 107-685, 107th Cong., 2d Sess. 235 (2002).

53. *Universal City Studios, Inc. v. Corley,* 273 F.3d 429 (2d Cir. 2001) (footnote omitted) (emphasis added).

54. *Universal City Studios, Inc. v. Corley,* 273 F.3d 429 (2d Cir. 2001) (footnote omitted) (emphasis added). See also *U.S. v. Elcom Ltd.,* 203 F.Supp. 2d 1111, 1131 (N.D. Cal. 2002) ("For example, nothing in the DMCA prevents anyone from *quoting from a work or comparing texts for the purpose of study or criticism.* It may be that from a

technological perspective, the fair user may find it more difficult to do so—*quoting may have to occur the old fashioned way, by hand or by re-typing*, rather than by 'cutting and pasting' from existing digital media. Nevertheless, the fair use is still available.") (emphasis added).

55. *In Re Aimster Copyright Litigation, 2003 U.S. App. LEXIS 13229* (7th Cir. 2003) ("The swappers, who are ignorant or more commonly disdainful of copyright and in any event discount the likelihood of being sued or prosecuted for copyright infringement, are the direct infringers."); *U.S. v. Elcom Ltd.*, 203 F.Supp. 2d 1111, 1135 (N.D. Cal. 2002) ("There is as yet no generally recognized right to make a copy of a protected work, regardless of its format, for personal noncommercial use.").

56. Congressional Developments: Peer-to-Peer Piracy on University Campuses, Hearing, Subcommittee on Courts, the Internet, and Intellectual Property, Committee on the Judiciary, U.S. House of Representatives, 108th Congress, 1st Session, February 26, 2003 ("FastTrack users trading from networks managed by U.S. educational institutions account for 10 percent of all users on FastTrack at any given moment. It's very unlikely that this amount of file-sharing activity is in furtherance of class assignments." Opening statement of Lamar Smith, Subcommittee Chair.) ("Unfortunately, colleges play a prominent role in contributing to P2P piracy. . . . [c]olleges can't expect Congress to continuously help them on intellectual property issues if they do not act as responsible members of the intellectual property system." Opening statement of Ranking Member Howard Berman.).

57. Contrast the quoted dicta from *Universal City Studios, Inc. v. Corley* with limits for use of the implicit digital-to-digital cutting and pasting limits of the Fair Use Guidelines for Educational Multimedia (reprinted in Arlene Bielefield and Lawrence Cheeseman, *Technology and Copyright Law: A Guidebook for the Library, Research, and Teaching Professions*, 92–102 [1997]), which allows educators and students to incorporate a digital copy of a photograph or a limited audio (30 seconds) or video (three minutes) clip into an educational multimedia work such as a PowerPoint presentation. This contrast underscores the tenuous nature of the guidelines as an accurate representation of fair use.

58. Section 108(c) states that "[t]he right of reproduction under this section applies to three copies or phonorecords of a published work duplicated solely for the purpose of replacement of a copy or phonorecord that is damaged, deteriorating, lost, or stolen, or if the existing format in which the work is stored has become obsolete, if—(1) the library or archives has, *after a reasonable effort, determined that an unused replacement cannot be obtained at a fair price*; and (2) any such copy or phonorecord that is reproduced in digital format is not made available to the public in that format outside the premises of the library or archives in lawful possession of such copy" (emphasis added).

59. Section 108(e) contains a similar market search requirement but the replacement copy need not be unused in order for it to prevent the reproduction and distribution rights of §108 from activating.

60. Conference Report, H. Rpt. No. 107-685, 107th Cong., 2d Sess. 226 (2002) ("In addition, section 1(b) requires the transmitting institution to apply certain technological protection measures to protect against retention of the work and further downstream dissemination.").

61. Kenneth D. Crews, Distance Education and Copyright Law: The Limits and Meaning of Copyright Policy, 27 *Journal of College and University Law* 15, 29 (2000) ("An overall difficulty of applying either section 110(1) or section 110(2) to the needs of education is that neither section permits the making of any copies whatsoever.").

62. H. Rpt. No. 94-1476, 94th Cong., 2d Sess. 103 (1976), reprinted in 5 United States Code Congressional and Administrative News 5659, 5718 (1976).

63. The phrase "in essence copied again" is used because the first is represented by the ephemeral recording under §112(f) made and loaded onto the institution's server to facilitate distance education; a second copy results from the ephemeral recording "embodying the performance or display to be used for making transmissions authorized under section 110(2)." This second copy is made when you capture the entire teaching encounter, to serve as an archive, for example, according to §112(b)(2).

64. Section 112(f)(1)(A) contains a prohibition against copying the copy; i.e., the ephemeral recording: "no further copies or phonorecords are reproduced from them, except as authorized under section 110(2)."

65. Conference Report, H. Rpt. No. 107-685, 107th Cong., 2d Sess. 234 (2002).

66. 17 U.S.C. 110.

7

Fair Use of Copyrighted Material in the Distance Education Classroom

FAIR USE IS A "GENERAL" LIMITATION on the exclusive rights of copyright owners. The limitation is general in the sense that "fair" can always apply to a use of copyrighted material, even when it appears that a more "specific" statute section also applies. For example, as discussed in detail in chapter 3, §110(2) covers the performance and display of material in the distance education environment. But what if an educator would like to perform more than a "reasonable and limited" version of an audiovisual work? Is this prohibited because it is outside the limits of §110(2)?

First, the specific statutory limitations on the exclusive rights of copyright owners do not operate as prohibitions; rather, a specific "limitation" section such as §110(2) articulates what is and what is not covered by the privilege granted by its language. Second, and more to the point, the use of the audiovisual work beyond the "reasonable and limited" portion of §110(2) would not necessarily be prohibited by the copyright law unless it would also fail to be a fair use of the material. In short, if a specific section of the copyright law does not appear to authorize use of the material, a fair use analysis can be undertaken in order to determine whether the use is nonetheless acceptable. Finally, a license agreement may also authorize uses beyond that privileged by a "specific" limitation on the exclusive rights such as §110 or the general limitation provided by fair use in §107. This underscores the need to review license "use" clauses to make sure that a full array of distance education use rights is included, such as performances and displays in the virtual classroom and reproductions for the virtual classroom, as well as digital library and e-reserve use (display or performance) and distributions to virtual library patrons.

Understanding Fair Use: A Crash Course

In order to draft a privilege provision that could apply to any use of copyrighted material, Congress made the language of §107, the fair use provision, purposefully vague, leaving interpretation and application of the principle to be developed by the courts on a case-by-case basis. Examining the language of §107 in conjunction with several court cases offers guidance in applying fair use in library and educational settings. However, fair use is an equitable concept, so courts refuse to establish bright-line tests, that is, a clear crossing of the line into infringing behavior. Thus, determining the limits of fair use is less about identifying "too much" or "too little" or "this side" or "that side" of the line than it is about understanding how the factors are applied in analogous cases and if any patterns or trends are signaled by those cases.

There are four fair use factors that need to be considered in any fair use assessment: "(1) the purpose and character of the use, including whether such use is of a commercial nature or is for nonprofit educational purposes; (2) the nature of the copyrighted work; (3) the amount and substantiality of the portion used in relation to the copyrighted work as a whole; and (4) the effect of the use upon the potential market for or value of the copyrighted work."[1] All factors are considered; none in theory is given more weight than another, as fair use is an equitable concept and its analysis by courts reflects as much. Since there is little case law on point (i.e., no library e-reserve case or distance education classroom case), the following analysis borrows from the existing library and classroom case law, which is itself scant, as well as recent digital fair use cases by analogy. It attempts to assess judicial trends, as difficult as the task might be and as tentative as the results offered. The reader should be reminded once again that the following is *not* meant to provide legal advice; rather, it considers some of the relevant concepts and recent precedent that a plaintiff copyright owner would surely use in making a case against a defendant school, college, university, or other educational entity.

The Purpose and Character of the Use

While an educational use is generally a "good" use as far as the fair use analysis is concerned, recent cases such as *A&M Records, Inc. v. Napster* remind copyright users that though a use might not be done for commercial gain it might still be deemed commercial if "repetitive and exploitative" and if done to avoid paying for lawful copies, as was the circumstances of file-swappers using Napster. The Supreme Court cautions against reading any sort of litmus test into the first prong of analysis:

The language of the statute makes clear that the commercial or nonprofit educational purpose of a work is only one element of the first factor enquiry into its purpose and character. . . . Accordingly, the mere fact that a use is educational and not for profit does not insulate it from a finding of infringement, any more than the commercial character of a use bars a finding of fairness. If, indeed, commerciality carried a presumptive force against a finding of fairness, the presumption would swallow nearly all of the illustrative causes listed in the preamble of paragraph of §107, including news reporting, comment criticism, teaching, scholarship, and research, since these activities are generally conducted for profit in this country.[2]

While placing a single article on a course website or e-reserve does not appear to be the sort of activity that courts like the Ninth Circuit in *A&M Records, Inc. v. Napster* are chastising, a court could conclude that an institution with a large enrollment that scans and loads, semester after semester, a copy of a required workbook or manual on basic computer or research skills into an e-reserve or course website for a class that all incoming freshman are required to take would be creating a substitute for purchase, and such posting might not be far from the repetitive and exploitative behavior the Ninth Circuit found so distressing. Constructing and using other copyrighted works in the same way and purpose, such a series of tests, articles, images, etc., so the institution and its students could avoid paying license or other book and materials fees, might lead a court to the same conclusion. Again, there is no magic number of users that makes a reproduction and distribution system repetitive and exploitative. Fair use requires looking at all factors. In a similar concept more directed at the fourth factor (market impact), courts also consider whether the use, if made widespread, would so undermine the market for the work as to drive the copyright creator-owner-producer from the market—a result contrary to the goal of the copyright law, which is to promote the creative arts.[3] In a recent Seventh Circuit opinion the court saw tremendous harm to the value of several tests printed in their entirety, without permission, in a local newsletter. While no revenue was lost because the texts were not available for purchase in the educational marketplace, the court held that publishing the complete tests in a newsletter eliminated their usefulness as valid measures of student performance and saw harm in what was not "a fair purpose."[4]

Recent case law focuses on "commercial exploitation" as opposed to the mere commercial nature of the use. This stands to reason, because most litigated uses are in conjunction with a commercial enterprise, as intimated by the *Campbell v. Acuff-Rose Music, Inc.* observation quoted above. "For profit" is *not* necessarily an obstacle to "fair use." In the words of one commentator: "The fact that defendant's book was sold for profit is not of itself determinative because if all uses for profit were to fail under this factor, practically no fair uses could be made at all."[5] On the other hand, "commercial use" need not encompass profit seeking. In the much publicized *A&M Records, Inc. v. Napster, Inc.*, the Ninth Circuit concluded that the purpose of individuals who participated in the sharing of music through Napster technology was indeed commercial. The court explained that "[d]irect economic benefit is not required to demonstrate a commercial use. Rather, repeated and exploitative copying of copyrighted works even if the copies are not offered for sale, may constitute a commercial use. . . . In the record before us, commercial use is demonstrated by a showing that repeated and exploitative unauthorized copies of copyrighted works were made *to save the expense of purchasing authorized copies.*"[6] This is significant for many libraries associated with educational institutions that make an extra copy in order to save the purchase price of a second or backup copy. A repeated pattern or practice of collection or reserve building across curriculums or degree programs might lead a court to a similar conclusion.

Courts also view transformative uses more favorably[7] than those that unnecessarily substitute the copy for the original or transpose the document to another medium or environment. This is why the "space shift" argument of the file-sharing community fails in the courts. Defendant file sharers look to the *Sony*[8] (Betamax) case and its acceptance of the time-shift concept as a fair use. Not available to watch the program now? Record it and watch it later. Could this argument by analogy apply to other types of copyrighted material, such as music? Burn a copy of a recording onto a CD because the car sound system is equipped without a cassette player. Rather than a time-shift, defendants sought to legitimize a space-shift, from analog to digital or from one digital platform to another, that is, CD to MP3 file. The space-shift argument is an attempt to apply the *Sony* ruling to the Internet. In a case of first impression, the makers of MP3 technology allowed users to listen to music lawfully acquired through purchase, but unlawfully loaded (copied) onto servers so customers could access music in a different space from the original compact disc technology, such as the space of a personal computer music driver. In determining that this space-shift copying was not a fair use, the court commented that the space-shifting argument "is simply another way of saying that the unauthorized copies are being retransmitted in another medium—an insufficient basis for any legitimate claim of transformation."[9]

However, when transformation does occur, some courts have found that this transformation overrides the otherwise commercial nature of a use: "[T]he more transformative the new work, the less will be the significance of other factors like commercialism, that may weigh against a finding of fair use."[10] The "transformation" must be more than a reproduction. For example, regarding a thumbnail index of pictures on a World Wide Web site, a court found the commercial nature of the site nonetheless transformative, as it "was also of a somewhat more incidental and less exploitative nature than more traditional types of 'commercial use.'"[11] Moreover, in *Kelly v. Arriba Soft Corp.* on appeal the Ninth Circuit found the index functional, thus transformative: "Arriba's search engine functions as a tool to help index and improve access to images on the internet and their related web sites."[12] Although the thumbnails were complete copies, they had been transformed into a new product, an index to information on the Internet, and "users are unlikely to enlarge the thumbnails and use them for artistic purposes because the thumbnails are of much lower-resolutions than the originals; any enlargement results in a significant loss of clarity of the image, making them inappropriate as display material."[13] As such "[t]he thumbnails would not be a substitute for the full-sized images because the thumbnails lose their clarity when enlarged."[14] Likewise, in comparing the use of excerpts from a song in a public television documentary versus the use of a poster of a quilt on the set of a television sit-com, the *Higgins v. Detroit Educational Television Foundation* court observed:

> The Court sees a marked distinction between the use of the poster in Ringgold [*Ringgold v. Black Entertainment Television. Inc.*, 126 F.3d 70 (2d Cir. 1997)] and the use of "Under the Gun" in "Stop the Fighting II." First, and foremost, whereas the clear purpose of the use in Ringgold was commercial, as discussed above, the purpose of the use of "Under the Gun" was educational. Second, whereas the poster in Ringgold was used for its express decorative purpose and was clearly seen—and sometimes used as the focal point for the action in the ROC church recital scene— only two barely discernible snippets of an instrumental portion of "Under the Gun" is heard as background music in "Stop the Violence II." "Stop the Fighting II" is not a musical composition, but is instead an audio-visual program that seeks to educate teenagers about conflict resolution and the dangers of drugs. Defendants *transformed* a small portion of "Under the Gun" to create a distinctly new work. Moreover, Defendants did not use "Under the Gun" to promote "Stop the Fighting II," nor is the song by any means the focal point of the action. Rather, it is used only as soft background music for less than twenty seconds of drug raid footage in a 5-minute feature on the DEA, with narration and dialogue superimposed over the music, and then again, barely audible, as background music while dialogue continued in the closing moments of the DEA feature.[15]

When courts look at "purpose and character," the first factor, they assess whether "the new work merely supersede[s] the objects of the original creation, or instead adds something new, with a further purpose or different character, altering the first with new expression, meaning, or message; it asks, in other words, whether and to what extent the new work is transformative."[16] Transformative works are encouraged, their production at the heart of the copyright incentive structure; fair use offers the "guarantee of breathing space within the confines of copyright and the more transformative the new work, the less will be the significance of other factors, like commercialism, that may weigh against a finding of fair use."[17]

Reproducing a series of articles or other copyrighted material (analog or digital) and handing them out in class or posting on a course website is not particularly transformative of the works it reproduces, whether by photocopy or scan, though it could be argued that a new work as a whole, an edited course reader, is created.[18] Likewise, making a copy for archival purposes (in a classroom vertical file or course website resource page) is also unlikely to be deemed transformative.[19] While it could be concluded that merely reproducing material for use in a classroom or course website is not transformative, courts have been more sympathetic to educators than to commercial copy shops and corporations. There is little transformative about copying the entirety or large portions of a work verbatim. In a recent case,[20] *Los Angeles Times v. Free Republic*, the entire texts of articles on newspapers' websites were posted on another website and registered members could add commentary. The newspapers sued, alleging copyright infringement. The court found that the copying was verbatim, encompassed large numbers of articles, and occurred on an almost daily basis. The evidence supported a finding that defendants engaged in extensive, systematic copying of the newspapers and was not able to demonstrate that verbatim copying of plaintiffs' articles was necessary to achieve their critical purpose.[21]

In contrast, there is support for this multiple and nontransformative educational copying even when multiple copying is involved. The Supreme Court in footnote 11 of the *Campbell v. Acuff-Rose Music, Inc.* decision refers to statutory support for this nontransformative but still fair purpose exception for educators: "The obvious statutory exception to this focus on transformative uses is the straight reproduction of multiple copies for classroom distribution."[22] The operative language of the Court's reference is the opening sentence of §107, which reads:

> Notwithstanding the provisions of sections 106 and 106A, the fair use of a copyrighted work, including such use by reproduction in copies or phonorecords or by any other means specified by that section, for purposes such as criticism, comment, news reporting, teaching (*including multiple copies for classroom use*), scholarship, or research, is not an infringement of copyright.[23]

This suggests that the transformative test of the first fair use factor will not be as stringently applied to the educational setting. The value of "prevailing" on the first fair use factor is that the copyright owner must demonstrate market harm; by the same token, since commercial uses are presumptively unfair, the defendant would need to show that there is no market harm.[24]

The Nature of the Work

The second fair use factor, dealing with the nature of the work, is likely to not favor the educational institution, because most works copied have some modicum of creativity and are thus protected by copyright. An important factor here is that, in the precedents involving copy shops and serial publications, courts have placed scientific and technical information—journal literature from the hard sciences, such as chemistry or physics, for example—on the far end of copyright protection (the so-called thin copyright), as opposed to poetry or works of fiction, on the opposite end of the spectrum or continuum (protected by a thick copyright of sorts). Of course, facts and figures are afforded no copyright protection whatsoever, though the incorporation of such information into an orderly pattern can be copyrighted as a compilation[25] (an example would be a database). In a compilation, what is protected is the creative nature of selection, coordination, and arrangement of the data, but the underlying unprotected data remain just that, unprotected. However, a license agreement governing an educational institution's use of the underlying data may be restricted beyond that under copyright by the term and conditions of the license. Again, it is essential to review the use clauses of a database license agreement to ensure that the institution has not contracted away its fair use or other "use" rights.

Recent precedent from the Seventh Circuit of *Assessment Technologies of WI, LLC v. Wiredata, Inc.*, consistent with other reverse engineering software[26] and "data extraction"[27] cases, suggests that intermediate copying of protected material in order to extract unprotected material is a fair use if the resulting product would not be in competition with the original product.

> Similarly, if the only way WIREdata could obtain public-domain data about properties in Wisconsin would be by copying the data in the municipalities' databases as embedded in Market Drive, so that it *would be copying the compilation and not just the compiled data* only because the data and the format in which they were organized could not be disentangled, it *would be privileged to make such a copy*, and likewise the municipalities.[28]

Here the vendor-plaintiff did not create the database. Rather, "it created only an empty database.... To try by contract or otherwise to prevent the municipalities from revealing their own data, especially when, as we have seen, the complete data are unavailable anywhere else, might constitute copyright misuse."[29] Unless prohibited by license terms and conditions, a strong fair use case could be made for copying in order to extract unprotected elements from a software program, database, or website for noncompeting educational uses.

Returning to the nature of content that is protected, in *American Geophysical Union v. Texaco*, the scientific journal articles photocopied were "essentially factual in nature"[30] but the content of excerpts (chapters from various books) used to compile course-packs in the *Princeton University Press v. Michigan Document Services*[31] and *Basic Books, Inc. v. Kinko's Graphics Corp.*[32] cases were "creative material." Scientific articles enjoy less protection than the creative excerpts. Newspaper articles pasted onto the electronic bulletin board in the *Los Angeles Times v. Free Republic* case were "predominantly factual. Consequently, defendants' fair use claim is stronger than it would be had the works been purely fictional."[33] Likewise, in a controversy concerning the copying of 4.3 percent of a "book [that] was essentially factual in nature," the court in *Maxtone-Graham v. Burtchaell*[34] observed that "[l]ike the biography, the interview is an invaluable source of material for social scientists, and later use of verbatim quotations within reason is both foreseeable and desirable."[35]

In *Kelly v. Arriba Soft Corp*, Arriba operated a visual search engine on the Internet. It used a "crawler" to gather approximately two million images by the time of trial. The engine created thumbnail images, including photographs taken by Leslie Kelly, a photographer specializing in California Gold Rush country. Although Arriba ultimately won the case, the second "fair use" factor, the nature of the work, weighed against the indexer because the photographs were creative, "artistic" work.[36] Depending on the nature of the material, this factor can help or hurt the educational institution.

Precedent also suggests that courts are more lenient with uses of published material than unpublished material, based on the reasoning that a copyright owner of an unpublished work has not had opportunity to reap the benefit of the marketplace, that is from sales of its works. This may be of concern to instructors who cut and paste from World Wide Web content often consisting of material posted on personal sites. Is this material published or unpublished? Though a recent district court concluded that posting material on a website is a publication for purposes of the copyright law,[37] whether other courts would conclude likewise is unclear.

In other circumstances, determining when publication occurs can be elusive. The concept of publication is not the same as that of distribution.[38] Under § 106, the exclusive right of the copyright owner to make public distributions includes such by "sale or other transfer of ownership, or by rental, lease, or lending" of "copies or phonorecords of the copyrighted work." Therefore all traditional publications such as sales by a bookstore or rentals by a public library are public distributions, but not all distributions in public settings are in fact publications, as one can distribute an unpublished work to the public.[39] Though not all publications require a clear commercial aspect; for example, a printed set of PowerPoint slides distributed to scholars at a conference is most likely not a publication, but leaving a stack of handouts at the information desk of the student union likely *is* a publication.[40]

The concept of "publication" is more important to the potential copyright plaintiff perhaps than to the educator as defendant, because the originator of the work must register the copyright to secure the full array of copyright damage options; otherwise statutory damages or attorney's fees are not available to the successful plaintiff under §412. Registration acts as a sort of "notice" to the world that the work is protected. If the work is published, registration must occur within three months of publication for plaintiffs to have the full array of damage options. In cases where the work is unpublished, registration must occur before infringement in order for the plaintiff to secure the right to claim statutory damages and attorney fees. This might explain why the court concluded that publication occurred when the website went "live" in the *Getaped.com v. Cangemi* case. The website went live in June, with infringement after that date and registration occurring sometime later that summer. Only by concluding the website was indeed published could the court secure for the plaintiff the full array of damages.

The Amount and Substantiality of the Portion Used in Relation to the Work as a Whole

In practice, the third fair use factor, the amount and substantiality of the portion used in relation to the copyrighted work as a whole may not favor the educator in the distance education environment because most items placed in a virtual classroom or posted on a course website constitute a complete taking of the work. A complete journal article or a substantial portion of a consumable work such as a test or workbook or other material such as an audiovisual work or textbook is likely beyond the limits of fair use. Of course, this factor can easily weigh in favor of the institution when a lesser portion of a work is taken. As Gasaway comments, though, such abridgement may not be pedagogically appropriate. "For example, a short excerpt of a motion picture may indeed give a flavor or create a mood, but educational videotapes are different. Many of these works are short, and their very nature makes them useless if less than the entire work is used."[41]

The fair use analysis does not end simply because entire work is copied. As the Ninth Circuit in *Worldwide Church of God v. Philadelphia Church of God* summarized it, "[w]hile 'wholesale copying does not preclude fair use per se,' copying an entire work 'militates against a finding of fair use.'"[42] However, courts have realized that at times a "100 percent" taking is necessary, as the First Circuit concluded in *Nunez v. Caribbean International News Corp.*, where a Puerto Rican newspaper published photographs of a nude Miss Universe contestant. Sixto Nunez, the photographer, had distributed them to the modeling community. The newspaper succeeded in its "fair use" defense, as the pictures were newsworthy. According to the court, "El Vocero admittedly copied the entire picture; however, to copy any less than that would have made the picture useless to the story. As a result, like the district court, we count this factor as of little consequence to our analysis."[43] The court concluded that this factor was "neutral," neither supporting nor weighing against a finding of fair use. However, as Melamut points out, the only Supreme Court decision to find fair use in the context of 100 percent taking was the *Sony* time-shift case.[44] Moreover, there are extensive limitations on the use of the 100 percent taking within the context of the *Sony Corp. of America, Inc. v. Universal City Studios* ruling, as the Seventh Circuit in the *Aimster* case recently reiterated.[45]

While there exist certain works that necessitate complete copying and use, such as photographs or other images, so that the work's effectiveness as a teaching tool might be reduced if less than a complete copy were made, a use of less than a complete copy could still be made in many circumstances of textual, musical, or audiovisual works. Educators would be hard-pressed to argue for the need to reproduce and then display or perform 100 percent of the work in such instances. Recall also the discussion of the dubious pedagogical necessity of using the "entire work" and performance of works other than nondramatic musical and literary works.

Courts have not established any bright line regarding how much copying is too much in the course-pack cases that would be the likely analogous litigation for a classroom or e-reserves scenario. Based upon the copy-shop case law,[46] it might be suggested that, once more than 5 to 10 percent of a work is taken, there is a danger that the amount of the taking could weigh in against a finding of fair use. In many of the cases mentioned in this chapter, courts found the third factor weighed against a finding of fair use: Copying a story from a newspaper onto a bulletin board,[47] photocopying an article from a journal (articles generally have their own copyright, apart from a copyright in the journal as a whole),[48] and scanning a photograph[49] are complete, 100 percent takings of works, though that finding was not determinative in all cases.

The third factor also looks at the substantiality of the portion used in relation to the copyrighted work as a whole. In other words, if the taking is of a small proportion of the work (measured quantitatively) but is nonetheless "substantial" to the work, this will weigh against a fair use. The seminal case in the area is the Supreme Court case *Harper & Row Publishers, Inc. v. Nation Enterprises*,[50] in which an excerpt from President Ford's memoirs was published in *The Nation* magazine. The excerpt was only a small proportion of the book, some three hundred words. However, it was "the heart" of the book: the discussion of President Ford's pardon of President Nixon. This, in addition to other factors in the case, led the Court to find that using the excerpt was not fair use.

In another demonstrative Supreme Court case, *Campbell v. Acuff-Rose Music, Inc.*, the holder of the copyright to Roy Orbison's "Pretty Woman" sued the musical group 2 Live Crew, which had copied the original's first line of lyrics and its signature opening musical hook, the original's "heart." The Court in that case found for fair use, because it was a parody. In order to have a successful parody, the heart was needed to "'conjure up' at least enough of the original work to make the object of its critical wit,"[51] the Orbison melody, unmistakable, that is, incorporating the opening signature guitar riff into the backing track.

However, the "distinction between potentially remediable displacement and unremediable disparagement is reflected in the rule that there is no protectable market for criticism. The market for potential derivative uses includes only those that creators of original works would in general develop or license others to develop. Yet the unlikelihood that creators of imaginative works will license critical reviews or lampoons of their own productions removes such uses from the very notion of a potential licensing market."[56] This comment would seem to support the use of material in educational settings as the subject of critique, a common use in scholarship, though the comment was made part of the general context of the *Campbell v. Acuff-Rose Music, Inc.*, decision, which involved parody, an unlikely use of copyrighted material for most educators.

These cases demonstrate several concepts in fair use. First, even a small taking can weigh against fair use in the proper circumstances, underscoring again the point that there is no bright-line test as to the third factor. Second, parody is an acceptable form of fair use, even if by necessity it means the creative heart of the work is used.

The Effect of the Use upon the Potential Market for or Value of the Work

The fourth fair use factor, the effect of the use upon the potential market for or value of the copyrighted work, in practice is often considered the most important factor. For example, in many of the cases discussed in this chapter, the court's overall conclusion of fair use aligned with a determination of whether the use negatively impacted the market for the work. When a library makes a copy, does that act replace making a purchase? Is the copy harming the potential for the work's sale in any way? While the Supreme Court has observed that all factors must be treated equally,[52] lower courts in the *Basic Book, Inc.*,[53] *Princeton University Press* copy-shop,[54] and *American Geophysical Union* library[55] cases have looked to the importance of the fourth factor.

The courts look not only at the impact on the market for the original work, but also on any secondary or residual market that has developed. In *American Geophysical Union*, the market harm was the key to a decision against *Texaco*. The researchers copied journal articles, not entire journal issues but each an individual work, thus reproducing an article represented a complete reproduction of the work. The court looked not only at the potential "sales of additional journal subscriptions, back issues and back volumes" but also potential "licensing revenues and fees."[57] In *American Geophysical Union,* the secondary market was already established through intermediary clearinghouses such as the Copyright Clearance Center. However, it is unclear whether the secondary market must be well established or at least developing or have only the potential to develop before it will be considered. The Supreme Court has stated:

> A challenge to a noncommercial use of a copyrighted work requires proof either that the particular use is harmful, or that if it should become widespread, it would adversely affect the potential market for the copyrighted work. . . . If the intended use is for commercial gain, that likelihood [of market harm] may be presumed. But if it is for a noncommercial purpose, the likelihood must be demonstrated.[58]

In a recent case involving a subject matter relevant to the present discussion, the Seven Circuit similarly predicted the result if the publication of standardized tests were to become widespread: "If ever a 'floodgates' argument had persuasive force, therefore, it is this case. . . . If Schmidt wins this case, it is goodbye to standardized tests in the Chicago public school system; Schmidt, his allies, and the federal courts will have wrested control of educational policy from the Chicago public school authorities."[59]

However, the recent *A&M Records, Inc. v. Napster* decision considered the future or potential not-yet-present secondary market and a copyright owner's plan to "monetize" a resource in the future.[60] The court recognized harm "related to Napster's deleterious effect on the present and future digital download market."[61] In addition, *Napster* suggests that a copying or "reproduction" to avoid the purchase of a bona fide copy does in fact impact the economic rights of the copyright owner.[62] This can be an important consideration in the educational environment, as many copyrighted materials are produced solely for the educational marketplace, so abuse among a few educators, if widespread, would more quickly destroy the market for a curricular item than one for which a general consumer market also existed. This may be especially true in the nascent distance education product market, and, as we have seen in the discussion of TEACH, Congress is vigilant to protect it. Moreover, there may be harm beyond that which is measurable by lost sales or other revenue as the Seventh Circuit recently observed, by destroying the "value" of the work.[63]

Depending on the category of copyrighted work and the use made of it, courts may or may not identify a harmed secondary market. In *Higgins v. Detroit Educational Television Foundation,* the court found that while videocassettes of a documentary program in which a portion of the plaintiff's copyrighted song was used were sold, "the program was not mass marketed; rather,

the distribution of the video program was limited to educational institutions.
. . . Nor, in this case, does the fact that one non-educational sale was made convert the non-profit nature of the video into a commercial one."[64] In the context of this comment, the court made specific reference to the secondary market (loss of licensing revenue from use of excerpts versus loss of revenue from sales of the recording itself, the primary market) "for textbooks and other educational books and music licensing":

> Unlike the defendants' copying business in *Princeton University Press v. Michigan Document Services* whose activities of intentionally copying the plaintiffs' copyrighted words for profit exploited the plaintiffs' licensing market, in this case, the Defendant's use in no way competes with Plaintiffs [*sic*] market. The market niche that the Defendants have filled is the educational videotape market. Clearly Plaintiff has no interest in occupying this market. . . .The fact remains that Plaintiff has not demonstrated that the value of his copyright interest in 'Under the Gun' has in any way been affected by the limited educational use of an insubstantial portion of the song by a not-for-profit entity.[65]

One drawback for educators is that, unlike the market for music excerpts in a PBS documentary film case, the secondary market for reproduction of text materials, performance of audiovisual works, and potentially other curricular material (such as artwork or photographs that an educator might want to use in a display) is well developed. There are fees for reproduction rights for text material and visual art, as well as for performance rights for the use of audiovisual works such as motion pictures. Moreover, the recent cases make the point that potential for "monetize-ation" of a work into a new market is still a market that can be nonetheless affected by extensive unauthorized uses. If schools across the country engaged in similar uses, market harm would surely be demonstrated.

Trends in Fair Use and Related Litigation and in the Educational Environment

The existing case law relating to educational environments can be grouped into three categories: the older copy-shop cases, other library or education cases, and recent cases that reference library or educational settings in explaining the boundaries of fair use in digital environs. Each set of cases has a lesson to offer. The copy-shop cases—not a fair use—suggest the limit of the concept and so reproduction and distribution systems in distance education programs should be designed to avoid the appearance of course-pack distribution, unless permission is sought, fees paid, or license terms and conditions allow for the inclusion of the documents in an e-course-pack. The related educational cases signal that the variety of materials educators seek to use is in fact protected by copyright and its use in nonprofit educational settings is no insulation from a successful claim of infringement. Third, the recent digital fair use cases suggest a disturbing trend, one that offers very little wiggle room for fair use in the cut-and-paste digital world of distance education. Of course, the last case grouping presents only dicta, but it is disturbing language nonetheless. Finally, all of the case groups to some extent contrast statements of the law with either common practice or "fair use" limits as presented in various fair use guidelines.

Lessons from the Copy-Shop Precedent

At this point in time, the copy-shop cases represent a fairly consistent body of precedents. Creating course-packs, in essence an anthology of readings, and re-producing the course-packs for distribution or sale to students is not a fair use. Though most of the cases involved commercial copy shops,[66] nonprofit educational entities are not beyond the reach of litigation.[67] As a result, prudent commercial and institutionally based copy-shop operations seek permissions, pay license fees, or stay within the so-called classroom guidelines (however questionable that practice might be[68]) when either making course-packs or multiple copies of copyrighted material for educational use. Likewise, in the distance education environment, the same practices would be prudent.

The question becomes, What products constitute an e-course-pack or multiple copying scenario and which are more like traditional library uses, such as building a reference collection or creating a reading reserve? For example, digitizing the entire readings of a class, placing them on a CD-ROM, and then distributing copies of the CD to distance education students would be the same as creating and distributing print course-packs. A publisher would certainly argue that placing the content of that CD-ROM on a course website or library e-reserve, so that students could print out the entire pack of readings with a few key strokes or mouse strokes, would be the same as printing and making available a course-pack with its own table of contents such that students could flip a few pages and locate the desired article. Of course the distinction between the latter and the former example is that with the course website it is the student who decides to download or print out the copy. This begs another question.

Is a collection of articles in a course e-reserve from which a student may download or print out selected articles the same as the unsupervised photocopier or other reproducing equipment that the library is allowed to make available without fear of contributory liability? Can the e-reserve be an extension of this concept? The likelihood of an affirmative answer to this question appears less likely when all the readings are collected in one place, as opposed to a course in which students must individually request each item. Use of warning notices is also prudent and attempts to duplicate online the §108(f)(1) privileges that qualifying libraries have. Section 108(f)(1) states that nothing in §108 "shall be construed to impose liability for copyright infringement upon a library or archives or its employees *for* the unsupervised use of reproducing equipment located on its premises: Provided, that such equipment displays a notice that making of a copy may be subject to the copyright law."[69] However, the most recent amendment of §108, by the DMCA in 1998, suggests that Congress is *not* in favor of using that provision to support digital libraries and, it could be argued, e-support services such as e-reserve.[70] Of course, those comments relate to subsections 108(b) and (c), and it could be argued that the same concern would also apply to another subsection, 108(f), containing the liability limitation.

Along these lines, placement of individual readings on the course website would not be prudent, as it is not consistent with TEACH. The course website should at most contain only those copyrighted items authorized by TEACH. Remember that TEACH is *not* about nor does it support (authorize) the use of "textbooks, course packs, other material in any media, copies or phonorecords of which are typically purchased or acquired by students" or "electronic course-packs, e-reserves, and digital library resources"; rather, TEACH is about teaching in the distance education classroom, not the provision (display, performance, distribution, or reproduction) of copyrighted materials in the virtual library, bookstore, or resource center. All other material should be accessed through the library. Not only does this centralize the use of copyrighted material; it also allows the library to operate within the spirit of the more extensive reproduction and distribution provisions granted under §108.

The issue of e-reserves is perhaps less settled. Unfortunately, there is no firm case law supporting the creation of e-reserves for either traditional or distance students. At least libraries would like to believe it is less settled, owing to the lack of on-point case law. The issue becomes murky in e-reserve systems, because of the ability of the library to package or present the system more in line with a course-pack distribution system, or in a scenario where the creation by students of the course-pack may be only a few clicks away. Though ease of service becomes the driving force behind e-reserve, Melamut suggests that this may be its undoing:

> With e-reserves, there is no longer any risk of physical damage, theft, or mutilation of the original materials. In fact, scanning makes it possible to remove unwanted notes and scribbles and even increase legibility. The library no longer has the problems attendant with physical storage of the material: the inevitable "lost" file or missing pages [the sorts of scenarios for which §108(b) and (c) were arguably intended].[71]

As a general rule, however: "[T]here is as yet *no generally recognized right to make a copy of a protected work*, regardless of its format, for personal noncommercial use."[72] These comments suggest caution when cutting and pasting digital content in educational environments. Moreover, it has become apparent that copyright owners are becoming more willing to pursue infringement actions against nonprofits, individuals, and educational institutions (see discussion below).

The statement closest to support of the creation of multiple copies of individual items for classroom use is the *Campbell v. Acuff-Rose Music* footnote discussed in the previous section regarding multiple copying for classroom use; this is in contrast to the copy-shop cases prohibiting such copying for collected items. An e-reserve for on-campus or distance students might fall somewhere in between, and so would a legal analysis. While an e-reserve falls short of actually handing out collections of reproduced materials, courts have a knack for looking through pretext. The point is, does an e-reserve exist where the vast majority of students do not end up printing out or downloading for later viewing on their own computers every item in every e-reserve? Does the fact that students undertake their conduct of their own accord place the conduct more in line with the use of unsupervised reproducing equipment, where the decision to copy is the students'? Of course this would be a different situation if the instructor said "have every article listed in the syllabus ready for possible reference during our live chat sessions." The result of the instructor's command would be to have a course-pack of the readings in the hands of each student. Given Congress's reluctance (expressed in the legislative history) to facilitate virtual library creation, a case could be made against the extensive use of e-reserve or at least the institution would need to evaluate each reading according to the four fair use factors with selection of "thin copyright" preferred over thick works as well as "less" better than "whole" takings of the item.[73] Of course, licensing can solve these quandaries by simply including the right to make e-course-packs and e-reserves with material downloaded from the subscribed-to online databases. However, this assumes that all items are available in the desired format.

Copyrighted Content in Libraries and Educational Settings

While the Supreme Court has not ruled on any cases under the 1976 copyright law, it has, in a split vote issued without opinion, decided a case involving the National Institutes of Health and National Library of Medicine's practice of operating a photocopy system that reproduced medical journals for staff; it was a vast organization-wide mechanism that resulted in over a hundred thousand copies a year. Though decided under the 1909 Copyright Act, the courts at that time had developed an intricate four-part fair use test.[74] Congress adopted the same four-factor fair use test when it enacted §107 as part of the 1976 Copyright Act; the same test is still in effect today. After one Supreme Court Justice recused himself from voting, the remaining justices split the vote, and since tie votes on appeal go to the winner at the previous level, the decision of the lower court in the case stood. What is telling about the entire case history is that, of the sixteen judges who heard the case (the eight Supreme Court Justices, the seven members of the United States Claims Court sitting en banc—four concluding the use fair, three concluding the photocopying unfair—and the original Claims Court judge, concluding the use was unfair), eight felt the photocopying service was fair and eight judges did not. Considering that the original judge also sat en banc, that vote counting twice in our informal tally, it would be more accurate to say eight concluded the use fair, while seven did not, the point being that many cases present close facts, with variance of opinion, even among the judiciary.

A more recent decision of the Fourth Circuit concluded that a nonprofit church library violated the copyright owner's exclusive right of distribution when the copies it made available in its collection "to the borrowing or browsing public" were bootleg or unlawful copies.[75] There have been a few cases involving fair use and educational materials. The use of text material was the focus in *Marcus v. Rowley*,[76] where a teacher and district were sued for reproduction (about half of the book *Cake Decorating Made Easy*) and repeat (term to term) distribution (not a fair use; and in excess of the "classroom" guidelines).[77] Audiovisual works, off-air tapes, figured in *Encyclopedia Britannica Educational Corp. v. Crooks*,[78] where the Board of Cooperative Educational Services of Erie County was sued for reproduction and distribution of off-air tapes. More recent cases have involved tests and other consumables: In *Chicago School Reform Board of Trustees v. Substance, Inc.*,[79] reprinting of tests in a professional education newsletter was held not a fair use. A similar result occurred in *Educational Testing Service v. Katzman*.[80] The point of these cases is that the array of material used by educators—text, A-V works, tests, workbooks—are in indeed protected by copyright, and the mere fact that the use is educational or nonprofit is not enough alone to swing the fair use analysis when the use represents a complete or substantial use of the work and the use occurs time and time again (*Marcus* and *Encyclopedia Britannica Educational Corp.* cases) or debilitates the market for the work, such as standardized tests (the *Chicago School Reform Board of Trustees* case).

A Narrow View of Fair Use in Digital Educational Environments: Comments from the Recent Section 1201 Cases

Most disturbing is the dictum in several cases involving the anti-circumvention and anti-trafficking rules of §1201. Section 1201 was another product of the now infamous DMCA. These early plaintiffs offered as a defense to their circumvention or trafficking that the eventual use of the material was protected by fair use. In a district court decision from the West Coast and an appellate decision from the Second Circuit (East Coast), courts made a clear rebuff to these arguments, upholding the application of the §1201 rules as a separate offense; that is, apart from the copyright infringement/fair use/ privilege defense analysis. Both courts saw no threat to fair use under the §1201 anti-circumvention and anti-trafficking rules discussed in chapter 4. Worse, and more to the point for the present discussion, in support of that position, both courts—either by design or by accident—presented a very limited view of educational fair use in the digital age. True, these are just two cases, and the comments are dicta, not the holding of the cases. Too, the comments were made not in the context of a fair use defense to a claim of copyright infringement but of an attempt by defendants to use fair use as a defense to a §1201 act of circumvention or trafficking, a separate offense under Title 17. Yet if these dicta represent an accurate presentation of fair use or at least signal a new trend in interpretations of fair use, these comments would represent a far different view of fair use being developed than what is in practice today by many institutions, and an even more limiting view than the position presented in fair use guidelines such as those created for use with multimedia works.[81]

First, the Second Circuit in *U.S. v. Elcom Ltd.* indicated that the fact that the content of copyrighted material is more malleable in digital environs does not reduce the strength or the owner's rights, or, said another way, does not suddenly expand the rights of users:

> The fact that the resulting copy will not be as perfect or as manipulable as a digital copy obtained by having direct access to the DVD movie in its digital form, provides no basis for a claim of unconstitutional limitation of fair use. A film critic making fair use of a movie by quoting selected lines of dialogue has no constitutionally valid claim that the review (in print or on television) would be technologically superior if the reviewer had not been prevented from using a movie camera in the theater, nor has an art student a valid constitutional claim to fair use of a painting by photographing it in a museum. Fair use has never been held to be a guarantee of access to copyrighted material in order to copy it by the fair user's preferred technique or in the format of the original.[82]

More startling is the court's elucidation of what might constitute a fair use of the digital content of a DVD movie, a use that might prove far more limiting than existing notions of fair use, as least as represented by various fair use standards such as represented by the Fair Use Guidelines for Educational Use of Multimedia Works[83]:

> Their examples of the fair uses that they believe others will be prevented from making all involve copying in a digital format those portions of a DVD movie

amenable to fair use, a copying that would enable the fair user to manipulate the digitally copied portions. Although the Appellants insisted at oral argument that they should not be relegated to a "horse and buggy" technique in making fair use of DVD movies, [footnote omitted] the DMCA does not impose even an arguable limitation on the opportunity to make a variety of *traditional fair uses of DVD movies, such as commenting on their content, quoting excerpts from their screenplays, and even recording portions of the video images and sounds on film or tape by pointing a camera, a camcorder, or a microphone at a monitor as it displays the DVD movie.*[84]

The fair use multimedia guidelines referenced above have never been given judicial imprimatur, so adherence to their provisions, arguably as with any of the other so-called educational fair use guidelines for classroom copying, off-air taping, or music, is questionable at best.[85] In spite of this caution, many institutions have nonetheless created compliance mechanisms based upon conformity to these standards,[86] a questionable practice that has not gone unnoticed by the U.S. Copyright Office.[87] The point is that developing judicial reflection suggests a serious revision of fair use in digital works, in contrast to its expression in these existing standards and the implementing practices of many educational institutions.

Similar discussion came from the district court of Northern California in *U.S. v. Elcom Ltd.*[88]:

> For example, nothing in the DMCA prevents anyone from *quoting from a work or comparing texts for the purpose of study or criticism.* It may be that from a technological perspective, the fair user may find it more difficult to do so—*quoting may have to occur the old fashioned way, by hand or by re-typing, rather than by 'cutting and pasting' from existing digital media.* Nevertheless, the fair use is still available.[89]

In an odd result, the copying of the digital content (DVD) might have to be nondigital, then reconverted back to digital for more convenient use in a Web-based distance education environment, but this is the emerging interpretation courts have been offering thus far.[90] Forcing educators and students to engage in these mechanisms of copying would be in stark contrast to the cut-and-paste world with which most people in distance education, or education in general, have become familiar.

Fair Use in the Distance Classroom: Beyond TEACH

Can the concept of fair use and its expression in relevant precedent be applied to the distance education environment to analyze those circumstances where TEACH would not support use of copyrighted material but the use is nonetheless a teaching-learning activity; that is, not "textbooks, course packs, other material in any media, copies or phonorecords of which are typically purchased or acquired by students" or "as electronic course-packs, e-reserves, and digital library resources"? Use of copyrighted material in the distance education classroom beyond the limit of §110(2) can still be permissible under a concept of fair use. Examples would be the performance of more than a "reasonable and limited" portion for works other than nondramatic musical or literary works, such as

- a complete performance of an audiovisual work, VHS, DVD, etc., beyond the "reasonable and limited" portion restriction of §110(2), or
- the digitalization (ephemeral recording) of more than a §110(2) authorized portion, a restriction imposed by §112(f)(2), or the display of an amount beyond what would be comparable to that which is typically displayed in the course of a live classroom session, or
- the display of material for purposes of background, such as an article not directly related or of material assistance to the teaching activity as interpreted by the legislative history

Suppose an educator desires to show an entire VHS videocassette to a distance education class, either by broadcasting or streaming it in synchronous session-time to students or by placing it on the course website for students to access asynchronously. The use of the entire VHS is beyond the "reasonable and limited" portion restriction placed on works other than nondramatic musical or literary works authorized by §110(2). In order to facilitate the 24/7 asynchronous access by students, a digital copy (ephemeral recording) would be needed as well and loaded on the server of the institution. However, as discussed in chapter 6, this conversion of the entire VHS tape would also be in excess of the ephemeral recording privilege granted in §112(f)(2). The fact that this analysis must occur at all is evidence that disparity still exists with respect to the rights of distance educators and students and their "live" face-to-face on-campus counterparts.

Let's analyze the reproduction conversion first. It is assumed that no performance right or additional right to reproduce or space- or format-shift is attached to the work. Certainly the use would be nonprofit educational, a use favored by the court. Also, there does not appear to be any sort of repetitive and exploitative process here, unless the institution is in the practice of converting every tape it possesses just in case it might be used at some point in distance education, thus creating a digital jukebox of converted VHS tapes for use by distance educators and students, quite contrary to the letter and spirit of §112(b) or §112(&) as discussed in chapter 6.

The second fair use factor might swing either way, depending on the nature of the audiovisual work. Is the videocassette a simple documentary or a more entertaining one akin to a Ken Burns production, or is it a theatrical film, thus subject to thick copyright protection?[91] The answer may shift the results of this factor's analysis. However, it could be argued that even a documentary would contain creative elements in the presentation of underlying facts, figures, etc. such that even the most basic documentary using,[92] for example, a collection of public domain archival footage would still be protected by copyright potentially as a compilation.[93] In a similar vein, in *Maxtone-Graham v. Burtchaell,* the taking of verbatim interviews for use in a subsequent book was fair use, as the interview is "essentially factual in nature." Moreover, "[l]ike the biography, the interview is an invaluable source of material for social scientists, and later use of verbatim quotations within reason is both foreseeable and desirable."[94]

Since the entire work is digitized, as in the *Nunez v. Caribbean International News Corp.* case, the best that could be hoped for in analysis of the third prong would be a neutral finding, but a more likely result of this factor would be a weighing against fair use, except perhaps in those cases, as it was in *Nunez,* where "to copy any less would have made the picture useless to the story."[95] Thus far there is one factor likely supporting the digitalization, and possibly two against (creative nature of work, 100 percent reproduction), or taking a nod from the *Nunez* case, might not be relevant to the analysis or, in the words of the court, "of little consequence."

When considering the fourth factor, both the primary and secondary market must be examined. It is assumed that the institution owns a lawful copy of the work. Often the argument is made that the market impact is not as great since at least one copy has been purchased.[96] Is a digital version available in the marketplace?[97] If so, then recall that §112(f)(2)(A) would not have allowed even a §110(2) portion of the work to be digitized. In any case, it would appear that a clear argument of negative market effect could be established, either for loss of sales or loss of license revenue. Then consider the market itself. While reproduction of a fact-oriented educational documentary might possibly favor fair use on the second factor, and the necessity of a 100 percent reproduction result in at best an inconsequential finding of the third factor based on the argument that a less than 100 percent is useless in the classroom, for example, demonstrating half of a lab procedure, under the fourth factor market harm might easily be established in the more insular and restricted educational video marketplace. The publisher, though, would have the burden of proving harm. Finally, suppose the video is not available in DVD. Recall that recent decisions such as *UMG Recordings v. MP3.com, Inc.* and *A&M Records, Inc. v. Napster, Inc.,* have stressed that space-shifting and the decision to move into secondary markets, CD versus MP3[98] or CD versus Web-based,[99] or, in our example, analog-VHS versus digital-DVD, is within the sole purview of the copyright owner. Underscoring this analysis is the fact that use of the VHS tape in analog, while perhaps inconvenient for purposes of distance education, is still possible. As the dicta from the *Universal City Studios, Inc. v. Corley* and *United States v. Elcom Ltd.* cases point out, there are still numerous fair uses of the VHS that could be made such as by pointing a camera, a camcorder, or a microphone at a monitor as it displays the VHS cassette as it is playing and streaming that content over the Internet movie if the institution so desired. Under this scenario, §112(b) would allow no more than thirty copies of the stream-broadcast to be made and rebroadcast for up to seven years after the first transmission, a very clumsy way indeed to get a digital after-the-fact copy of the VHS documentary. (Of course, any §112(b) ephemeral recording of a particular transmission program embodying a §110(2) performance would need to be within the portion limits of §110(2).) It seems that, under the fourth factor, market harm of either the primary or secondary market (for which permission or license to space-shift would be needed) or perhaps both would be demonstrated.

An institution might also be tempted to convert and then "hold" the VHS tape in reserve, but only use (perform) one of the versions at any one time with the argument that it paid for one copy and no more than one copy is used at a time. This rationalization, while attractive to the educational institution, is likely not to succeed with a court, as the space-shift case precedent makes clear. Fair users do not get to choose the medium in which to enjoy the work. Acquiring a lawfully made copy provides the purchaser with certain dominion rights over that copy that attach to the *copy of the work*, not to the copyrighted work itself, as might be the case with a license based upon the numbers of users versus the number of machines on which a copy is loaded (depending, of course, on the terms and conditions of the license).

Where does that leave the analysis? The first factor, nature of use, would favor the institution in making the recording, unless the conversion is part of a widespread digitalization process or a digital version is available for sale, then conversion would tend to demonstrate a nontransformative desire to avoid paying for a second copy. The second factor would depend on the nature of the work. The third, as noted above, would be neutral at best. The fourth factor would not favor fair use.

In the scenarios described above and in other likely variations, a fair use analysis of a VHS-to-digital copy of the entire video would lead to the conclusion that the digitalization would not be a fair use or at most would be a questionable fair use. As a result, the copy that is made is not a lawfully made copy, and any rights under §110 to make use of it, even within the limits of that section, would fail. Recall the lawfully made requirement for audiovisual works under §110(1) and all works under §110(2) (see table 7.1).

This position is underscored in situations where the primary market for the protected work *is* the school, library, or other nonprofit marketplace. Al-

TABLE 7.1
Making a Performance of an Audiovisual Work, in Excess of the Section 110(2) Limitation

	Documentary film VHS or DVD in a science class	Theatrical film VHS or DVD in a film class
Purpose of use	fair this assumes no repetitive and exploitative pattern	fair in addition, this assumes the performance is not for recreation or entertainment
Nature of work	fair? this conclusion assumes that the court concludes the documentary is "thin" copyright	not fair
Amount (performance of the entire film)	not fair or neutral at best	not fair or neutral at best, though in a film class there may be a greater need to perform the entire work
Market impact	not fair the educational market may be more sensitive than one for which a general consumer also exists	not fair
Result	arguably a fair use?	likely not a fair use?

Note: For purposes of this analysis, assume the school, college, university, or other educational entity has purchased or otherwise acquired a lawfully made copy of both films in either VHS or DVD.

though in *Hotaling v. Church of Latter Day Saints*[100] the statute of limitations (three years) for infringement based upon unauthorized reproduction had passed, the plaintiff claimed that the distribution was ongoing, as the unlawfully copied work was made available to members of the public through the holdings of the church library. The court observed: "When a public library adds a work to its collection, lists the work in its index or catalog system, and makes the work available to the borrowing or browsing public, it has completed all the steps necessary for distribution to the public."[101] Because the library had unlawfully made a complete cover-to-cover copy of one of the plaintiff's books, the distribution of that material was also unlawful because it no longer complied with the first sale public distribution right conferred by § 109. Application of this holding to distance environments suggests that, once material is posted unlawfully to a course website, it would continue to violate the exclusive right of distribution or perhaps performance or display for every day it remains on that site and accessible by students as part of a class session.

Thus a turn toward fair use to support the performance or display must be made. Or, in the alternative, assume that fair use or some other mechanism, a license perhaps—though it is far less likely that a license would be in place for the film's digitalization rather than its performance—would authorize the digitalization. However, §110(2) does not allow the performance of the entire amount irrespective of whether the work is lawfully made or not. In a more likely scenario, in which the institution possesses a DVD and does not need to copy the film because it plans to stream the content synchronously, the DVD would be performed directly from disk during the class session. The point is that the institution may still need to justify under fair use the performance of an amount greater than the "reasonable and limited" amount authorized under §110(2).

A similar analysis in the performance of the VHS or DVD can also be undertaken here as well. Certainly the use would be nonprofit educational, a use favored by courts. Also, there does not appear to be any sort of repetitive and exploitative process here, unless the institution is in the practice of performing large amounts of audiovisual works in its courses. The fact that this might be pedagogically unsound should not matter in a fair use analysis per se, as that is rather a factor for a §110(2) analysis as discussed in chapter 3. Likewise, the nature of the work might also favor a fair use for a documentary film, that like the scientific article, would be subject to their copyright, but this might not be the result with the performance of a more creative theatrical film. However, as the precedent suggests that even the most basic documentary, of juxtaposed public domain material, would still be copyrightable as a compilation. The entire video is shown, so that factor does not favor fair use. However, the stronger the case for the need to show an entire film, the more likely a court might conclude that 100 percent would still favor a fair use, especially if the film is a short documentary, or at least consider that it does not weigh much in either direction, fair or unfair.[102] On the other hand, while a botany student can learn about botany without having to watch audiovisual content of the subject matter in the form of a VHS or DVD documentary, a budding student film editor might be hard-pressed to learn his or her craft without viewing complete examples of the product.

While it is clear that fair use will apply to those circumstances beyond the §110(2) limits, Congress could have easily amended §110(2) to include the right to perform 100 percent of other than nondramatic literary or musical works. It did not, and a court might view this as significant and conclude that, while fair use might be seen to support something more than a reasonable and limited amount of an audiovisual work, it might not support a performance of the entire work. Again, as with the digitalization, this factor might be neutral at best.

Fair use is an equitable doctrine, not one of pluses and minuses. While conversion of the documentary VHS tape would appear to favor fair use, a court could easily conclude that the market for documentary educational material is so sensitive that digitizing the entire tape would be unfair. Further, it might lead a court to hedge its analysis elsewhere, such as the second factor, and conclude that the documentary film, as a compilation, still merits protection, with the result that two factors would not favor fair use, with a possible additional factor, the third, not favoring the use either or at best being not determinative. This is not to suggest that courts engage in arbitrary decision making. Rather, with an equitable analysis such as fair use, the proper result might first be determined then the analysis constructed to reach the chosen result.

In the case of the theatrical film, it is assumed that the use is not recreational but a part of a teaching activity, so the use would weigh in favor of fair use. However, the nature of the work is clearly creative and subject to "thick" copyright protection. Again, the amount used is likely not fair, though for some subject areas a strong argument could be made of a 100 percent performance of its content. Is the film *Saving Private Ryan* shown in a history class to reinforce the topic of D-Day, or is it part of a Modern Film class? In the former, an entire screening might not be necessary. As with the fourth factor, the market for a theatrical film is obviously worth more, but in terms of the copyright incentive structure a court might conclude that the market is more sensitive for a documentary or, in this case, a newly released independent film as opposed to a major blockbuster that has played the theaters and been out on DVD for some time. In a case where the market harm could be demonstrated as small and the need to use 100 percent as great, there might be a slight weight in favor of fair use, but in most circumstances, this use would also not likely be fair.

The impact on the market will depend on several considerations. Here the uniqueness of the market may work against the institution. Showing *The Lord of the Rings* in a Literature in Translation course, when it is likely that everyone in the class has already seen the film, may not impact rentals of the DVD, nor would it be as likely to impact sales of the DVD boxed set with additional footage, because showing (performing) the film alone is not a substitute for that special package set. By the same token, showing *The Life Cycle of the Brown Tree Fungus* might not impact a student's decision to buy the DVD, either. If the institution has not purchased the DVD or somehow paid for its use—perhaps obtained it from the local public library without charge—the market is impacted, because there is lost the limited opportunity for the copyright owners to seek revenues from the performance fee attendent to such material. The educational market for some subject matters (the brown tree fungus being a case in point), is arguably rather limited, and every revenue dollar is critical to the future of new productions. Thus a court might view the incentive structure of the copyright law best served when institutions are encouraged to contribute revenue to copyright owners instead of performing entire works in the distance education classroom without revenue contributing, as would result from a positive fair use finding. As observed by one commentator:

> In short, no litigated case exists to date regarding a distance learning program. A court would likely place special emphasis on the fourth factor of §107, focusing on whether the digital transmission of an article, picture, or musical composition resulted in an undercutting of the inherent value in the author's works and a corresponding thwart of the author's incentive to create new works. There is certainly a strong argument that if a large segment of students began taking online courses using digital material, rather than traditional classes with textbooks, the potential market for these protected works could be adversely affected. Specifically, a court could potentially look towards whether the distance learning education institution made any attempt to seek permission of copyright holders, seek licensing arrangement, or use copyright clearinghouses.[103]

Combine this observation with recent court comments regarding use of even excerpts of DVD works short of specific statutory privilege and the necessity of looking beyond fair use in support of distance education performances appears obvious, if not to §110(2) and §112(b) or (f), then to license.

An alternative is to license the use of the film. Many institutions now license on a per-student basis, though for tertiary institutions with thousands of students this can be rather expensive. If this is an option, make sure that distance education rights are included. As more and more content is acquired by license, it is imperative that agreements not only allow for use in supporting capacities such as e-course-packs and e-reserves but also include all categories of copyrighted material (audiovisual, sound recordings, dramatic literary and musical works, etc.) and reach a variety of uses such as reproduction, distribution, performance, and display. Review the existing performance right purchased with existing material to make sure that online rights are included. Digitalization rights might be needed in addition to online performance rights, unless the institution plans to broadcast or stream the showing (performance) of the audiovisual work as it is shown.

Notes

1. 17 U.S.C. 107.

2. *Campbell v. Acuff-Rose Music*, 510 U.S. 569, 579 (1994) (quotation marks and citation omitted).

3. *Campbell v. Acuff-Rose Music, Inc.*, 510 U.S. 569, 590 (1994).

4. *Chicago Board of Education v. Substance, Inc.*, 354 F.3d 624, 627 (7th Cir. 2003) ("There is no analytical difference between destroying the market for a copyrighted work by producing and selling cheap copies and destroying the subsequent years' market for a standardized test by blowing its cover. In the newspaper that he edits, Schmidt

published six of the tests given in January 1999. He did this because he thought them bad tests and that he could best demonstrate this by publishing them in full.").

5. Stephen Fraser, The Conflict Between the First Amendment and Copyright Law and Its Impact on the Internet, 16 *Cardozo Arts & Entertainment Law Journal* 1, 25 (1998).

6. *A&M Records, Inc. v. Napster, Inc.*, 239 F.3d. 1004 (9th Cir. 2001) (emphasis added).

7. *Kelly v. Arriba Soft Corp.*, 77 F. Supp. 2d 1116 (C.D. Calif. 1999), aff'd 280 F.3d 934 (9th Cir. 2002) (Web thumbnail index was transformative, fair use, in-line link or frame violates display right.), prior opinion withdrawn, aff'd in part, rev'd in part, 336 F.3d 811 (9th Cir. 2003) (framing issue not discussed) ("Courts have been reluctant to find fair use when an original work is merely retransmitted in a different medium." Id. at 819, footnote to *Infinity Broadcasting Corp. v. Kirkwood*, 150 F.3d 104, 108 (2d Cir. 1998) (radio broadcast over telephone line); *UMG Recordings, Inc. v. MP3.com, Inc.*, 92 F. Supp. 2d 349, 351 (S.D.N.Y. 2000) (CD audio into computer MP3); *Los Angeles News Service v. Reuters Television International Ltd.*, 149 F.3d 987, 993 (9th Cir. 1998) (news footage without editing).

8. *Sony Corporation of America, Inc. v. Universal City Studios, Inc.*, 363 U.S. 417 (1984).

9. *UMG Recordings, Inc. vs. MP3.com, Inc.*, 92 F. Supp. 2d 349, 351 (S.D.N.Y. 2000).

10. *Campbell v. Acuff-Rose Music*, 510 U.S. 569, 579 (1994) (citation omitted).

11. *Kelly v. Arriba Soft Corp.*, 77 F. Supp. 2d 1116, 1119 (C.D. Cal. 1999), aff'd in part, rev'd in part, 336 F.3d 881 (9th Cir. 2003) citing to *A&M Records, Inc. v. Napster, Inc.*, 239 F.3d 1004, 1015 (9th Cir. 2001).

12. *Kelly v. Arriba Soft Corp.*, 336 F.3d 811, 818 (9th Cir. 2003).

13. *Kelly v. Arriba Soft Corp.*, 336 F.3d 811, 818 (9th Cir. 2003).

14. *Kelly v. Arriba Soft Corp.*, 336 F.3d 811, 821 (9th Cir. 2003).

15. *Higgins v. Detroit Educational Television Foundation*, 4 F. Supp. 2d 701, 706-707 (S.D. Mich. 1998) (emphasis added).

16. *Campbell v. Acuff-Rose Music*, 510 U.S. 569, 579 (1994) (internal quotation markings and citations omitted).

17. *Campbell v. Acuff-Rose Music*, 510 U.S. 569, 579 (1994) (citation omitted).

18. *Princeton University Press v. Michigan Document Services*, 99 F.3d 1381, 1388–1389 (6th Cir. 1996).

19. *American Geophysical Union v. Texaco, Inc.*, 60 F.3d 913, 922-924 (2d Cir. 1993).

20. *Los Angeles Times v. Free Republic*, 2000 U.S. Dist. LEXIS 5669 (C.D. Cal. 2000).

21. *Los Angeles Times v. Free Republic*, 2000 U.S. Dist. LEXIS, at *24 (C.D. Cal. 2000). ("Since the first posting of an article to the Free Republic site often contains little or no commentary, it does not significantly transform plaintiffs' work." Id. at *30).

22. *Campbell v. Acuff-Rose Music*, 510 U.S. 569, 579 (1994).

23. 17 U.S.C. 107 (emphasis added).

24. John W. Hazard Jr. Copyright Law in Business and Practice §8:3, at 8–12 (2004).

25. 17 U.S.C. 101 ("A 'compilation' is a work formed by the collection and assembling of preexisting materials or of data that are selected, coordinated, or arranged in such a way that the resulting work as a whole constitutes an original work of authorship. The term 'compilation' includes collective works.").

26. *Sega Enterprises Ltd. v. Accolade, Inc.*, 977 F.2d 1510 (9th Cir. 1992); *Atari Games Corp. v. Nintendo of America, Inc.*, 975 F.2d 832 (Fed. Cir. 1992), both cited in *Assessment Technologies of WI, LLC. v. Wiredata, Inc.*, 350 F.3d 640, 645 (7th Cir. 2003).

27. *Ticketmaster Corp. v. Tickets.com,* 2000 U.S. Dist. LEXIS 12987 (C.D. Calif. 2000) ("Reverse engineering" applied to factual extraction of material from website if necessary to access unprotected material. It need not be the only way, but the most efficient way to extract the data.).

28. *Assessment Technologies of WI, LLC. v. Wiredata, Inc.*, 350 F.3d 640, 645 (7th Cir. 2003) (first and second emphasis added).

29. *Assessment Technologies of WI, LLC. v. Wiredata, Inc.*, 350 F.3d 640, 646-647 (7th Cir. 2003).

30. *American Geophysical Union v. Texaco, Inc.*, 60 F.3d 913, 925 (2d Cir. 1993).

31. *Princeton University Press v. Michigan Document Services*, 99 F.3d 1381, 1389 (6th Cir. 1996) ("The second statutory factor, 'the nature of the copyrighted work,' is not in dispute here. The defendants acknowledge that the excerpts copied for the coursepacks contained creative material, or 'expression'; it was certainly not telephone book listings that the defendants were reproducing. This factor too cuts against a finding of fair use.").

32. *Basic Books, Inc. v. Kinko's Graphics Corp.*, 758 F. Supp. 1522, 1532–1533 (S.D.N.Y. 1991) ("Factual works, such as biographies, reviews, criticism and commentary, are believed to have a greater public value and, therefore, uses of them may be better tolerated by the copyright law. Works containing information in the public interest may require less protection. Fictional works, on the other hand, are often based closely on the author's subjective impressions and, therefore, require more protection. These are general rules of thumb. The books infringed in suit were factual in nature. This factor weighs in favor of defendant.") (citations omitted).

33. *Los Angeles Times v. Free Republic,* 2000 U.S. Dist. LEXIS, at *55 (C.D. Cal. 2000).

34. *Maxtone-Graham v. Burtchaell,* 803 F.2d 1253 (2d Cir. 1986).

35. *Maxtone-Graham v. Burtchaell,* 803 F.2d 1253, 1263 (2d Cir. 1986).

36. *Kelly v. Arriba Soft Corp.*, 77 F. Supp. 2d 1116, 1120 (C.D. Cal. 1999).

37. *Getaped.com v. Cangemi,* 188 F. Supp. 2d 398 (S.D.N.Y. 2002) (Posting a website on the Internet constitutes publication for purposes of triggering ownership rights. In order to receive statutory damages and attorney fees registration must occur before infringement of unpublished works, or registration must occur within three months of infringement for published works.).

38. Traditionally, courts have interpreted distribution to require some sort of "commercial" enterprise, tied to the formal publication of the work. The description of distribution in Section 106 is almost identical to the definition of "publication" in Section 101 ("'publication' is the distribution of copies or phonorecords of a work to the public by sale or other transfer of ownership, or by rental, lease, or *lending*" (emphasis added)). In addition, the legislative history refers to the Section 106 "distribution" right as "publication." H.R. Rep. No. 94-1476, 94th Cong. 2d Sess. 61–62 (1976), reprinted in 1976 U.S. Code Congressional & Administrative News, 5659, 5674–5675.

39. Two famous copyright cases involved distribution of unpublished or prepublication works. See *Salinger v. Random House, Inc.*, 881 F.2d 90 (2d Cir.), cert. den. 493

U.S. 1094 (1987) (unpublished letters of author J. D. Salinger); *Harper & Row Publishers, Inc. v. Nation Enterprises*, 471 U.S. 539 (1985) (prepublication excerpt of President Ford's memoirs); see also *Estate of Martin Luther King, Jr. v. CBS, Inc.*, 194 F.3d 1121 (11th 1999) ("I Have a Dream" speech of Dr. Martin Luther King heard by thousands and broadcast to thousands more was not a publication). Moreover, "[t]here must be multiple copies available for distribution, transfer, rent, lease, or lending. Thus, publication occurs only if the single item is one of many copies available for distribution." John W. Hazard Jr., Copyright Law in Business and Practice § 1:5, at 1-10 (2004). "An offering must also be to a 'group of persons,' not just to a single individual, and the offering must be for the purpose of further distribution. If the manufacturer of the greetings cards in the example above offered to distribute the cards for private display only, no publication would occur, because the offer must be made for further distribution, public performance, or public display." Id., at § 1:7, pp. 1-11–1-12.

40. See U.S. Copyright Office, Compendium II, U.S. Copyright Office Practices, § 905.01 (1984) (leaving copies in a public place for anyone to take is a publication, but distributing text at a seminar for use only by the recipients is ordinarily not a publication); and discussion in John W. Hazard Jr., Copyright Law in Business and Practice § 1:5, at 1-8–1-12 (1999) (discussing the concept of publication).

41. Laura N. Gasaway, Impasse: Distance Learning and Copyright, 62 *Ohio State Law Journal* 783, 814 (2001).

42. *Worldwide Church of God v. Philadelphia Church of God*, 227 F.3d 1110, 1118 (9th Cir. 2000), quoting *Hustler Magazine, Inc. v. Moral Majority, Inc.*, 796 F.2d 1148, 1155 (9th Cir. 1986).

43. *Nunez v. Caribbean International News Corp.*, 235 F.3d 18, 24 (1st Cir. 2000).

44. Steven J. Melamut, Pursuing Fair Use, Law Libraries, and Electronic Reserves, 92 *Law Library Journal* 157, 170 (2000).

45. *In Re Aimster Copyright Litigation*, 334 F.3d 643 (7th Cir. 2003) (interpreting fair uses of off-air taping under *Sony Corp. of America, Inc. v. Universal City Studios*, 363 U.S. 417 (1984)) the Seventh Circuit observed the following was a fair use:

Sony's Betamax video recorder was used for three principal purposes, as Sony was well aware (a fourth, playing home movies, involved no copying). The first, which the majority opinion emphasized, was time shifting, that is, recording a television program that was being shown at a time inconvenient for the owner of the Betamax for later watching at a convenient time. The second was "library building," that is, making copies of programs to retain permanently. The third was skipping commercials by taping a program before watching it and then, while watching the tape, using the fast-forward button on the recorder to skip over the commercials. The first use the Court held was a fair use (and hence not infringing) because it enlarged the audience for the program. The copying involved in the second and third uses was *unquestionably infringing* to the extent that the programs copied were under copyright and the taping of them was not authorized by the copyright owners—but not all fell in either category. Subject to this qualification, *building a library of taped programs* was infringing because it was the *equivalent of borrowing a copyrighted book from a public library, making a copy of it for one's personal library, then returning the original to the public library.* The third use, commercial-skipping, amounted to creating an unauthorized derivative work, [citations omitted] namely a commercial-free copy that would reduce the copyright owner's income from his original program, since 'free' television programs are financed by the purchase of commercials by advertisers (all emphasis added). (Id. at 647–648)

46. *Princeton University Press v. Michigan Document Services,* 99 F. 3d 1381 (6th Cir. 1996); *Basic Books, Inc. v. Kinko's Graphics Corp.,* 758 F. Supp. 1522 (S.D.N.Y. 1983); *Addison-Wesley Publishing v. New York University,* Copyright L. Rptr. (CCH) ¶25,544 (S.D.N.Y. 1983); *Harper & Row, Publishers, Inc. v. Tyco Copy Service,* Copyright L. Rptr. (CCH) ¶25,230 (D. Conn. 1981); Basic *Books, Inc. v. Gnomon Corp.,* Copyright L. Rptr. (CCH) ¶25,145 (D. Conn. 1981).

47. *Los Angeles Times v. Free Republic,* 2000 U.S. Dist. LEXIS 5669 (C.D. Cal. 2000).

48. *American Geophysical Union v. Texaco,* 60 F. 3d 913 (2d Cir. 1994).

49. *Kelly v. Arriba Soft Corp.,* 336 F.3d 811, 821 (9th Cir. 2003) (photograph on website); *Nunez v. Caribbean International News Corp.,* 235 F. 3d 18 (1st Cir. 2000) (photograph in newspaper).

50. *Harper & Row, Inc. v. Nation Enterprises,* 471 U.S. 539, 564–566 (1985).

51. See *Campbell v. Acuff-Rose Music,* 510 U.S. 569, 588 (1994) ("Parody needs to mimic an original to make its point, and so has some claim to use the creation of its victim's (or collective victims') imagination, whereas satire can stand on its own two feet and so requires justification for the very act of borrowing." Id. at 580–581.).

52. *Campbell v. Acuff-Rose Music,* 510 U.S. 569, 577–578 (1994).

53. *Campbell v. Acuff-Rose Music,* 510 U.S. 569, 592 (1994).

54. *Basic Books, Inc. v. Kinko's Graphics Corp.,* 758 F. Supp. 1522, 1534 (S.D.N.Y. 1991) citing *Harper & Row, Inc.,* 471 U.S. at 566.

55. *Princeton University Press v. Michigan Document Services,* 99 F. 3d 1381, 1389–1391 (6th Cir. 1996).

56. *American Geophysical Union v. Texaco* 60 F.3d 913, 926 citing *Harper & Row, Inc.,* 471 U.S. at 566, 37 F. 3d 881 (2d Cir. 1994).

57. *American Geophysical Union v. Texaco, Inc.,* 60 F.3d 913, 927–931 (2d Cir. 1993).

58. *Sony Corporation of America v. Universal City Studios, Inc.,* 464 U.S. 417, 451 (1984).

59. *Chicago Board of Education v. Substance, Inc.,* 354 F.3d 624, 630-631 (7th Cir. 2003).

60. *A& M Records, Inc. v. Napster, Inc.,* 114 F. Supp. 2d. 896 (N.D. Cal. 2000) *aff'd* 239 F. 3d. 1004 (9th Cir. 2001).

61. *A& M Records, Inc. v. Napster, Inc.,* 239 F. 3d. 1004, 1017 (9th Cir. 2001).

62. *A& M Records, Inc. v. Napster, Inc.,* 239 F. 3d. 1004, 1018 (9th Cir. 2001).

63. *Chicago Board of Education v. Substance, Inc.,* 354 F.3d 624, 630 (7th Cir. 2003) ("The memorandum argues that the school board does not intend to sell the tests, and so Schmidt isn't eating into their market by publishing the tests. This is true, but irrelevant, because he is destroying the value of the tests and the fact that it's not a market value has no significance once the right to copyright unpublished works is conceded, as it must be. The memorandum argues that expert testimony would establish that there is no educational value in publishing the exact same exam year after year. No one supposes there is; the argument rather is that some questions must be carried over to future years in order to validate the exam.").

64. *Higgins v. Detroit Educational Television Foundation*, 4 F. Supp. 2d 701, 704 (footnote omitted), 705 (E.D. Mich. 1998).

65. *Higgins v. Detroit Educational Television Foundation*, 4 F. Supp. 2d 701, 710 (E.D. Mich. 1998).

66. *Princeton University Press v. Michigan Document Services*, 99 F. 3d 1381 (6th Cir. 1996); *Basic Books, Inc. v. Kinko's Graphics Corp.*, 758 F. Supp. 1522 (S.D.N.Y. 1983); *Harper & Row, Publishers, Inc. v. Tyco Copy Service*, Copyright L. Rptr. (CCH) ¶ 25,230, at 16,363 (D. Conn. 1981); *Basic Books, Inc. v. Gnomon Corp.*, Copyright L. Rptr. (CCH) ¶ 25,145, at 15,849 (D. Conn. 1980).

67. *Addison-Wesley Publishing v. New York University*, Copyright L. Rptr. (CCH) 25,544 (S.D.N.Y. 1983).

68. Kenneth D. Crews, The Law of Fair Use and the Illusion of Fair-Use Guidelines, 62 *Ohio State Law Journal* 599 (2001).

69. 17 U.S.C. 108(f)(1).

70. Pub. L. No. 105-304, 112 Stat. 2869 (1998) (Digital Millennium Copyright Act or DMCA). For example, in providing qualifying libraries and archives the right to digitalize unpublished works for purposes of "preservation and security" in § 108(b) and if a published work is "damaged, deteriorating, lost, or stolen, or if the existing format in which the work is stored has become obsolete" in § 108(c), Congress also limited the use of that digital copy to in-house use only, as both § 108(b) and (c) contain the proviso: "is not made available to the public in that format outside the premises of the library or archives in lawful possession of such copy." Congress explained its rationale and concern, as the DMCA Senate Report cautioned: "This proviso is necessary to ensure that the amendment strikes the appropriate balance, permitting the use of digital technology by libraries and archives while guarding against the potential harm to the copyright owners' market from patrons obtaining unlimited access to digital copies from any location." S. Rep. 105-190, 105th Cong., 2d Sess. 61–62 (1998). The DMCA Senate Report trod carefully into the digital age, unwilling to endorse the concept of the digital library and drawing a distinction between traditional and virtual libraries, in spite of developments within the library and archive community to move precisely in the direction of the transparency of information and library and archive services: "Although online interactive digital networks have since given birth to online digital 'libraries' and 'archives' that exist only in the virtual (rather than physical) sense on Web sites, bulletin boards and home pages across the Internet, it is not the Committee's intent that section 108 as revised apply to such collections of information. . . . The extension of the application of section 108 to all such sites is tantamount to creating an exception to the exclusive rights of copyright holders that would permit any person who has an online Web site, bulletin boards, or a home page to freely reproduce and distribute copyrighted works. Such an exemption would *swallow the general rule and severely impair the copyright owner's right and ability to commercially exploit their copyrighted works.*" S. Rep. 105-190, 105th Cong., 2d Sess. 62 (1998) (emphasis added). As with TEACH, the DMCA Congress did not trust human nature or technologies to control infringing events once material is digitally available beyond the confines of the library or archives or, in a similar concern of TEACH, beyond the doors of the educational institution.

71. Steven J. Melamut, Pursuing Fair Use, Law Libraries, and Electronic Reserves, 92 *Law Library Journal* 157, 160 (2000).

72. *U.S. v. Elcom Ltd.*, 203 F. Supp. 2d 1111, 1131 (N.D. Cal. 2002) (emphasis added). The *Elcom* court observed that (*RIAA v. Diamond Multimedia Systems*, 180 F.3d 1072 (9th Cir. 1999), did not hold "that the right to make a copy for personal use is protected as fair use," *Elcom*, 203 F. Supp. 2d. at 1135. AHRA (Audio Home Recording Act), i.e., the *RIAA* case, offers statutory exemption for home taping of "all noncommercial copying by consumers of digital and analog musical recordings." Id. "Making a back-up copy of an ebook, for personal noncommercial use would likely be upheld as a non-infringing use," id., referring to software copying under 17 U.S.C. 117, arguably limited to §117 scenarios?).

73. See also ACRL (Association of College & Research Libraries) Statement on fair use and electronic reserves (http://www.ala.org/ala/acrl/acrlpubs/whitepapers/statementfair.htm) which suggests institutions consider both the nature of the work ("Librarians take the character of the materials into consideration in the overall balancing of interests.") and the amount of the work placed on e-reserve, both qualitatively ("Librarians consider the relationship of the amount used to the whole of the copyright owner's work.") and quantitatively ("Because the amount that a faculty member assigns depends on many factors, such as relevance to the teaching objective and the overall amount of material assigned, librarians may also consider whether the amount, even the entire work, is appropriate to support the lesson or make the point.").

74. *Williams & Wilkins Co. v. United States*, 172 U.S.P.Q. 670 (Ct. Cl. 1972), rev'd 487 F.2d 1345, 1352 (Ct. Cl. 1973), aff'd 420 U.S. 376 (1975).

75. *Hotaling v. Church of Latter Day Saints*, 128 F. 3d 199, 203 (4th Cir. 1997). For a detailed discussion of §109 distribution right, see Mary Minow and Tomas A. Lipinski's *The Library's Legal Answer Book* (Chicago: American Library Association, 2003), 54–57.

76. *Marcus v. Rowley*, 695 F.2d 1171 (9th Cir. 1983).

77. In a commercial educational fair use case, when the court concluded that the defendant's having "copied or directed her students to copy plaintiff's copyrighted materials [literary works and sound recordings] as part of a 'Dynamism' course which she offered for sale" was not a fair use, the court cited *Marcus v. Rowley* and noted that the copying "was not limited and spontaneous, but was extensive and methodical, and consisted of copying from the same author, time after time. This is clearly not within the letter or spirit of the Congressional guidelines." *Bridge Publications, Inc. v. Vien*, 827 F. Supp. 629, 636 (S.D. Cal. 1993).

78. *Encyclopedia Britannica Educational Corp. v. Crooks*, 447 F. Supp. 243 (W.D.N.Y. 1978).

79. *Chicago School Reform Board of Trustees v. Substance, Inc.*, 354 F.3d 624 (7th Cir. 2003).

80. *Educational Testing Service v. Katzman*, 793 F.2d 533 (3d Cir. 1986).

81. Moreover, certain categories of work are statutorily recognized to be more sensitive of digital sampling. See *Bridgeport Music, Inc. v. Dimension Films*, _F.3d_, 2004 WL 1960167 (6th Cir. 2004) (court refused to apply a de minimus standard to a two-second unrecognizable sample of a George Clinton Jr. song; under §114(b) a sound recording owner has the exclusive right to sample his or her own work: "world is free to imitate or simulate the creative work fixed in the sound recording so long as an actual copy of the sound recording itself is not made" Id. at *5).

82. *Universal City Studios, Inc. v. Corley*, 273 F.3d 429, 459 (2d Cir. 2001) (footnote omitted).

83. The guidelines are reprinted in Arlene Bielefield and Lawrence Cheeseman, *Technology and Copyright Law: A Guidebook for the Library, Research, and Teaching Professions* 92–102 (1997).

84. *Universal City Studios, Inc. v. Corley*, 273 F.3d 429, 459 (2d Cir. 2001) (emphasis added).

85. Kenneth D. Crews, The Law of Fair Use and the Illusion of Fair-Use Guidelines, 62 *Ohio State Law Journal* 599 (2001).

86. U.S. Copyright Office, Report on Copyright and Digital Distance Education 115 (1999) ("Many educational institutions across the country at both the K–12 and post-secondary levels are using them [Educational Multimedia Fair Use Guidelines] as a reference or link to them on their websites." (footnote omitted)).

87. U.S. Copyright Office, Report on Copyright and Digital Distance Education xxii (1999) ("Finally, the relationship of guidelines to fair use and other statutory defenses should be clarified. The public should understand that guidelines are intended as a safe harbor, rather than a ceiling on what is permitted.").

88. *U.S. v. Elcom Ltd.*, 203 F. Supp. 2d 1111 (N.D. Cal. 2002).

89. *U.S. v. Elcom Ltd.*, 203 F. Supp. 2d 1111, 1131 (N.D. Cal. 2002) (emphasis added).

90. *321 Studios v. Metro Goldwyn Mayer Studios, Inc.*, 307 F. Supp. 2d 1085, 1101 (N.D. Cal. 2004) ("Fair use is still possible under the DMCA, although such copying will not be as easy, as exact, or as digitally manipulable as plaintiff desires. Furthermore, as both Corley and 321 itself stated, users can copy DVDs, including any of the material on them that is unavailable elsewhere, by non-digital means.").

91. Even the commercial use of small portions of a theatrical film, in creating trailers, can infringe copyright. See *Video Pipeline, Inc. v. Buena Vista Home Entertainment, Inc.*, 342 F.3d 191 (3d Cir. 2003). In its fair use analysis the court characterized the nature of the theatrical films: "But the second statutory factor does not necessarily weigh in favor of finding fair use simply because the public already has access to the original work. Rather, that Disney's movies and trailers contain mainly creative expression, not factual material, suggests that the use is not fair regardless of the published or unpublished status of the original." Id. at 201. Remaining fair use analysis: "Although the clips are copied from Disney's original rather than its derivative works, it is highly relevant to our inquiry here that the clips will likely serve as substitutes for those derivatives." (nature of the use factor, not fair) Id. at 199. "Disney has not claimed, for instance, that any of the clips 'give away' the ending of a movie, or ruin other intended surprises for viewers of the full-length films. Moreover, as advertisements, the clip previews are meant to whet the customer's appetite, not to sate it; accordingly, they are not designed to reveal the 'heart' of the movies. Simply put, we have no reason to believe that the two-minute clips manage in so brief a time, or even intend, to appropriate the 'heart' of the movies." (portion taken factor, fair) Id. at 201. "In light of Video Pipeline's commercial use of the clip previews and Disney's use of its trailers as described by the record evidence, we easily conclude that there is a sufficient market for, or other value in, movie previews such that the use of an infringing work could have a harmful effect cognizable under the fourth factor." (market impact factor, not fair) Id. at 202.

92. Documentaries of public doman material may also be the subject of copyright. See *Dastar Corporation v. Twentieth Century Fox Film Corporation*, 539 U.S. 23, 123 S. Ct. 2041 (2003) ("In 1948 . . . General Dwight D. Eisenhower completed *Crusade in Europe*,

his written account of the allied campaign in Europe during World War II. Doubleday published the book, registered it with the Copyright Office in 1948, and granted exclusive rights to an affiliate of respondent Twentieth Century Fox Film Corporation (Fox). . . . The television series, consisting of 26 episodes, was first broadcast in 1949. It combined a soundtrack based on a narration of the book with film footage from the United States Army, Navy, and Coast Guard, the British Ministry of Information and War Office, the National Film Board of Canada, and unidentified 'Newsreel Pool Cameramen'. . . . Fox, however, did not renew the copyright on the *Crusade* television series, which expired in 1977, leaving the television series in the public domain." 123 S. Ct. at 2044. Federal fair trade law prohibits acts likely to cause confusion as to the "origin" of goods among consumers. The question before the Court was whether the failure to "attribute" the recent series to the original 1949 series violated this requirement. The Court characterized the original 26-episode documentary as follows: "Dastar's alleged wrongdoing, however, is vastly different: it took a *creative* work in the public domain—the *Crusade* television series—copied it, made modification (arguably minor), and produced its very own series of videotapes." Id. at 2046–2047 (emphasis added).).

93. *Dastar Corporation v. Twentieth Century Fox Film Corporation*, 539 U.S. 23, 123 S. Ct. 2041 (2003). "The original film footage used in the *Crusade* television series could have been copyrighted, *as was copyrighted (as a compilation) the Crusade television series*, see 17 U.S.C. §102(a)(6) even though it included material from the public domain [i.e., in the archival film footage]. Had Fox renewed the copyright in the *Crusade* television series, it would have had an easy claim of copyright infringement, see §103(a)." Id. at 2049 (emphasis added).).

94. *Maxtone-Graham v. Burtchaell*, 803 F.2d 1253, 1263 (2d Cir. 1986).

95. *Nunez v. Caribbean International News Corp.*, 235 F.3d 18, 24 (1st Cir. 2000).

96. Laura N. Gasaway, Impasse: Distance Learning and Copyright, 62 *Ohio State Law Journal* 783, 789 (2001) ("One could argue that if the educational institution has purchased or lawfully acquired a work it seeks to perform in a distance learning course, then there should be no adverse impact on the market.").

97. The fact that a work is out of print may impact the analysis as well: "We also note that *Pregnant by Mistake* was out of print when *Rachel Weeping* was published. While this factor is not essential to our affirmance of the district court's finding of fair use, it certainly supports our determination." *Maxtone-Graham v. Burtchaell*, 803 F.2d 1253, 1264 (2d Cir. 1986).

98. *UMG Recordings v. MP3.com, Inc.*, 92 F. Supp. 2d 349, 351 (S.D.N.Y. 2000).

99. *A&M Records, Inc. v. Napster, Inc.*, 239 F. 3d 1004, 1019 (9th Cir. 2001).

100. *Hotaling v. Church of Latter Day Saints*, 118 F.3d 199, 203 (4th Cir. 1997).

101. *Hotaling v. Church of Latter Day Saints*, 118 F.3d 199, 203 (4th Cir. 1997).

102. Laura N. Gasaway, Impasse: Distance Learning and Copyright, 62 *Ohio State Law Journal* 783, 814 (2001) ("The work was meant to be shown in its entirety to teach the content.").

103. Robert Thornburg, The Impact of Copyright Law on Distance Education Programs: How Fair Use and the CONFU Guidelines May Shape the Future of Academia, 27 *Southern Illinois University Law Journal* 321, 354 (2003) (footnotes omitted).

Appendix A

A TEACH Q&A Compliance Audit

Limitations on Materials

1. *Does the performance consist of the entire work, other than the performance of an entire nondramatic literary or entire nondramatic musical work, such as an audiovisual work (VHS video or DVD movie) or a dramatic literary or dramatic musical work (a play or an opera, respectively)?*

If so, performances of all categories of copyrighted works other than a nondramatic literary or nondramatic musical work are limited to "reasonable and limited portions" of the work by statute. 17 U.S.C. §110(2). The Conference Report suggests an amount "less than the entire work" is acceptable but two factors, the "nature of the market for that type of work and the pedagogical purposes of the performance," should be considered in determining what constitutes that acceptable amount. Conference Report, H. Rpt. No. 107-685, 107th Cong., 2d Sess. 227 (2002). This is in contrast to the market for a particular work itself; i.e., a particular type of work might be more prone to unauthorized performances than another type of work, an audiovisual work such as a Hollywood motion picture more so than a dramatic musical work such as a Broadway musical.

2. *Is the teacher displaying a greater portion of a copyrighted work in a distance education setting than he or she would normally use in "the course of a live classroom session"?*

The use of any work to which the display right applies is limited by statute to "an amount comparable to that which is typically displayed in the course of a live classroom session." 17 U.S.C. §110(2).

"[A]lthough it is possible to display an entire textbook or extensive coursepack material through an e-book reader or similar device or computer application, this type of use of such materials as supplemental reading would *not be analogous* to the type of display that would take place in the classroom, and therefore would not be authorized under the exemption." Conference Report, H. Rpt. No. 107-685, 107th Cong., 2d Sess. 229 (2002)(emphasis added). Congress did not want the expanded rights of educators in distance settings to be a cart blanche for the inclusion of vast amounts of digital content into online instructional settings. If an instructor would not actually use (perform or display) the material in a live classroom, he or she should not add it to the online curriculum just because distance or other technology renders it so easy to scan, load, and post it on the course website.

3. *Regardless of these limitations, is the work one that is produced "primarily for performance or display as part of mediated instructional activities transmitted via digital networks"?*

If so, the work is excluded by the opening proviso of 17 U.S.C. §110(2).

The exclusion is not intended to apply generally to all educational material or to all materials having educational value. The exclusion is limited to materials whose primary market is "mediated instructional activities," i.e., materials performed or displayed as an integral part of the class experience, analogous to the type of performance or display that would take place in a live classroom setting. At the same time, the reference to "digital networks" is intended to limit the exclusion to materials whose primary market is the digital network environment, not instructional materials developed and marketed for use in the physical classroom. Conference Report, H. Rpt. No. 107-685, 107th Cong., 2d Sess. 227 (2002).

These items could best be described as curricular materials designed for the online class environment.

4. *Is the material used supplemental to the lesson in any way?*

According to the legislative history, 17 U.S.C. §110(2) does not "address other uses of copyrighted works in the course of digital distance education, including student use of supplemental or research materials in digital form, such as electronic course packs, e-reserves, and digital library resources. Such activities do not involve uses analogous to the performance and displays currently addressed in section 110(2)." Conference Report, H. Rpt. No. 107-685, 107th Cong., 2d Sess. 229 (2002).

5. *Is the copy of the material used in the performance or display a lawfully made copy?*

17 U.S.C. § 110(2) prohibits the use of the material if "the nonprofit educational institution knew or had reason to believe [that the copy] was not lawfully made and acquired."

Unlike the 17 U.S.C. § 110(1) "unlawfully made" copy proviso, which is triggered when the "person responsible for the performance [i.e., the teacher or student or guest lecturer] knew or had reason to believe" the copy of the work used was not lawfully made, revised § 110(2) now places the emphasis on the institution as a whole, with arguably the actual knowledge ("knew") or suspicion ("had reason to believe") of every employee imputed upwards to its administrators, that is, the institution. This arguably imposes a responsibility that is *institution-wide* and that extends to *all* TEACH § 110(2) uses (performances and displays). It differs from the § 110(1) face-to-face teaching "lawfully made" requirement, which applies only to a limited category of copyrighted material ("in the case of a motion picture or other audiovisual work, the performance, or the display of individual images").

Instructional Requirements

6. *Is the performance or display of copyrighted material made by the instructor at his or her direction or under the actual supervision of the instructor?*

See 17 U.S.C. § 110(2)(A). This requirement, according to the legislative history, allows for both synchronous and asynchronous instruction, but the supervision must be "actual" and "not in name or theory only." Conference Report, H. Rpt. No. 107-685, 107th Cong., 2d Sess. 228–229 (2002).

7. *Is the performance or display an integral part of the class session?*

See 17 U.S.C. § 110(2)(A). According to the legislative history, the use "must be part of a class itself, rather than ancillary to it." Conference Report, H. Rpt. No. 107-685, 107th Cong., 2d Sess. 229 (2002).

8. *Is the class session part of the "systematic mediated instructional activities" of the institution?*

This is required by 17 U.S.C. § 110(2)(A). MIA [mediated instructional activities] with respect to the performance or display of a work by digital transmission refers to activities that use copyrighted works (1) as an integral part of the class experience, where the work is (2) controlled by or under the actual supervision of the instructor, and (3) analogous to the type of performance or display that would take place in a live classroom setting. See 17 U.S.C. §110(2) (defining MIA). These three requirements are similar but not identical to the three provisos of 17 U.S.C. §110(2)(A): (1) "integral part of a class session," (2) "made by, at direction of, or under the actual supervision of an instructor" and (3) part of systematic mediated instructional activities," arguably making the language somewhat redundant.

"This latter concept [mediated instructional activities by digital transmission] is intended to require the performance or display to be analogous to the type of performance or display that would take place in a live classroom setting. Thus, although it is possible to display an entire textbook or extensive course-pack material through an e-book reader or similar device or computer application, this type of use of such materials as supplemental reading would *not be analogous* to the type of display that would take place in the classroom, and therefore would not be authorized under the exemption." Conference Report, H. Rpt. No. 107-685, 107th Cong., 2d Sess. 229 (2002). The difference between the use of MIA here in subsection (2)(A) Q8 in contrast with its use in the exclusion of MIA provision in Q3 is that the "former relates to the nature of the exempt activity; the latter limits the relevant materials by excluding those primarily produced and marketed for the exempt activity." Conference Report, H. Rpt. No. 107-685, 107th Cong., 2d Sess. 229 (2002).

9. *Is the material performed or displayed directly related and of material assistance to the teaching content of the transmission?*

This is required by 17 U.S.C. §110(2)(B). According to the legislative history, which also makes reference to a similar point made by the Register's Report (U.S. Copyright Office, Report on Copyright and Digital Distance Education 89 (1999)) and relates it to the same language in the pre-TEACH §110(2)(B) requirement, "this test of relevance and materiality connects the copyrighted work to the curriculum, and it means that the portion performed or displayed may not be performed or displayed for the mere entertainment of the students, or as unrelated background material." Conference Report, H. Rpt. No. 107-685, 107th Cong., 2d Sess. 230 (2002).

10. *Is the transmission of the performance or display made solely for, and to the extent technologically feasible the reception is limited to, students officially enrolled in the course for which the transmission is made?*

This is required by 17 U.S.C. §110(2)(C)(i). There can be no other purpose to the transmission; that is, it must be made "solely for . . . students officially enrolled in the course for which the transmission is made." If others in addition to those students officially enrolled receive the transmission (e.g., by hacking into the system), the performance or display may still be covered by the "reception is limited to" statutory exception as long as the institution attempted to make a limitation on such reception; however, it must make that limitation "to the extent technologically feasible," e.g., by using state-of-the-art network software.

"This requirement is not intended to impose a general requirement of network security. Rather, it is intended to require only that the students or employees authorized to be recipients of the transmission should be identified, and the transmission should be technologically limited to such identified authorized recipients through systems such as password access or other similar measures." Conference Report, H. Rpt. No. 107-685, 107th Cong., 2d Sess. 230 (2002).

11. *Is the nonprofit educational institution seeking to use the statutory exemption accredited?*

If not, the rights granted by 17 U.S.C. §110(2) do not apply. Accreditation refers to the institution, not a particular program. In the case of K-12 entities, accreditation "shall be as recognized by the applicable state certification or licensing procedures" and for post-secondary entities, accreditation "shall be as determined by a regional or national accrediting agency recognized by the Council on Higher Education Accreditation or the United States Department of Education." See 17 U.S.C. §110(2) (defining accreditation).

Compliance Requirements

12. *Has your school, college, university, or institution adopted copyright policies regarding various aspects of the copyright law?*

This is required by 17 U.S.C. §110(2)(D)(i). The statute requires that the transmitting educational institution "institutes policies regarding copyright." The statute uses the plural "policies." However, the legislative history is silent as to the content of such policies, though the range of possibilities is not limited to distance education matters alone. As to the purpose of the three §(2)(D)(i) requirements (policies, informational materials, and copyright notice relating to the course), the Conference Report offers the following comment: "These requirements are intended to promote an environment of compliance with the law, inform recipients of their responsibilities under copyright law and decrease the likelihood of unintended and uniformed acts of infringement." Conference Report, H. Rpt. No. 107-685, 107th Cong., 2d Sess. 230 (2002). This might suggest by logic that instructors, staff, and students be informed of the contents of the policies and that there be some measure of enforcement and recognize in a manner consistent with other institutional policies.

13. *Has your school, college, university, or institution developed and distributed "informational materials that accurately describes and promotes compliance with the copyright laws of the United States to faculty, students and relevant staff members"?*

This is also required by 17 U.S.C. §110(2)(D)(i). See Q12, above, and response. The statute uses the word "provides," so it is arguable that a copyright in-service would serve as an appropriate vehicle to fulfill the command of §110(2)(D)(i). Also, since statutory language is normally interpreted not to be superfluous, this second proviso is in addition to and distinct from the first proviso of §110(2)(D)(i) requiring the formulation of copyright policies. The informational materials consist then of items different from and in addition to the copyright policies the school or district develops in response to the first proviso, such as posters, flyers, a "copyright column" in the staff newsletter, PowerPoint slides from an annual in-service, etc.

14. *Has the school, college, university, or institution provided notice to students that materials used in connection with courses may be subject to copyright protection?*

This too is required by 17 U.S.C. 110(2)(D)(i). See Qs12 and 13, above, and response.

The statutory use of "*the* course" instead of "*a* course" may suggest that the notice provision applies only to a §110(2) (distance education) course and perhaps not to all courses offered by the institution, whereas the policy and informational materials provisions appear to apply throughout the entire school or district. In the alternative, it may simply indicate the nature of the notice, that when the required "notice" is provided to students (nondistance and distance alike) it must inform students that materials used in conjunction with the course may be protected by copyright. In any event, institutions will need to notify students in some fashion that course materials may be subject to copyright law. The precise manner and content of the notice provided is indeterminable in either the statute or its legislative history. However, the notice could be modeled after those already in use for interlibrary loan of software circulation. See 17 U.S.C. §108(f)(1) and 37 C.F.R. at §201.14 (warnings of copyright for use by certain libraries and archives); 17 U.S.C. §109(b)(2)(A) and 37 C.F.R. at §201.24 (warning of copyright for software lending by nonprofit libraries). Placement could be in student handbooks, as a preface to course syllabi, or as part of a distance education course website log-on screen or home page.

While the TEACH revision to §110(2) does not require the institution to provide training and in-service sessions, it does require extensive documentation of policies and informational material to be developed for teachers, students, and staff. There is no requirement per se that the institution make any assessment of whether faculty, students, and staff have a basic level of understanding of the material so developed and distributed in order to see whether its compliance efforts are effective. However, it would appear that such training and assessment components should be part of any effective copyright compliance program. Moreover, since the goal of copyright compliance is now formalized within the educational institution by the statute requiring adoption of copyright policies, informational materials, and notice one could assume, or at least hope, that known breaches of any such policy or general attitudes of noncompliance so adopted would be dealt with by the institution, as would similar violations of its policies regarding other issues such as sexual harassment.

Additional Requirements for Works in a Digital Transmission

15. *If the performance or display consists of material made available via digital transmission, has the school applied technological measures that prevent both (1) the retention of the work (in the computer of the recipient of a transmission) in accessible (unencrypted) form for longer than the class session, and (2) the unauthorized further dissemination of the work in accessible (unencrypted) form?*

These two requirements are found in 17 U.S.C. §110(2)(D)(ii)(I)(aa) and (bb), respectively.

According to the legislative history, there is an adaptable definition of "class session": "The duration of a 'class session' in asynchronous distance education would generally be that period during which a student is logged on to the server." Conference Report, H. Rpt. No. 107-685, 107th Cong., 2d Sess. 231 (2002). However, this distance class session is not without limit: "It does not mean the duration of a particular course (i.e., a semester or term), but rather is intended to describe the equivalent of an actual face-to-face mediated class session." Conference Report, H. Rpt. No. 107-685, 107th Cong., 2d Sess. 231 (2002).

In addition, "the technological protection measure in subparagraph (2)(D)(ii) refers only to retention of a copy or phonorecord *in the computer of the recipient* of a transmission." Conference Report, H. Rpt. No. 107-685, 107th Cong., 2d Sess. 231 (2002). Apparently, other retentions not in the "computer of the student," that is, the "recipient of a transmission," are acceptable. Retention in the form of a printout or even retention on a disk separate from the computer would not appear to pose a problem from the perspective of the legislative history. However, "an encrypted file would still be considered to be in 'accessible form' if the body or institution provides the recipient with a key for use beyond the class session." H. (Conf.) Rpt. No. 107-685, 107th Cong., 2d Sess. 232 (2002).

"Further, it is possible that, as times passes, a technological protection measure may cease to reasonably prevent retention of the work in accessible form for longer than the class session and further dissemination of the work either due to the evolution of technology or to the widespread availability of a hack that can be readily used by the public." Conference Report, H. Rpt. No. 107-685, 107th Cong., 2d Sess. 232 (2002). Thus an educational institution must be cognizant of both the abilities and tendencies of its students, as well as developing industry standards and monitor its network for possible abuse to ensure that use of the most up-to-date protection protocols are in place.

The Conference Report indicates this is an "objectively reasonable standard regarding the ability of a technology protection measure to achieve its purpose." Conference Report, H. Rpt. No. 107-685, 107th Cong., 2d Sess. 232 (2002). It does not have to work perfectly and prevent each and every retention and dissemination, but the technology protection measure must do something and by the language of the statute must do it reasonably well.

The Conference Report offers this additional observation: "Examples of technological protection measures that exist today and would reasonably prevent retention and further dissemination, include measures used in connection with streaming to prevent the copying of streamed material, such as the Real Player 'Secret Handshake/Copy Switch' technology discussed in *Real Networks v. Streambox*, 2000 WL 127311 [*Real Networks, Inc. v. Streambox, Inc.*, 2000 U.S. Dist. LEXIS 1889 (W.D. Wash. 2000) (preliminary injunction)], or digital rights management systems that limit access to or use encrypted material downloaded onto a computer." Conference Report, H. Rpt. No. 107-685, 107th Cong., 2d Sess. 232 (2002).

16. *Has the school engaged in conduct that could reasonably be expected to interfere with the technological measures used by copyright owners to prevent such retention or further dissemination?*

This conduct is prohibited by 17 U.S.C. §110(2)(D)(ii)(II).

A second condition of using copyrighted works in a digital transmission is §110(2)(D)(ii)(II), which states that the institution may "not engage in conduct that could reasonably be expected to interfere with technological measures" used by copyright owners to prevent such further retention or dissemination (as discussed above in Q15). This is what might be termed an anti-interference provision. While it is not identical to other recent amendments to the copyright law, it is nonetheless consistent. See 17 U.S.C. §1201. (In short, §1201(a)(1) prevents circumvention of an access control (writing a code, i.e., a hack, that breaks the access control, e.g., restricting the work to a single technological platform), §1201(a)(2) prevents transfer (trafficking) of that access protocol (posting the hack-script), and §1201(b) prevents transfer (also trafficking) of a technological use control or device or mechanism, such as a code sequence that allows DVD viewers to fast forward past ("operation prohibited") advertising.)

"[L]ike the other provisions under paragraph (2)(D)(ii), the requirement [the anti-interference provision of §(2)(D)(ii)(II)] has no legal effect other than as a condition of eligibility for the §110(2) exemption. Thus it is not otherwise enforceable to preclude or prohibit conduct." Conference Report, H. Rpt. No. 107-685, 107th Cong., 2d Sess. 231 (2002). However, such interference might indeed violate the anti-circumvention rule or precede a violation of the anti-trafficking rules of §1201 as well as foreclose the application of TEACH. By the same token, it also means that because a §110(2)(D)(ii)(II) interference is not the same as a §1201 violation, institutional "interfere[nce]" with a "technological [protection] measure" need not rise to a level meeting the requirements of the §1201 rules for that interference to render inapplicable the exemption granted by TEACH §110(2). In this way the §110(2)(D)(ii)(II) anti-interference provision is broader than §1201, as §1201 applies only if an actual event of circumvention (access control) or trafficking (access or use control) occurs, whereas §110(2)(D)(ii)(II) is triggered by conduct that can "reasonably be expected to interfere with" those measures even if that interference is not ultimately successful.

Expansion of the Ephemeral Recording Right to Make Digital Copies or Phonorecords

17. In order to facilitate a performance or display of copyrighted material in accordance with 17 U.S.C. §110(2), was a copy or phonorecord (analog or digital) made of material that is initially in digital form?

"Under new subsection 112(f)(1), transmitting organizations authorized to transmit performances or displays under section 110(2) may load on their servers copies or phonorecords of the performance or display authorized to be transmitted under section 110(2) to be used for making such transmissions. The subsection recognizes that it often is necessary to make more than one ephemeral recording in order to efficiently carry out digital transmissions, and authorizes the making of such copies or phonorecords." Conference Report, H. Rpt. No. 107-685, Cong., 2d Sess. 234 (2002). Section 112(&) is best viewed as a before-the-fact provision, authorizing the ephemeral recording in anticipation and in order to facilitate an authorized §110(2) performance or display. This is in contrast to the ephemeral recording privilege of §112(b), an after-the-fact provision that authorizes the capture (recording: phonocopy or record) "of a particular transmission program embodying the performance or display" of a "nonprofit organization entitled to transmit a performance or display." 17 U.S.C. §112(b). However, if a copy or phonorecord (the ephemeral recording) is made "of a work that is in digital form," the use of such copies is subject to three requirements.

First, the copies must be "retained and used solely by the educational institution that made them." 17 U.S.C. §112(f)(1)(A). This means that copies of material made by one school district could not be transferred to another school district for use in its distance course, even if that use would likewise be authorized under §110(2).

Second, "no further copies [can be] reproduced from them, except as authorized under §110(2)." 17 U.S.C. §112(f)(1)(A). This provision limits any further reproduction by the educational institution that initiated the §112(f) copying (the ephemeral recording), even if for another bona fide use under the copyright law such as a fair use under §107 in the creation of an e-reserve, for example, as those uses are not authorized under §110(2) (see Q4 and response). However, transient or temporary copies are also allowed. See §110(2): "no accredited educational institution shall be liable for infringement by reason of the transient or temporary storage of material carried out through the automatic technical process of a digital transmission of the performance or display of that material as authorized under paragraph (2)." This might be best understood as a no "copies of a copy" rule.

Finally, the use of copies or phonorecords are limited to "transmissions authorized under 110(2)." 17 U.S.C. §112(f)(1)(B). Suppose that instead of making a further copy of a copy to use on the school's e-reserve server, the instructor after the semester is concluded transfers the copy to the library for use as an e-reserve by another teacher in another course. This use would be prohibited by §112(f)(1)(B) because an e-reserve is not a use authorized by §110(2) (see Q4 and response), even though the use is made of the same copy by the same institution (meeting the requirements of §112(f)(1)(A)) and its use in an e-reserve might otherwise constitute a fair use under §107.

18. *If a copy or phonorecord is made, was the work copied from an analog format; i.e., the copying by the educational institution involved digitalization of a work originally in analog form?*

If so, then the copying (digitalization) can proceed only if one of the following two conditions exist: (1) no digital version of the work is available to the institution, or (2) a digital version is available but it is "subject to technological protection measures that prevent its use for section 110(2)." 17 U.S.C. §112(f)(2)(A) and (B), respectively. In addition, both subsection (f)(1)(A) (retention and use and further copy) and subsection (f)(1)(B) (sole use) provisos apply. See Q17 and response.

In addition, § 112(f)(2) authorizes the conversion from an analog version, but only "with respect to the amount of such works that are authorized to be performed or displayed under section 110(2)." 17 U.S.C. § 112(f)(2). The impact of this limitation on the digitalization of analog materials in support of distance education is demonstrated with the following example. Suppose a teacher would like to show a movie to his or her distance students. The school owns a lawfully made copy of the movie on 16mm film or VHS cassette, either recording being in analog form. Assuming the other instructional requirements of § 110(2) are met (see Qs 6–11 and 17 and responses) then only a "reasonable and limited portion" of the film can be digitized. This is because performances of a work other than the performance of an entire nondramatic literary or entire nondramatic musical work, such as an audiovisual work (video or DVD movie) or a dramatic literary or dramatic musical work (a play or an opera, respectively) are limited by statute to "reasonable and limited portions" of the work. See Q1 and response—even though it might be easier to digitize the entire movie and then cut or clip the "reasonable and limited portion . . ." authorized by § 110(2), or have a copy of the entire movie digitized for later use when different "reasonable and limited portions" might be a better fit for a different lesson. The only "conversion of point or other analog versions of works into digital formats permitted hereunder, [is limited] . . . to the amount of such works authorized to be performed or displayed under section 110(2)." 17 U.S.C. § 112(f)(2). Any digitalization under the ephemeral recording provision of § 112(f) is limited to that amount which can be legitimately performed or displayed under § 110(2).

For purposes of § 112(f)(2), the legislative history is silent as to what the concept of "available to the institution" means. Two interpretations are possible: one narrow, the other broad. Does "available to the institution" mean a physical embodiment of a copyrighted work in analog form actually owned (e.g., the institution purchased an analog version [videocassette] but not the digital [DVD] version) or otherwise under the physical control of the institution (e.g., a CD-ROM governed by license agreement)? In the alternative, does it refer to any available version, such as a version available for purchase in the marketplace similar to the § 108(c) requirement that applies to the replacement of works that are damaged, deteriorating, lost, or stolen, or where the technology necessary to render the work usable is obsolete (e.g., an 8-track analog cassette tape) and an unused replacement copy is unavailable at a fair price? A broad view of "available" might also apply to some other mechanism of access, through interlibrary loan, for example. Arguably, using a broader view of "available to the institution" would mean that the institution would need to acquire (purchase) or at least make arrangements to borrow the work in its digital form, often at some or perhaps significant real or administrative cost, rather than simply convert an analog version it does possess. Yet this limited analog-to-digital conversion right is consistent with the legislative history and the statute: "This subsection does not authorize the conversion of print or other analog versions of works into digital formats, except. . . ." 17 U.S.C. §112(f)(2). Using a broader view increases the burden on the institution and means that unless a digital version is not available through any means whatsoever, or, according to TEACH §112(f)(2)(B), is available but is also subject to technological protection measures that prevent its use for TEACH §110(2), digitalization of an analog version cannot be made. While not explicit in the text of the statute, that interpretation would be consistent with other provisions of the copyright law and of TEACH and heightened ("fear" of infringement with respect to works in digital form), as expressed in its legislative history.

Appendix B

Model Distance Education Copyright Policy

Use of Copyrighted Material in the Distance Education Classroom

IT IS THE POLICY OF [name of institution] to comply with the copyright laws of the United States of America, and foster a respect for the copyright of others among administrators and instructional and support staff and students.

This policy governs the use of copyrighted material in the distance education classroom. This policy implements § 110(2) and §§ 112(b) and (f) of the copyright laws of the United States, Title 17, United States Code.

Copyrighted material may be performed or displayed in a distance education teaching session by synchronous or asynchronous means.

All uses not governed by this policy may nonetheless be authorized by specific permission obtained from the copyright owner, by general license agreement with the publisher or authorized distributor of the copyrighted content, or by a general concept of fair use. See [institution's policy on obtaining permission from copyright owners, policy on licensing, and policy on fair use if available].

Licensing of Copyrighted and Other Content

Where possible the following clause shall be incorporated into license agreements that [name of institution] enters into regarding copyrighted or other material that may be performed or displayed in a distance education class session:

[optional paragraph] The licensee shall have the right to make an ephemeral recording or recordings of any content that is the subject of this agreement. Provided that all ephemeral recordings are limited to works that are the subject of a performance or display or of a class session embodying such a performance or display, and when made in the course of a face-to-face teaching activity consisting solely of enrolled students of the course or when made in a distance education teaching activity, to the extent technologically feasible, consisting solely of enrolled students of a course.

The licensee shall have the right to perform or display any content that is the subject of this agreement. Provided that the performance or display is made solely in conjunction with its use in a face-to-face teaching activity limited to enrolled students of a course or distance education teaching activity limited to the extent technologically feasible to enrolled students of a course.

[Author's note: The following sentence will likely *prevent* instructors from taking a recorded class session along with them when they move to another educational employer, but this or a similar clause might be desired by either the institution or content licensor.] In the case of an ephemeral recording made under this clause, the licensee or its employees shall not transfer or otherwise distribute the ephemeral recording to any other person or school, college, university, or other educational entity. What is granted is a right to take in essence recorded lectures that might contain copyrighted material. Except that the individual instructor responsible for the performance or display may retain and use the ephemeral recording embodying a performance or display for a period of not more than [insert agreed-upon limit] in his or her non-commercial educational activities. [Author's note: The previous sentence mitigates somewhat the harshness of the preceding sentence, but does not allow the transfer of all ephemeral recordings, only those that are recorded as part of a teaching session, in essence a §112(b) recording, but *not* the digitized content files made under §112(f) or similar license provision. Of course, the sentence could be modified to include that right as well.]

General Requirements

Instructors, guest lecturers, or students may perform or display copyrighted material in a distance education class session, but in the case of guest lecturers and students, the performance or display must be at the direction of or under the actual supervision of an instructor, and direction or supervision must not be in name only.

The performance or display of copyrighted material must be an integral part of a class session and part of systematic mediated instructional activities. The performance or display must be part of actual instruction, not ancillary to it.

The performance or display must be directly related and of material assistance to the teaching content of the transmission. The performance or display must be relevant to actual instruction, not for purposes of entertainment or as unrelated background material or of a general cultural nature.

The transmission of the distance education teaching session is made solely for students officially enrolled in the course.

To the extent technologically feasible, receipt of the transmission of the distance education teaching session is limited to students officially enrolled in the course.

Compliance Requirements

[Name of institution] shall adopt and implement a *Use of Copyrighted Material in the Distance Education Classroom* Policy. The following person or persons are responsible for enforcement and periodic review of the *Use of Copyrighted Material in the Distance Education Classroom* Policy: [list appropriate institutional committee, administrator, etc. and approval process as needed].

[Name of institution] shall develop and distribute informational materials to faculty, students, and relevant staff members, including administrators, that accurately describe, and promote compliance with, the copyright laws of the United States. The following person or persons are responsible for the creation, dissemination, and periodic review of all informational materials made available to faculty, students, and relevant staff members, including administrators, that accurately describe, and promote compliance with, the copyright laws of the United States: [list appropriate institutional committee, administrator, etc. and approval process as needed].

All course syllabi and all distance education course websites of [name of institution] shall provide notice to students that materials used in connection with the course may be subject to copyright protection. The following notice shall appear on the first page of all syllabi and on the home page of a distance education course website:

[Optional Notice No. 1 (long version)] NOTICE: All materials that under United States Copyright law would be considered the normal work product of the instructor, pursuant to the class or lecture note exception to the work-for-hire doctrine, are under the sole ownership of the instructor. This work product includes but is not limited to outlines, exercises, and discussion questions. See *Hays v. Sony Corp of America*, 847 F.2d 412 (7th Cir. 1988); and *Weinstein v. University of Illinois*, 811 F. 2d 1091 (7th Cir. 1987). Regarding websites, the instructor, the university, and the website designer share the copyright in the "look and feel" of the site. The underlying software that generates the website is also protected by copyright. Documents and other material appearing on the website or by link from the site may also be protected by copyright.

This site is maintained for educational purposes only. Your viewing of the material posted here does not imply any right to reproduce, to distribute, or to redisplay it other than for your own personal or educational noncommercial use. Links to other sites are provided for the convenience of the site user (staff or student) or visitor and do not imply any affiliation or endorsement of the other site owner or a guarantee of the quality or veracity of information contained on the linked site, nor should links be viewed as any form of implied license to use material found on the linked site in excess of fair use. As a student, your ability to post or link to copyrighted material is also governed by United States Copyright law. This instructor and/or other staff of the institution reserve the right to delete or disable your post or link, or to deny access to any material if, in their judgment, the post or link would involve violation of copyright law. In addition, repeat instances requiring the institution to delete content or disable access may result in the denial of access to the institution's distance education networks or other information communication technologies.

[Optional Notice No. 2 (short version)] Copyright Notice. All materials used in connection with this course may be protected by copyright law.

Compliance Requirements for Digital Transmissions

When a distance education class session involves the performance or display of digital content, administrators and instructional and support staff shall apply technological measures that reasonably prevent (1) the retention of the work in accessible form by recipients of the transmission for longer than the class session, and (2) unauthorized further dissemination of the work in accessible form by such recipients to others.

The following technological measures will fulfill the obligations of this provision:

- Real Player "Secret Handshake/Copy Switch" technology discussed in *Real Networks v. Streambox, Inc.*, 2000 WL 127311, 2000 U.S. Dist. LEXIS 1889 (W.D. Wash. 2000).

- Digital rights management systems that limit access to or use encrypted material downloaded onto a computer [such as (provide example or mechanism if appropriate)].
- [list other technological measures as appropriate].

When a distance education class session involves the performance or display of digital content, administrators and instructional and support staff shall not engage in any conduct that could reasonably be expected to interfere with technological measures used by copyright owners to prevent such retention or unauthorized further dissemination, even if that conduct does not actually result in interference with technological measures used by copyright owners to prevent such retention or unauthorized further dissemination.

Portion Limitations

As long as the other provisions of this Policy are met, the performance of a nondramatic literary or nondramatic musical may be made without limit. This would include reading an entire short story or singing an entire song.

The performance of any other work is limited to a reasonable and limited portion of the work. In determining what is a reasonable and limited portion, consider the pedagogical purposes for the performance and the market for that type of copyrighted work. The following questions may be of assistance in making this determination:

- How much of the work is needed in order for the performance to achieve acceptable pedagogical goals or standards?
- Is the market for that type of copyrighted work particularly sensitive to lost performance revenue?

All displays of copyrighted material are limited to an amount comparable to that typically displayed in the course of a live classroom session. This amount will vary from display to display. The significant question is whether the instructor is displaying a greater portion than is necessary or would be displayed in a face-to-face teaching session merely because it is easier to display a greater portion of the work in a distance education teaching session. This may be particularly the case with displays of works in digital form.

Material Not Governed by the *Use of Copyrighted Material in the Distance Education Classroom* Policy

All uses not governed by this policy may nonetheless be authorized by specific permission obtained from the copyright owner, by general license agreement with the publisher or authorized distributor of the copyrighted content, or by a general concept of fair use. See [institution's policy on obtaining permission from copyright owners, policy on licensing, policy on fair use].

The following are not part of the distance education teaching session:

- Curricular materials produced or marketed by third parties primarily for performance or display in the distance education classroom, i.e., as part of mediated instructional activities. These curricular materials may be obtained by license. See [institution's policy on licensing].
- Copyrighted material that administrators and instructional and support staff know or have reason to know consists of a copy or phonorecord not lawfully made or acquired under the copyright law.
- Copyrighted material that is supplemental to the distance education teaching activity such as textbooks and workbooks, course readings, etc. This includes material that is not an integral part of the class experience, controlled by or under the actual supervision of the instructor, and analogous to the type of performance or display that would take place in a live classroom setting. Instructional and support staff and students should access such material through the institution's e-bookstore or e-library or e-reserve, and not through the distance education course website. See [institution's policy on textbook provision, course packs, e-reserves].

Reproduction in Preparation for a Distance Education Teaching Session

In order to facilitate a performance or display of copyrighted material by instructors or students authorized under this policy, it may be desirable to have ready access to such materials in digital form. In order to facilitate that ready access, it may be necessary to make a copy or phonorecord of the copyrighted material so it may be loaded on servers, computers, etc. At times more than one copy or phonorecord may be necessary. This section authorizes the making of those copies or phonorecords, known in the copyright law as "ephemeral recordings."

General Requirements

All copies or phonorecords must be retained and used solely by instructional and support staff of [name of institution].

All copies or phonorecords must be used solely for performances or displays authorized under this policy.

No further copies or phonorecords may be reproduced from the "ephemeral" copies or phonorecords, except for the transient or temporary storage of material carried out through the automatic technical process of a digital distance education teaching session, provided that access to material stored on any system or network controlled or operated by [name of institution] shall be limited to students officially enrolled in the course and for a period no longer than is reasonably necessary to facilitate the transmission of the distance education teaching session.

Permissible Copies or Phonorecords

Copies or phonorecords can be made of a work in digital form.

Digital copies or phonorecords (conversion) of a work in analog form can be made, if no more of the work is recorded than can be performed or displayed under this policy (see Portion Limitations, above) and one of the two following circumstances exist: (1) no digital version of the work is available to [name of institution], or (2) the digital version of the work that is available to the institution is subject to technological protection measures that prevent its use under this policy.

[optional provision] A digital work is considered available to [name of institution] when it can be purchased, licensed, rented, etc. in the general consumer or educational marketplace.

This provision does not authorize the making of an analog copy or phonorecord of a work that is in analog form.

Reproduction of the Distance Education Teaching Session

A distance education teaching session incorporating a performance or display authorized under this policy may be recorded in either analog or digital form. The recording known in the copyright law as an "ephemeral recording" may include the performance or display of copyrighted material authorized under this policy.

Permissible Copies or Phonorecords and Uses

Up to thirty copies or phonorecords of the ephemeral recording may be made.

A copy or phonorecord of the ephemeral recording may be transferred to one or more qualifying institution(s) for use in its distance education teaching, i.e., as a rebroadcast of the ephemeral recording.

One copy or phonorecord of the ephemeral recording may be preserved exclusively for archival purposes.

Impermissible Copies or Phonorecords and Uses

No further copies or phonorecords of the ephemeral recording may be reproduced from the copies or phonorecords.

All other copies or phonorecords of the ephemeral recording(s) must be destroyed within seven years from the date the performance or display was first made to students in a distance education teaching session, except as above.

Appendix C

Copyright Statute Sections (Selected)

Selected Sections of the U.S. Copyright Law, Title 17, United States Code

Section 101: Definitions.
Section 106: Exclusive rights in copyrighted works.
Section 107: Limitations on exclusive rights: Fair use.
Section 110(1) and (2): Limitations on exclusive rights: Exemption of certain performances and displays.
Section 112(b) and (f): Limitations on exclusive rights: Ephemeral recordings.
Section 201(a), (b), and (d): Ownership of copyright.
Section 204: Execution of transfers of copyright ownership.

Section 101: Definitions (Selected Provisions)

Except as otherwise provided in this title, as used in this title, the following terms and their variant forms mean the following:

"Audiovisual works" are works that consist of a series of related images which are intrinsically intended to be shown by the use of machines or devices such as projectors, viewers, or electronic equipment, together with accompanying sounds, if any, regardless of the nature of the material objects, such as films or tapes, in which the works are embodied.

A "derivative work" is a work based upon one or more preexisting works, such as a translation, musical arrangement, dramatization, fictionalization, motion picture version, sound recording, art reproduction, abridgment, condensation, or any other form in which a work may be recast, transformed, or adapted. A work consisting of editorial revisions, annotations, elaborations, or other modifications which, as a whole, represent an original work of authorship, is a "derivative work."

A "digital transmission" is a transmission in whole or in part in a digital or other non-analog format.

To "display" a work means to show a copy of it, either directly or by means of a film, slide, television image, or any other device or process or, in the case of a motion picture or other audiovisual work, to show individual images nonsequentially.

The term "financial gain" includes receipt, or expectation of receipt, of anything of value, including the receipt of other copyrighted works.

"Literary works" are works, other than audiovisual works, expressed in words, numbers, or other verbal or numerical symbols or indicia, regardless of the nature of the material objects, such as books, periodicals, manuscripts, phonorecords, film, tapes, disks, or cards, in which they are embodied.

"Motion pictures" are audiovisual works consisting of a series of related images which, when shown in succession, impart an impression of motion, together with accompanying sounds, if any.

To "perform" a work means to recite, render, play, dance, or act it, either directly or by means of any device or process or, in the case of a motion picture or other audiovisual work, to show its images in any sequence or to make the sounds accompanying it audible.

"Phonorecords" are material objects in which sounds, other than those accompanying a motion picture or other audiovisual work, are fixed by any method now known or later developed, and from which the sounds can be perceived, reproduced, or otherwise communicated, either directly or with the aid of a machine or device. The term "phonorecords" includes the material object in which the sounds are first fixed.

"Pictorial, graphic, and sculptural works" include two-dimensional and three-dimensional works of fine, graphic, and applied art, photographs, prints and art reproductions, maps, globes, charts, diagrams, models, and technical drawings, including architectural plans. Such works shall include works of artistic craftsmanship insofar as their form but not their mechanical or utilitarian aspects are concerned; the design of a useful article, as defined in this section, shall be considered a pictorial, graphic, or sculptural work only if, and only to the extent that, such design incorporates pictorial, graphic, or sculptural features that can be identified separately from, and are capable of existing independently of, the utilitarian aspects of the article.

"Publication" is the distribution of copies or phonorecords of a work to the public by sale or other transfer of ownership, or by rental, lease, or lending. The offering to distribute copies or phonorecords to a group of persons for purposes of further distribution, public performance, or public display, constitutes publication. A public performance or display of a work does not of itself constitute publication.

To perform or display a work "publicly" means (1) to perform or display it at a place open to the public or at any place where a substantial number of persons outside of a normal circle of a family and its social acquaintances is gathered; or (2) to transmit or otherwise communicate a performance or display of the work to a place specified by clause (1) or to the public, by means of any device or process, whether the members of the public capable of receiving the performance or display receive it in the same place or in separate places and at the same time or at different times.

"Sound recordings" are works that result from the fixation of a series of musical, spoken, or other sounds, but not including the sounds accompanying a motion picture or other audiovisual work, regardless of the nature of the material objects, such as disks, tapes, or other phonorecords, in which they are embodied.

To "transmit" a performance or display is to communicate it by any device or process whereby images or sounds are received beyond the place from which they are sent.

A "work made for hire" is (1) a work prepared by an employee within the scope of his or her employment; or (2) a work specially ordered or commissioned for use as a contribution to a collective work, as a part of a motion picture or other audiovisual work, as a translation, as a supplementary work, as a compilation, as an instructional text, as a test, as answer material for a test, or as an atlas, if the parties expressly agree in a written instrument signed by them that the work shall be considered a work made for hire. For the purpose of the foregoing sentence, a "supplementary work" is a work prepared for publication as a secondary adjunct to a work by another author for the purpose of introducing, concluding, illustrating, explaining, revising, commenting upon, or assisting in the use of the other work, such as forewords, afterwords, pictorial illustrations, maps, charts, tables, editorial notes, musical arrangements, answer material for tests, bibliographies, appendixes, and indexes, and an "instructional text" is a literary, pictorial, or graphic work prepared for publication and with the purpose of use in systematic instructional activities. . . .

Section 106: Exclusive Rights in Copyrighted Works

Subject to sections 107 through 121, the owner of a copyright under this title has the exclusive rights to do and to authorize any of the following: (1) to reproduce the copyrighted work in copies or phonorecords; (2) to prepare derivative works based upon the copyrighted work; (3) to distribute copies or phonorecords of the copyrighted work to the public by sale or other transfer of ownership, or by rental, lease, or lending; (4) in the case of literary, musical, dramatic, and choreographic works, pantomimes, and motion pictures and other audiovisual works, to perform the copyrighted work publicly; (5) in the case of literary, musical, dramatic, and choreographic works, pantomimes, and pictorial, graphic, or sculptural works, including the individual images of a motion picture or other audiovisual work, to display the copyrighted work publicly; and (6) in the case of sound recordings, to perform the copyrighted work publicly by means of a digital audio transmission.

Section 107: Limitations on Exclusive Rights: Fair Use

Notwithstanding the provisions of sections 106 and 106A, the fair use of a copyrighted work, including such use by reproduction in copies or phonorecords or by any other means specified by that section, for purposes such as criticism, comment, news reporting, teaching (including multiple copies for classroom use), scholarship, or research, is not an infringement of copyright. In determining whether the use made of a work in any particular case is a fair use the factors to be considered shall include (1) the purpose and character of the use, including whether such use is of a commercial nature or is for nonprofit educational purposes; (2) the nature of the copyrighted work; (3) the amount and substantiality of the portion used in relation to the copyrighted work as a whole; and (4) the effect of the use upon the potential market for or value of the copyrighted work.

The fact that a work is unpublished shall not itself bar a finding of fair use if such finding is made upon consideration of all the above factors.

Section 110(1) and (2) and definitions: Limitations on Exclusive rights: Exemption of Certain Performances and Displays

Notwithstanding the provisions of section 106, the following are not infringements of copyright:

(1) performance or display of a work by instructors or pupils in the course of face-to-face teaching activities of a nonprofit educational institution, in a classroom or similar place devoted to instruction, unless, in the case of a motion picture or other audiovisual work, the performance, or the display of individual images, is given by means of a copy that was not lawfully made under this title, and that the person responsible for the performance knew or had reason to believe was not lawfully made;

(2) except with respect to a work produced or marketed primarily for performance or display as part of mediated instructional activities transmitted via digital networks, or a performance or display that is given by means of a copy or phonorecord that is not lawfully made and acquired under this title, and the transmitting government body or accredited nonprofit educational institution knew or had reason to believe was not lawfully made and acquired, the performance of a nondramatic literary or musical work or reasonable and limited portions of any other work, or display of a work in an amount comparable to that which is typically displayed in the course of a live classroom session, by or in the course of a transmission, if

(A) the performance or display is made by, at the direction of, or under the actual supervision of an instructor as an integral part of a class session offered as a regular part of the systematic mediated instructional activities of a governmental body or an accredited nonprofit educational institution;

(B) the performance or display is directly related and of material assistance to the teaching content of the transmission;

(C) the transmission is made solely for, and, to the extent technologically feasible, the reception of such transmission is limited to (i) students officially enrolled in the course for which the transmission is made; or (ii) officers or employees of governmental bodies as a part of their official duties or employment; and

(D) the transmitting body or institution (i) institutes policies regarding copyright, provides informational materials to faculty, students, and relevant staff members that accurately describe, and promote compliance with, the laws of the United States relating to copyright, and provides notice to students that materials used in connection with the course may be subject to copyright protection; and (ii) in the case of digital transmissions (I) applies technological measures that reasonably prevent (aa) retention of the work in accessible form by recipients of the transmission from the transmitting body or institution for longer than the class session; and (bb) unauthorized further dissemination of the work in accessible form by such recipients to others; and (II) does not engage in conduct that could reasonably be expected to interfere with technological measures used by copyright owners to prevent such retention or unauthorized further dissemination.

In paragraph (2), the term "mediated instructional activities" with respect to the performance or display of a work by digital transmission under this section refers to activities that use such work as an integral part of the class experience, controlled by or under the actual supervision of the instructor and analogous to the type of performance or display that would take place in a live classroom setting. The term does not refer to activities that use, in one or more class sessions of a single course, such works as textbooks, course packs, or other material in any media, copies or phonorecords of which are typically purchased or acquired by the students in higher education for their independent use and retention or are typically purchased or acquired for elementary and secondary students for their possession and independent use.

For purposes of paragraph (2), accreditation (A) with respect to an institution providing post-secondary education, shall be as determined by a regional or national accrediting agency recognized by the Council on Higher Education Accreditation or the United States Department of Education; and (B) with respect to an institution providing elementary or secondary education, shall be as recognized by the applicable state certification or licensing procedures.

For purposes of paragraph (2), no governmental body or accredited nonprofit educational institution shall be liable for infringement by reason of the transient or temporary storage of material carried out through the automatic technical process of a digital transmission of the performance or display of that material as authorized under paragraph (2). No such material stored on the system or network controlled or operated by the transmitting body or institution under this paragraph shall be maintained on such system or network in a manner ordinarily accessible to anyone other than anticipated recipients. No such copy shall be maintained on the system or network in a manner ordinarily accessible to such anticipated recipients for a longer period than is reasonably necessary to facilitate the transmissions for which it was made.

Section 112(b) and (f): Limitations on Exclusive Rights: Ephemeral Recordings

(b) Notwithstanding the provisions of section 106, it is not an infringement of copyright for a governmental body or other nonprofit organization entitled to transmit a performance or display of a work, under section 110(2) or under the limitations on exclusive rights in sound recordings specified by section 114(a), to make no more than thirty copies or phonorecords of a particular transmission program embodying the performance or display, if (1) no further copies or phonorecords are reproduced from the copies or phonorecords made under this clause; and (2) except for one copy or phonorecord that may be preserved exclusively for archival purposes, the copies or phonorecords are destroyed within seven years from the date the transmission program was first transmitted to the public.

(f)(1) Notwithstanding the provisions of section 106, and without limiting the application of subsection (b), it is not an infringement of copyright for a governmental body or other nonprofit educational institution entitled under section 110(2) to transmit a performance or display to make copies or phonorecords of a work that is in digital form and, solely to the extent permitted in paragraph (2), of a work that is in analog form, embodying the performance or display to be used for making transmissions authorized under section 110(2), if (A) such copies or phonorecords are retained and used solely by the body or institution that made them, and no further copies or phonorecords are reproduced from them, except as authorized under section 110(2); and (B) such copies or phonorecords are used solely for transmissions authorized under section 110(2).

(2) This subsection does not authorize the conversion of print or other analog versions of works into digital formats, except that such conversion is permitted hereunder, only with respect to the amount of such works authorized to be performed or displayed under section 110(2), if (A) no digital version of the work is available to the institution; or (B) the digital version if the work that is available to the institution is subject to technological protection measures that prevent its use for section 110(2).

Section 201(a), (b), and (d): Ownership of Copyright

(a) Initial ownership. Copyright in a work protected under this title vests initially in the author or authors of the work. The authors of a joint work are co-owners of copyright in the work.

(b) Works made for hire. In the case of a work made for hire, the employer or other person for whom the work was prepared is considered the author for purposes of this title, and, unless the parties have expressly agreed otherwise in a written instrument signed by them, owns all of the rights comprised in the copyright.

(d) Transfer of ownership. (1) The ownership of a copyright may be transferred in whole or in part by any means of conveyance or by operation of law, and may be bequeathed by will or pass as personal property by the applicable laws of intestate succession. (2) Any of the exclusive rights comprised in a copyright, including any subdivision of any of the rights specified by section 106, may be transferred as provided by clause (1) and owned separately. The owner of any particular exclusive right is entitled, to the extent of that right, to all of the protection and remedies accorded to the copyright owner by this title.

Section 204: Execution of Transfers of Copyright Ownership

(a) A transfer of copyright ownership, other than by operation of law, is not valid unless an instrument of conveyance, or a note or memorandum of the transfer, is in writing and signed by the owner of the rights conveyed or such owner's duly authorized agent.

(b) A certificate of acknowledgement is not required for the validity of a transfer, but is prima facie evidence of the execution of the transfer if— (1) in the case of a transfer executed in the United States, the certificate is issued by a person authorized to administer oaths within the United States; or (2) in the case of a transfer executed in a foreign country, the certificate is issued by a diplomatic or consular officer of the United States, or by a person authorized to administer oaths whose authority is proved by a certificate of such an officer.

Selected Bibliography

General Copyright Law

Bielefield, Arlene, and Lawrence Cheeseman. *Technology and Copyright Law: A Guidebook for the Library, Research, and Teaching Professions.* New York: Neal-Schuman, 1997.

Crews, Kenneth D. *Copyright Essentials for Librarians and Educators.* Chicago: American Library Association, 2000.

Howie, Margaret-Ann F. *Copyright Issues in Schools: Learn How to Protect Yourself and Your School from Violating Copyright Law.* Horsham, Pa.: LRP Publications, 1997.

McCord Hoffman, Gretchen. *Copyright Issues in Cyberspace: Questions and Answers for Librarians.* New York: Neal-Schuman, 2001.

Simpson, Carol. *Copyright for Schools: A Practical Guide.* 3rd ed. Worthington, Ohio: Linworth, 2001.

Fair Use in Education

Besej, June M. Copyright: What Makes a Use "Fair"? *Educause Review,* November/December 2003, at 12.

Crews, Kenneth D. The Law of Fair Use and the Illusion of Fair-Use Guidelines. 62 *Ohio State Law Journal* 599 (2001).

———. Copyright and Fair-Use Guidelines for Education and Libraries. *Journal of the American Society for Information Science* 1304 (1999).

Thornburg, Robert. The Impact of Copyright Law on Distance Education Programs: How Fair Use and the CONFU Guidelines May Shape the Future of Academia. 27 *Southern Illinois University Law Journal* 321 (2003).

Ownership Issues: Faculty

Borow, Todd A. Copyright Ownership of Scholarly Works Created by University Faculty and Posted on School-Provided Web Pages. 7 *University of Miami Business Law Review* 149 (1998).

Daniel, Philip T. K., and Patrick D. Pauken. The Impact of the Electronic Media on Instructor Creativity and Institutional Ownership within Copyright Law. 132 *Education Law Reporter* [1] (April 1, 1999).

Holmes, Georgia, and Daniel A. Levin. Who Owns Course Materials Prepared by a Teacher or Professor? The Application of Copyright Law to Teaching Materials in the Internet Age, 2000. *Brigham Young University Education and Law Journal* 165 (2000).

Kulkarni, Sunil R. All Professors Create Equally: Why Faculty Should Have Complete Control over the Intellectual Property Rights in Their Creations. 47 *Hastings Law Journal* 221 (1995).

Kwall, Roberta Rosenthal. Copyright Issues in Online Courses: Ownership, Authorship and Conflict, 18 *Santa Clara Computer & High Technology Law Journal* 1 (2001).

Laughlin, Gregory Kent. Who Owns the Copyright to Faculty-Created Web Sites?: The Work-for-Hire Doctrine's Applicability to Internet Resources Created for Distance Learning and Traditional Classroom Courses, 41 *Boston College Law Review* 549 (2000).

Le Moal-Gray, Michele J. Distance Education and Intellectual Property: The Realities of Copyright Law and the Culture of Higher Education. 16 *Touro Law Review* 981 (2000).

Packard, Ashley. Copyright or Copy Wrong: An Analysis of University Claims to Faculty Work. 7 *Communications Law & Policy* 275 (2002).

Pate, Sandip H. Graduate Students' Ownership and Attribution Rights in Intellectual Property. 71 *Indiana Law Journal* 481 (1996).

Seele, Stephanie L. Are Classroom Lectures Protected by Copyright Laws? The Case for Professors' Intellectual Property Rights. 51 *Syracuse Law Review* 163 (2001).

Townsend, Elizabeth. Legal and Policy Responses to the Disappearing 'Teacher Exception,' or Copyright Ownership in the 21st Century University. 4 *Minnesota Intellectual Property Review* 209 (2003).

Wadley, James B., and JoLynn M. Brown. Working between the Lines of *Ried*: Teachers, Copyrights, Work-for-Hire and a New Washburn University Policy. 38 *Washburn Law Journal* 385 (1999).

Distance Education: Pre-TEACH

Crews, Kenneth D. Distance Education and Copyright Law: The Limits and Meaning of Copyright Policy. 27 *Journal of College and University Law* 15 (2000).

Douvanis, Gus. Copyright Law and Distance Learning Technology: Fair Use in Far Classrooms. *International Journal for Instructional Media* 299 (1997).

Gasaway, Laura N. Distance Learning and Copyright. 62 *Ohio State Law Journal* 783 (2001).

Lipinski, Tomas A. An Argument for the Application of Copyright Law to Distance Education. *American Journal of Distance Education* 3, at 7 (1999).

Distance Education: Post-TEACH

Crews, Kenneth D. Copyright and Distance Education: Making Sense of the TEACH Act. *Change,* November/December 2003, at 34.

Lipinski, Tomas A. The Climate of Distance Education in the 21st Century: Understanding and Surviving the Changes Brought by the TEACH (Technology, Education, and Copyright Harmonization) Act of 2002, 29 *Journal of Academic Librarianship* 362 (2003).

———. Legal Reform in an Electronic Age: Analysis and Critique of the Construction and Operation of S. 487, the Technology, Education and Copyright Harmonization (TEACH) Act of 2001. 2003 *Brigham Young University Education and Law Journal* 95 (2003).

Licensing

Alford, Duncan E. Negotiating and Analyzing Electronic License Agreements. 94 *Law Library Journal* 621 (2002).

Bielefield, Arlene, and Lawrence Cheeseman. *Interpreting and Negotiating License Agreements: A Guidebook for the Library, Research and Teaching Professionals* (1999). New York: Neal-Schuman.

Harris, Lesley Ellen. *Licensing Digital Content: A Practical Guide for Librarians* (2002). Chicago: American Library Association.

Pike, George H. The Delicate Dance of Database Licenses, Copyright, and Fair Use. *Computers in Libraries,* May 2002, at 12.

Webb, John P. Managing Licensed Networked Electronic Resources in a University Library. *Information Technology and Libraries,* December 1998, at 198.

Case Index

321 Studios v. Metro Goldwyn Mayer Studios, Inc., 307 F. Supp. 2d 1085 (N.D. Cal. 2004), 107n29, 186n90

A&M Records, Inc. v. Napster, Inc., 239 F. 3d 1004 (9th Cir. 2001), 146n3, 156–58, 166, 175, 181n6, 181n11, 184n60, 184n61, 184n62, 188n99
Addison-Wesley Publishing v. New York University, Copyright L. Rptr. (CCH) 25,544 (S.D.N.Y. 1983), 184n46, 185n67
American Geophysical Union v. Texaco, Inc., 60 F.3d 913 (2nd Cir. 1993), 161, 165–66, 181n19, 182n30, 184n48, 184n56, 184n57
Assessment Technologies of WI, LLC. v. Wiredata, Inc., 350 F.3d 640 (7th Cir. 2003), 25n2, 161, 182n26, 182n28, 182n29
Atari Games Corp. v. Nintendo of America, Inc., 975 F.2d 832 (Fed Cir. 1992), 182n26
Avtec Systems, Inc. v. Pfeiffer, 805 F. Supp. 1312 (E.D. Va. 1992), aff'd in part, rev'd in part and remanded, 21 F.3d 568 (4th Cir. 1994), 28n26

Basic Books, Inc. v. Gnomon Corp., Copyright L. Rptr. (CCH) ¶ 25,145 (D. Conn. 1981), 184n46, 185n66
Basic Books, Inc. v. Kinko's Graphics Corp., 758 F. Supp. 1522 (S.D.N.Y. 1983); 162, 182n32, 184n46, 184n54, 185n66
Bridge Publications, Inc. v. Vien, 827 F. Supp. 629, 636 (S.D. Cal. 1993), 186n77
Bridgeport Music, Inc. v. Dimension Films, __ F.3d __, 2004 WL 1960167 (6th Cir. 2004), 186n81

Campbell v. Acuff-Rose Music, Inc., 510 U.S. 569 (1994), 147n11, 157, 160, 165, 170, 180n2, 180n3, 181n10, 181n16, 181n17, 181n22, 184n51, 184n52, 184n53
Chicago School Reform Board of Trustees v. Substance, Inc., 354 F.3d 624 (7th Cir. 2003), 171, 180n4, 184n59, 184n63, 186n79

Community for Creative Nonviolence v. Reid, 490 U.S. 730 (1989), 10, 27n21

Dastar Corporation v. Twentieth Century Fox Film Corporation, 539 U.S. 23, 123 S. Ct. 2041 (2003), 187n92, 188n93

Educational Testing Service v. Katzman, 793 F.2d 533 (3rd Cir. 1986), 171, 186n80

Encyclopedia Britannica Educational Corp. v. Crooks, 447 F. Supp. 243 (W.D.N.Y. 1978), 171, 186n78

Estate of Martin Luther King Jr. v. CBS, Inc., 194 F.3d 1121 (11th 1999), 182n39

Foraste v. Brown University, 290 F. Sup. 2d 234 (D.R.I 2003), 11, 15–16, 28n31, 29n37, 30n49, 30n50, 30n51

Getaped.com v. Cangemi, 188 F.Supp.2d 398 (S.D.N.Y. 2002), 163, 182n37

Harper & Row Publishers, Inc. v. Nation Enterprises, 471 U.S. 539 (1985), 164, 182n39, 184n50

Harper & Row Publishers, Inc. v. Tyco Copy Service, Copyright L. Rptr. (CCH) ¶ 25,230 (D. Conn. 1981), 184n46, 185n66

Hays v. Sony Corporation of America, 847 F.2d 412(7th Cir, 1988), 14, 28n29, 29n37, 30n46, 92, 204

Higgins v. Detroit Educational Television Foundation, 4 F. Supp. 2d 701, 704 (footnote omitted), 705 (E.D. Mich. 1998), 159, 166, 181n15, 185n64, 185n65

Hotaling v. Church of Latter Day Saints, 118 F.3d 199 (4th Cir. 1997), 177, 186n75, 188n100, 188n101

Hustler Magazine, Inc. v. Moral Majority, Inc., 796 F.2d 1148, 1155 (9th Cir. 1986), 183n42

In Re Aimster Copyright Litigation, 334 F.3d 643 (7th Cir. 2003), 146n5, 152n55, 164, 183n45

In re Simplified Information Systems, Inc., 89 Bankr. 538 (W.D. Pa. 1988), 28n26

Intellectual Reserve, Inc. v. Utah Lighthouse Ministry, Inc., 75 F. Supp. 2d 1290 (Dist. Utah 1999), 108n36

Kelly v. Arriba Soft Corp., 77 F. Supp. 2d 1116 (C.D. Calif. 1999), aff'd 280 F.3d 934 (9th Cir. 2002), 159, 162, 181n7, 181n11, 181n12, 181n13, 181n14, 182n36, 184n49

Lexmark International, Inc. v. Static ControlComponents, Inc., 253 F. Supp. 2d 943 (E.D. Ky. 2003), 50n21

Los Angeles Times v. Free Republic, 2000 U.S. Dist. LEXIS 5669 (C.D. Cal. 2000), 160, 162, 181n20, 181n21, 182n33, 184n47

Marcus v. Rowley, 695 F.2d 1171 (9th Cir. 1983), 171, 186n76, 186n77

Marshall v. Miles Laboratory, Inc., 647 F.Supp. 1326 (N.D. Ind. 1986), 27n23, 28n25, 28n26

Maxtone-Graham v. Burtchaell, 803 F.2d 1253 (2nd Cir. 1986), 162, 175, 182n34, 182n35, 188n94, 188n97

Metro-Goldwyn Studios, Inc. v Grokster, Ltd., 259 F. Supp. 2d 1029 (C.D. Calif. 2003), aff'd __ F.3d __, 2004 WL 1853717 (9th Cir. 2004), 146n4

New York Times Co., Inc. vs. Tasini, 533 U.S. 483 (2001), 30n47

Nunez v. Caribbean International News Corp., 235 F.3d 18, 24 (1st Cir. 2000), 163, 175, 183n43, 184n49, 188n95

Princeton University Press v. Michigan Document Services, 99 F. 3d 1381 (6th

Cir. 1996), 162, 167, 181n18, 182n31, 184n46, 184n55, 185n66

Real Networks, Inc. v. Streambox, Inc., 2000 U.S. Dist. LEXIS 1889 (W.D. Wash. 2000), 49n19, 50n27, 95, 107n29, 196, 204

RIAA v. Diamond Multimedia Systems, 180 F.3d 1072 (9th Cir. 1999), 186n72

Ringgold v. Black Entertainment Television, Inc., 126 F.3d 79 (2d Cir. 1997), 159

Salinger v. Random House, Inc., 881 F.2d 90 (2nd Cir.), cert. denied 493 U.S. 1094 (1987), 182n39

Sega Enterprises Ltd. v. Accolade, Inc., 977 F.2d 1510 (9th Cir. 1992), 182n26

Sherrill v. Grieves, 57 Wash. L. Rep. 286 (D.C. 1929), 28n27

Sony Computer Entertainment v. Connectix Corp., 203 F.3d 596 (9th Cir. 200), 25n3

Sony Computer Entertainment America, Inc. v. Gamemasters, Inc., 87 F. Supp. 2d 976 (N.D. Cal. 1999), 50n20

Sony Corp. of America, Inc. v. Universal City Studios, 363 U.S. 417 (1984), 158, 164, 181n8, 183n45, 184n58

Ticketmaster, Corp. v. Tickets.com, 2000 U.S. Dist. LEXIS 12987 (C.D. Calif. 2000), 25n3, 182n27

UMG Recordings v. MP3.com, Inc., 92 F. Supp. 2d 349 (S.D.N.Y. 2000), 146n2, 175, 181n7, 181n9, 188n98

Universal City Studios, Inc. v. Corley, 273 F.3d 429 (2d Cir. 2001), 49n18, 50n25, 107n29, 152n53, 152n54, 153n57, 176, 186n82, 187n84

Universal City Studios, Inc. v. Reimerdes, 82 F. Supp. 2d 211 (S.D.N.Y. 2000), 107n29

University of Colorado v. American Cyanamid, 880 F. Supp. 1387 (D. Colo 1995), 11, 28n29, 29n34

United States v. Elcom Ltd., 203 F.Supp. 2d 1111 (N.D. Cal. 2002), 51n31, 107n29, 152n54, 153n55, 172, 173, 176, 186n72, 187n88, 187n89

Vanderhurst v. Colorado Mountain College District, 16 F. Supp. 2d 1297 (D. Colo. 1998), 11, 28n29, 29n36

Video Pipeline, Inc. v. Buena Vista Home Entertainment, Inc., 342 F.3d 191 (3d Cir. 2003), 187n91

Weinstein v. University of Illinois, 881 F.2d 1091 (7th Cir. 1987), 13, 28n29, 29n37, 30n44, 30n45, 92, 204

Williams v. Weisser, 273 Cal. App. 2d 726, 78 Cal. Rptr. 542, 544 (1969), 29n40

Williams & Wilkins Co. v. United States, 172 U.S.P.Q. 670 (Ct. Cl. 1972), rev'd 487 F.2d 1345 (ct. Cl. 1973), aff'd 420 U.S. 376 (1975), 186n74

Worldwide Church of God v. Philadelphia Church of God, 227 F.3d 1110, 1118 (9th Cir. 2000), 163, 183n42

Subject Index

anti-circumvention and anti-trafficking rules, 43–45. *See also* fair use, defense to anti-circumvention and anti-trafficking
audiovisual works, 22, 43–47, 59–60, 123–25, 137, 171–80; defined, 5

derivative work, defined, 26n5
Digital Performance Right in Sound Recordings Act, 66, 68–73; exemptions for qualifying transmissions, 68–72
display, 20, 61–64; amount allowed in distance education, 61–64; defined, 19, 26n7; §109(c) right, 20–22;
distance education teaching (§110(2)): accreditation requirement, 77–78; compliance audit, Q&A, 189–200; compliance requirements (policies, informational material, notices), 89–93; digital transmissions and technological protection measures, 93–99; interference with technological protection measures prohibited, 99–103; lawfully made requirement, 43, 46–48; material

excluded from, 38–44, 78–79; pre-TEACH law, 22–25; teaching activity defined, 73–77; transient copies or phonorecords permitted, 103–4; transmission and reception made solely for enrolled students requirement, 79–84. *See also* ephemeral recordings; fair use, distance education classroom
DPRSRA. *See* Digital Performance Right in Sound Recordings Act

ephemeral recording, 116–17; comparison of §112(b) and §112(f), 125–27; digitalization of analog works, 132–36; exclusive rights of copyright owner, 4, 35; fair use or other rights and relationship to, 136–38; format and portion limitations, 126–27; meaning of available to the institution discussed, 138–42; nature of the recording, 122–24; portion limitations under §112(f), 128–30; post-session, pre-TEACH §112(b), 117–22, 134–35, 142–45; pre-session, TEACH §112(f),

131–32, 134–38; sound recordings,
64–66

face-to-face teaching (§110(1)), 16–20;
lawfully made requirement, 19–20;
transmission contrasted, 19
fair use, 155–56; amount and portion
factor, 163–65; copy shop cases,
168–70; defense to anti-
circumvention and anti-trafficking,
171–73; distance education
classroom, 173–80; educational
entities, 170–71; 173–80; effect on
market factor, 165–67
four factor test, 156–67; libraries,
169–71; nature of work factor,
161–63; purpose and character of use
factor, 156–60;

independent contractor, 9
informational materials regarding
copyright, 90–91
interference with technological
protection measures, 99–102

literary work, defined, 9

Mediated Instructional Activities, 36–42;
defined, 38
MIA. *See* Mediated Instructional
Activities
musical works, 54–56, 64–68

notice of copyright, 92–93

ownership of copyrighted works. *See*
work-for-hire doctrine

performance: amount allowed in
distance education, 53–61; defined,
17; reasonable and limited amount,
53–61
phonorecord, defined, 6
pictorial, graphic and sculptural works,
defined, 26n9
policies: Model Distance Education
Copyright Policy, 201–8; new
compliance requirement, 90–91;
transfer of copyrighted works
between faculty and institution,
13–15. *See also* work-for-hire
doctrine
public performance or display,
classroom, 26n15
purposes of recreation or entertainment,
73–74, 78–79

sound recording: contrasted with
musical works, 64–68; defined,
27n17, 86n18; performance right in
digital audio transmission, 68–73

technological protection measures,
99–103; anti-circumvention
distinguished, 99, 102
transfer of copyright, requirements,
14–16
transient copies, 103–4; ephemeral
recordings distinguished, 104, 142–45

work-for-hire doctrine: defined, 28n28;
employee defined for purposes of,
7–8; exception for educators, 10–12;
independent contractor distinguished
from, 9; policies, 13–15

About the Author

Tomas A. Lipinski was born in Milwaukee in 1958. After completing his JD from Marquette University Law School in Milwaukee, he received his LLM from the John Marshall Law School in Chicago and PhD from the University of Illinois at Urbana–Champaign. Mr. Lipinski has worked in a variety of legal settings, including the private, public, and nonprofit sectors. He has taught at the American Institute for Paralegal Studies and at Syracuse University College of Law. In summers he is a visiting associate professor at the Graduate School of Library and Information Science, University of Illinois at Urbana–Champaign, and from 1999 to 2003 at the Department of Information Science, School of Information Technology, at the University of Pretoria, South Africa.

Associate Professor Lipinski currently teaches, researches, and speaks frequently on various topics within the areas of information law and policy, especially copyright, privacy, and First Amendment issues in schools and libraries, and serves as codirector of the Center for Information Policy Research at the School of Information Studies, University of Wisconsin–Milwaukee. Publications in 2003 include *The Library's Legal Answer Book* (ALA), coauthored with Mary Minow.